CHINA IN FOCUS: ECONOMIC, POLITICAL AND EDUCATIONAL ISSUES

China in Focus: Economic, Political and Educational Issues

Ernest P. Nolan

Editor

Nova Science Publishers, Inc.

New York

Copyright © 2007 by Nova Science Publishers, Inc.

All rights reserved. No part of this book may be reproduced, stored in a retrieval system or transmitted in any form or by any means: electronic, electrostatic, magnetic, tape, mechanical photocopying, recording or otherwise without the written permission of the Publisher.

For permission to use material from this book please contact us:
Telephone 631-231-7269; Fax 631-231-8175
Web Site: http://www.novapublishers.com

NOTICE TO THE READER

The Publisher has taken reasonable care in the preparation of this book, but makes no expressed or implied warranty of any kind and assumes no responsibility for any errors or omissions. No liability is assumed for incidental or consequential damages in connection with or arising out of information contained in this book. The Publisher shall not be liable for any special, consequential, or exemplary damages resulting, in whole or in part, from the readers' use of, or reliance upon, this material.

Independent verification should be sought for any data, advice or recommendations contained in this book. In addition, no responsibility is assumed by the publisher for any injury and/or damage to persons or property arising from any methods, products, instructions, ideas or otherwise contained in this publication.

This publication is designed to provide accurate and authoritative information with regard to the subject matter covered herein. It is sold with the clear understanding that the Publisher is not engaged in rendering legal or any other professional services. If legal or any other expert assistance is required, the services of a competent person should be sought. FROM A DECLARATION OF PARTICIPANTS JOINTLY ADOPTED BY A COMMITTEE OF THE AMERICAN BAR ASSOCIATION AND A COMMITTEE OF PUBLISHERS.

LIBRARY OF CONGRESS CATALOGING-IN-PUBLICATION DATA
China in focus : economic, political and educational issues / editor: Ernest P. Nolan.
p. cm.
Includes index.
ISBN-13: 978-1-60021-543-8 (hardcover)
ISBN-10: 1-60021-543-2 (hardcover)
1. China--Economic conditions--2000- 2. China--Politics and government--2002- 3. Education--China. 4. Twenty-first century--Forecasts. I. Nolan, Ernest P.
HC427.95.C443 2008
330.951--dc22
2007031789

Published by Nova Science Publishers, Inc. ✦ New York

CONTENTS

PREFACE

China is blossoming as a world power. In the process, her economic, political and educational issues have become of interest to countries all over the globe. This new book presents in-depth analyses of such issues as foreign policy, FDI, military plans, school reform, currency policies, and overall economic developments

Chapter 1 - Over the last decade, Japan's evolution towards the status of a normal nation; namely, striving to put the image of a small political power behind it by expanding the mandate of the Self Defense Forces; pushing for a permanent seat on the UNSC; and strengthening its alliance with the U.S. is fueling China's Japan threat perception. Meanwhile, China's rapid economic growth and increasing military power fuels Japan's China threat perceptions. China's rise represents a challenge not only for Japan but other powers as well. Moreover, China and Japan both harbor mutual mistrust and misperceptions concerning their political, economic and military asymmetries, exemplified clearly by various tensions between 1995-2005. It is beyond the scope of this paper to examine all of these issues. In the new millennium, however, it is still important to analyze whether the Sino-Japanese competing political influence can further foster mutual misperceptions and or threat perceptions which are conducive to conflict in N.E. Asia. The author's paper analyzes this dynamic, concluding that such potential does exist. At the same time, the author also concludes that both powers can ameliorate possible conflict through various mechanisms for a constructive relationship in the new millennium.

Chapter 2 - One of the most important challenges facing China since the mid-1990s is how to address the rising foreign concerns over its increased international presence. Confronted with China's rapid economic development and growing international influence, some critics have begun to revive discussions concerning historical disorders and wars associated with the growth of great power (Bernstein & Munro, 1997; Kristof, 1993; *Economist*, 1992). Others have come up with a worrying image of a communist power, backed by virtually unlimited economic potential, challenging the western way of life (Chanda, 1996: 20). Still others working on strictly technical issues have predicted the potentially disastrous impact that a modernising China would have on the world's supplies of food, energy, minerals and other resources, as well as on the globe's ecological balance (Brown, 1994).

Chapter 3 – China has emerged as the most dynamic FDI-host country, and the contributions of FDI to the Chinese economy have burgeoned in ways that no one anticipated. Although considerable studies on the role of FDI in Chinese economy have appeared in recent years, a systematic treatment of the issue is still limited. This study first identifies several features of FDI in China, such as the export-oriented FDI strategy and the massive predominance of FDI from Hong Kong. After providing an analytical framework about determinants of FDI, its economic impact, and host countries' bargaining power, the paper explores factors behind China's success in attracting FDI and utilizing it to foster economic growth. These factors include China's huge country-size, effective FDI strategies, overseas Chinese investors, and a strong central government.

Chapter 4 - This paper presents a picture of administrative barriers to foreign direct investment (FDI) in China –its current situation, manifestations, causes, damaging effect and related measures to curb it. China is in a transition from a closed economy to an open market economy. Administrative barriers to FDI in China is reflected largely in investment restriction, non-transparent and inaccessible FDI rule and regulation, as well as bureaucratic interference in terms of the distortion of FDI operation behavior and the preclusion of market competition. They have become a pressing issue facing foreign investors in making decision to invest in china. China has made great effort to develop a regulation framework on incentive FDI, but this framework currently appears weak and powerless in the face of the administrative barriers. However, the construction of a complete legal framework for FDI and rebuild the government administrative system will be undoubtedly helpful in removing excessive administrative barriers.

Chapter 5 - This study mainly draws upon Robert Putnam (1993)'s framework, which focuses the effect of civil organization on civic culture, to evaluate the impacts of China's civil organizations on its democratic transition. The result indicates that: 1) there is a positive relation between civil organizational engagement and social trust, however such relation is not strong and significant; 2) participation in all types of civil organizations tends to decrease parochial culture of familism and have a weak relation with one's desire for authority; 3) all types of civil organization participation have a highly significant positive relationship with political discussion but a weak positive relation with one's political interest. These findings support the semi-civil society model of Chinese civil organizations. Chinese civil organizations are still far from developing. When more Chinese people are more active in civil participation, measured by the percentage of membership in more than 2 civil organizations, and when more public interest organizations emerge, the impacts of China's civil organizations on its civic culture will be more positive, and the implication for democratic transitions will be more significant.

Chapter 6 - There has been a dramatic increase in recent years in the numbers of international students undertaking undergraduate and postgraduate study in the United Kingdom. This has been as a direct result of the huge influx of students coming from the Far East, and in particular from China. This paper presents the findings of an exploratory questionnaire produced in order to reach a better understanding of the needs and expectations of international students in the university community. The paper concludes that this expansion of China into the global educational arena has serious implications for student provision and education both within the United Kingdom and beyond.

Chapter 7 - During the past twenty-five years, China has experienced and is still experiencing rapid and deep transformative change and, in this process, Chinese school education has also undergone unprecedented development. With the adoption of the policy of economic reform and opening up to the outside world in 1978, basic education in China entered a new era of progress. From that time to the mid-1980s, conscious efforts were made by the government to adjust the educational structure, increase the educational budget and raise the social status of teachers.

Chapter 8 - Hargreaves and Fullan asserted, "Beyond the walls of our schools, the world is changing dramatically; and it is pushing and pressing down hard on those who work within" (Hargreaves and Fullan, 1998: v). There is always a close connection between schooling and social changes in a country. Educational authorities and educators should devote themselves to improving their schools and to coping with the change. Taiwan has made these same endeavors.

In order to meet the great challenge of social-political change since martial law was lifted in 1987, Taiwan has been striving to launch many educational reforms to improve her schooling. The 1990s were a critical era for rapid reforms to education in Taiwan. Reacting to the conservative education policy and the chronologically accumulated dissatisfaction with the performance of schools, Taiwan not only has put decentralization of educational policy and deregulation into action, moving away from improper governance and domination of central authority, but also empowered schools and teachers to expand their professional autonomy.

Chapter 9 - In response to international pressure over its policy of pegging its currency (the yuan) to the U.S. dollar, the Chinese government on July 21, 2005, announced it would immediately appreciate the yuan to the dollar by 2.1% and adopt a currency policy based on a basket of currencies (including the dollar). Many Members have long charged that China "manipulates" its currency in order to make its exports cheaper and imports into China more expensive than they would be under free market conditions. They further contend that this policy is responsible for the large and growing U.S. trade deficits with China and the loss of U.S. manufacturing jobs. China's July 2005 reforms have done little to lessen congressional concerns. Several bills addressing China's currency have been introduced in Congress, including S. 295, which would raise U.S. tariffs on Chinese goods by an additional 27.5% unless China appreciated its currency.

Chapter 10 - Since the initiation of economic reforms in 1979, China has become one of the world's fastest-growing economies. From 1979 to 2005 China's real GDP grew at an average annual rate of 9.7%; it grew by 9.9% in 2005. Many economists speculate that China could become the world's largest exporter within the next few years and the largest economy within a few decades, provided that the government is able to continue and deepen economic reforms, particularly in regard to its inefficient state-owned enterprises (SOEs) and the state banking system. In addition, China faces several other difficult challenges, such as pollution and growing income inequality, that threaten social stability.

Trade continues to play a major role in China's booming economy. In 2005, exports rose by 28.4% to $762 billion, while imports grew by 17.6% to $660 billion, producing a $102 billion trade surplus. China is now the world's third-largest trading economy after the United States and Germany. China's trade boom is largely the result of large inflows of foreign direct investment (FDI) into China, which totaled $60 billion in 2005. Over half of China's trade is accounted for by foreign-invested firms in China.

China's economy continues to be a concern to U.S. policymakers. On the one hand, China's economic growth presents huge opportunities for U.S. exporters. On the other hand, the surge in Chinese exports to the United States has put competitive pressures on various U.S. industries. Many U.S. policy-makers have argued that greater efforts should be made to pressure China to fully implement its WTO commitments (especially in terms of protecting

U.S. intellectual property rights) and change various economic policies deemed harmful to U.S. economic interests, such as its currency policy and its use of subsidies to support its state-owned firms. In addition, recent bids by Chinese state-owned firms to purchase various U.S. firms have raised concerns among Members over the impact such acquisitions could have on U.S. national and economic security.

Chapter 11 - In recent years, the United States and other countries have expressed considerable concern that China's national currency (the yuan or renminbi) is seriously undervalued. Some analysts say the yuan needs to rise by as much as 40% in order to reflect its equilibrium value. Critics say that China's undervalued currency provides it with an unfair trade advantage that has seriously injured the manufacturing sector in the United States. Chinese officials counter that they have not pegged the yuan to the dollar in order to gain trade advantages. Rather, they say the fixed rate promotes economic stability that is vital for the functioning of its domestic economy.

On July 21, 2005, China announced a new foreign exchange system which is intended to allow more flexibility and to permit the international value of the yuan to be established by market forces. The yuan was increased in value by 2% and a "managed float" was introduced. However, the value of the yuan has changed little since then. Despite the publication of many studies, scholars do not agree whether or by what percent the yuan is undervalued. The wide range of estimates suggests that there is no reason to believe that any particular figure is correct. It is not clear that the U.S. trade deficit would be lower or U.S. manufacturers would benefit if China raised the value of the yuan. In the short run, U.S. producers might be able to sell higher-priced products to U.S. consumers if the inflow of Chinese goods were reduced. In the long run, though, as long as the United States is a net importer of capital, it will have a trade deficit and other countries will ultimately replace China as suppliers of low-cost goods to the U.S. market.

The Treasury Department has strongly urged China in recent years to adopt procedures that would allow the yuan to rise in value. Congress is considering legislation that would penalize China if its currency is not revalued. The United States has pursued the yuan-dollar exchange rate issue as a bilateral U.S.-China issue. Other countries are also affected by the presumably undervalued yuan — some more than the U.S. — but they have allowed the United States to take the lead.

There are at least five ways the United States could deal with the yuan exchange rate issue. Some of these would involve other countries more explicitly in the process. First, the United States could continue pressing China publicly to raise the value of the yuan on the assumption that change will not occur without foreign pressure. Second, it could stop pressing China publicly, on the expectation that China might move more rapidly towards reform if it is not pressured. Third, the United States could restrict imports from China pending action to revalue the yuan. Fourth, the U.S. could ask the IMF to declare that China is manipulating its currency in violation of IMF rules. Fifth, the United States could refer the issue to the World Trade Organization (WTO), asserting that the United States has been injured by unfair trade practices linked to the undervaluation of China's currency. The WTO, in turn, could authorize trade remedies (tariffs on Chinese goods, for example) aimed at correcting this abuse. This report will be updated as new developments arise.

In: China in Focus Economic, Political and Educational Issues
Editor: Ernest P. Nolan, pp. 1-16

ISBN 1-60021-543-8
© 2007 Nova Science Publishers, Inc.

Chapter 1

Towards a Constructive Sino-Japanese Relationship in the New Millennium

*Stephanie A. Weston**

Fukuoka University, Law Faculty, Nanakuma 8-19-1,
Jonan ku, Fukuoka 814-0180

Abstract

Over the last decade, Japan's evolution towards the status of a normal nation; namely, striving to put the image of a small political power behind.it by expanding the mandate of the Self Defense Forces; pushing for a permanent seat on the UNSC; and strengthening its alliance with the U.S. is fueling China's Japan threat perception. Meanwhile, China's rapid economic growth and increasing military power fuels Japan's China threat perceptions. China's rise represents a challenge not only for Japan but other powers as well. Moreover, China and Japan both harbor mutual mistrust and misperceptions concerning their political, economic and military asymmetries, exemplified clearly by various tensions between 1995-2005. It is beyond the scope of this paper to examine all of these issues. In the new millennium, however, it is still important to analyze whether the Sino-Japanese competing political influence can further foster mutual misperceptions and or threat perceptions which are conducive to conflict in N.E. Asia. My paper analyzes this dynamic, concluding that such potential does exist. At the same time, I also conclude that both powers can ameliorate possible conflict through various mechanisms for a constructive relationship in the new millennium.

Introduction

Over the last decade, Japan's evolution towards the status of a normal nation; namely, striving to put the image of a small political power behind it by expanding the mandate of the Self Defense Forces; pushing for a permanent seat on the UNSC; and strengthening its

---

* Contact: *saweston@jcom.home.ne.jp*

alliance with the U.S. is fueling China's Japan threat perception. Meanwhile, China's rapid economic growth and increasing military power fuels Japan's China threat perceptions. China's rise represents a challenge not only for Japan but other powers as well. Moreover, China and Japan both harbor mutual mistrust and misperceptions concerning their political, economic and military asymmetries[1], exemplified clearly by various tensions between 1995-2005. It is beyond the scope of this paper to examine all of these issues. In addition, many studies[2] have already analyzed the ambivalent and conflicting post-cold war Sino-Japanese relationship; especially in the last decade of the 20th century. In the new millennium, however, it is still important to analyze whether the Sino-Japanese competing political influence can further foster mutual misperceptions and or threat perceptions which are conducive to conflict in N.E. Asia. My paper analyzes this dynamic, concluding that such potential does exist. At the same time, I also conclude that both powers can ameliorate possible conflict through various mechanisms for a constructive relationship in the new millennium.

This analysis is important because this potential for Sino-Japanese conflict, besides undermining the bilateral relationship, could impact negatively on regional stability and prosperity. The path as well to peaceful coexistence among regional actors in Asia also requires a better understanding of mutual dissonance concerning perceptions and misperceptions in terms of soft and hard power. Finally, to build a constructive asymmetry, China and Japan must move beyond misperceptions of threat linked to problems rooted in the 19th and 20th centuries.

SINO-JAPANESE ASYMMETRIES-
MISPERCEPTIONS AND THREAT PERCEPTIONS

In order to build a more constructive Sino-Japanese relationship in the 21st century, it is important to understand existing Sino-Japanese misperceptions and threat perceptions underlying the relationship. The China threat perception, underneath the rhetoric, still exists in Japan due to China's growing economic, political and military power. China also sees Japan as a threat as the latter moves towards normal nation status and strives for greater political influence regionally and globally. According to one Chinese analyst, "Although Beijing long realized the asymmetry between economic and political dimensions in Sino-

---

[1] The concept of asymmetry relates to the relative strength or weakness of national power. As Hans Morgenthau states, "Power in international relations is the capacity of a nation to use its tangible and intangible resources-quantitative or qualitative – in such a way to affect the behavior of other nations.' A nation's power is also dependent on its self perception or others' perceptions of that power. Hans J. Morgenthau, *Politics Among Nations The Struggle for Power and Peace* (New York: Alfred Knopf, 1973), 104-49.

[2] Richard K. Betts, " Wealth, Power and Instability-East Asia and the United States after the Cold War," in *East Asian Security-An International Security Reader*, ed. Michael E. Brown, Sean M. Lynn-Jones and Steven E. Miller (Cambridge: The MIT Press, 1996); Reinhard Drifte, *Japan's Security Relations with China since 1989: From Balancing to Bandwagoning* (London: Routledge Curzon, 2003); Peter Drysdale and Dong Zhang, *Japan and China –Rivalry or Cooperation in East Asia?* (Australia: Australia-Japan Research Centre, 2000); Gilbert Rozman, " China's Changing Images of Japan, 1989-2001: The Struggle to Balance Partnership and Rivalry," *International Relations of Asia Pacific*, 2002; Neil E. Silver, *The United States, Japan and China-Setting the Course* (New York: Council on Foreign Relations, 2000); Gerald Segal, "The Coming Confrontation between China and Japan?," *World Policy Journal*, 1993: 27-32; Allen S. Whiting, *China Eyes Japan* (Berkeley: University of California Press, 1989.

Japanese relations, it felt more comfortable when Japan was economically generous but politically inactive. An economically centered and political trouble free relationship, however, is only possible when Japan remains an economic giant but a political and military dwarf."[3] On the other hand, in Japan, 'according to officials in the Foreign Ministry, the Ministry of Economy, Trade and Industry and the Japan Defense Agency (JDA), China's strategic challenge is Tokyo's most urgent concern.[4]

Related to these dynamics, as one China Japan specialist maintains, 'there is some cold in the hot and some hot in the cold concerning Japan-China relations.'[5] This latter observation particularly rings true when we look at the developments from 1995 to 2005. PM Koizumi has referred to 'Japan-China as one of the most important bilateral relationships'[6] and emphasizes the importance of a "future oriented relationship." Also, in 1998, China and Japan importantly concluded the third pillar of their present relationship–Japan-China Joint Declaration on Building a Partnership of Friendship and Cooperation for Peace and Development.[7] In addition, both countries have not only deepened their mutual economic ties but also fostered high level political, military exchanges, technical and cultural exchanges.

Concurrently, 1995-1996 is often considered to be the peak of terrible Sino-Japanese relations in the nineties due to escalating cross strait frictions; China's nuclear testing and Japan's subsequent suspension of ODA; the new U.S.-Japan guidelines; and overall strengthening of the U.S.–Japan alliance. Tensions continued throughout the latter half of the nineties into the 21st century with disputes over the Senkaku islands; Jiang Zemin's visit to Japan; Japanese PMs visits to Yasukuni Shrine; Chinese submarine, naval vessels or research ships incursions into Japan's EEZ; expansion of naval activity in the E. China Sea; the forcible seizure of North Koreans inside the grounds of the Japanese Consulate General in Shenyang; trade frictions; historical issues; the issuance of visas to Lee Teng-hui, the former President of Republic of China, to visit Japan as well as demonstrations in the spring of 2005 for several weeks in China over Japan's UNSC bid and a newly revised Japanese textbook. Last spring as well, Japan approval of a plan to grant Japanese firms the right to test drill in waters disputed with China in the East China Sea close to Japan's EEZ added to the litany of Chinese discontent. In addition, China enactment of the Anti-Secession Law in March of 2005, as one way to "formalize" the prevention of Taiwan's moves towards independence, generated opposition in the U.S., Japan and Taiwan. Prior to that, the U.S. and Japan, in a joint declaration, emphasized for the first time that 'Taiwan was a common security concern.'[8] This also generated a negative response from China.

These kinds of tensions impact on both countries' political regional capital. Both China and Japan need the trust and recognition of other Asian nations to enhance their political positions and prestige in the region. They also need to come to terms respectively with their changing regional roles. Although the PRC, under Jiang Zemin, started to engage more

---

[3] Michael D. Swaine and Alastair Ian Johnston, "China and Arms Control Institutions," in *China Joins the World*, ed. Elizabeth C. Economy and Michel Oskenberg (New York: Council on Foreign Relations, 1999), p. 91.

[4] Benjamin Self, "China and Japan: A Façade of Friendship," *The Washington Quarterly*, 2002, p. 85.

[5] Interview with Professor Wu Guangyi, Institute of World Economies and Politics, Chinese Academy of Social Science, Beijing, China, December 28, 2004.

[6] Ministry of Foreign Affairs of Japan, General Policy Speech by PM Junichiro Koizumi and the 159th Session of the Diet at *http://www.kantei.go-jp/foreign/koizumispeech/2004/01/19.sisei_e.html*

[7] Related to this declaration, 30 different agreements were also signed between both nations to further mutual cooperation.

[8] "China Expresses "Serious Concern" over U.S.-Japan Statement for Taiwan," at *http://en.chinabroadcast.cn/144/2005-2-21/88@208384.htm*

actively in 'great power and multilateral diplomacy,'[9] China resists the idea of Japan playing a lead strategic role regionally and globally.[10] China also questions Japan's right to be a "normal nation" without clearing the slate about the latter's past concerning other Asian nations. China sees changes in Japan's defense policies as movement towards the latter's possible remilitarization. Moreover, China views a "normal" Japan as a potential obstacle to China's assuming its rightful place in the regional and or global political order.

Although Japan like China asserts that its goal is not to become a global military power, Japan seeks to enhance its political position and influence bilaterally, regionally and globally. At the same time, Japan has shown it is still unable to come to terms with the past. Conflicts last year with its ASEAN-3[11] partners, exemplified this, while casting a shadow over the East Asian community talks held in December of 2005. As a matter of national interest, Japan feels it can no longer afford not to participate actively in the global community. Like other nations post 9/11, Japan must be adequately prepared to handle asymmetrical threats, transnational issues and homeland defense. Consequently, post 9/11, Japan has steadily expanded the parameters of its "defensive defense", by created security legislation for contingencies; enhancing its logistical support within the U.S.-Japan alliance; increasing SDF peace building and peacekeeping activities; contributing to the U.S. global war on terrorism; and and implementing a joint TMD system with its ally.

Besides these political differences, economic factors also enhance an atmosphere between the two nations more conducive to misperceptions about mutual disparities. China's economic rise with an over 9% growth rate poses a challenge as well as an opportunity for Japan. However, there is a "growing perception both in Japan and abroad that Japan and China may be trading places in terms of economic momentum and regional political influence."[12] For example, although Japanese exports to China increased for the sixth straight year in the first part of 2004 and China's imports from Japan also increased for the second straight year in 2004, the share of Japanese foreign direct investment [FDI] and trade in the Chinese economy has relatively decreased.[13] In addition, China rather than Japan first concluded an economic partnership agreement with ASEAN; is hosting of the six party talks and has become a member as well of G-20, ASEM, ASEAN-ARF and ASEAN + 3.

Added to the above dynamics, negative economic trends make it easier for China and Japan to engage in political performances on both sides which stroke historical resentments and or expand rhetoric concerning mutual threat perceptions. Some these trends include Sino-Japanese trade disputes involving intellectual property issues; some Chinese agricultural exports to Japan; and the quality of some Japanese products exported to China. In addition, the CCP, while maintaining its rule, must manage local discontent concerning the socio-economic gap between the developing coastal regions and the hinterland areas; failing state enterprises, rising crime and unemployment; energy and food shortages as well as corruption. In Japan, PM Koizumi's reform and restructuring policies have yielded some positive results. Growing trade with China has also stimulated the Japanese economy in some sectors.

[9] Lowell Dittmer, " Leadership Change in Chinese Political Development," *The China Quarterly*, 176(2003) : 918.

[10] Greg Austin and Stuart Harris, *Japan and Greater China Political Economy and Military Power in the Asian Century* (London: C. Hurst and Co., London, 20019, 98, 287.

[11] In the spring of 2005, demonstrations in Korea also occurred over Japan's UNSC permanent seat bid; the revised textbook problem as well as a territorial dispute over Takeshima Island involving Shimane prefecture in Japan and South Korea.

[12] Neil Silver, "U.S., Japan and China Setting the Course," (2000):325 at *http*://www.ciaonet.org/wps/sin01/

[13] Brad Glosserman, "Japan-China Mind Games," *The Japan Times* (2004):13.

However, Japan still needs more 'decentralization, deregulation, corporate restructuring, reform of government-affiliated corporations, and further disposal of non-performing loans.'[14]

China's growing economic capacities, as well, allows it to invest more in military modernization. While militarily, the Chinese are qualitatively behind the West in terms of equipment, integrated infrastructure, offshore capability and C4I[15] capacities, China is still a major nuclear power with growing defense expenditures. China sustained double digit increases in its announced defense budget from 1990 to 2002 as well as an 11.6 % increase in its 2004 defense budget.'[16] Chinese publicly released military budget figures, however, do not 'include total defense profits from weapons and service sales or People's Liberation Army [PLA] commercial activities; the cost of major weapons acquisitions funded from other budget accounts nor that of weapons research, pensions, nuclear weapons development, or the cost of the People's Armed Police."[17] In addition, while China's lacks a true blue water naval capacity, its overall military forces outnumber Japan's; its military disadvantages with Taiwan are diminishing and its missiles can target Japan or the U.S. at anytime. China too is 'focusing on how to use asymmetric strategies to defeat unnamed stronger opponents.'[18]

These trends as well as China's "strategic ambiguity" concerning the use of force to protect its national sovereignty and the upgrading of the PLA qualitatively and quantitatively enhance Japanese threat perceptions of China. These perceptions are further reinforced by Chinese submarines frequent penetration in the Japanese EEZ; 'the exploratory drilling in the East China Sea right at the edge of Japan's EEZ;' and the non transparency of the Chinese military expenditures.[19] Moreover, how China is using Japanese ODA and whether some these funds are being rolled over into military expenditures also worries Japan. This kind of concern is amplified when Japan sees China's successful space launch, export of weapons and increased weapon procurement.

While Japan and China's political, economic and military capacities are shifting in the new millennium, mutual pride makes the resolution of historical issues between the two nations difficult. Japan's growing confidence, for example, in its global political role and China's rise has also encouraged less Japanese appeasement of Chinese demands.[20]

Both countries younger policymakers as well with no memories of WWII or direct involvement in the normalization of Sino-Japanese relations, are less willingly to bend political will to suit each others' national needs.

Given the above dynamics, Japan has become increasingly blind towards China's emphasis on the resolution of historical problems. In addition, Japan feels it has already

---

[14] Junichiro Koizumi, "Asia in a New Century-Challenge and Opportunity," at *http://www.mofa.go.jp/region/asia-paci/china/boao0204/speech.html*

[15] The PLA has been devoted to C4I=command, control, communications, computers and intelligence (C4I) modernization and automation over the past quarter of a decade.

[16] *U.S. Secretary of Defense FY04 Report to Congress on PRC Military Power*, at *http://www.defenselinl.mil/pubs/d20040528PRC.pdf*

[17] Harvey J. Feldman, "The United States-PRC Relationship," in *The Security Environment in the Asia Pacific*, ed. Hung Mao Tien and Tun-Jen Cheng (Armonk, New York: M.E. Sharpe, 2000),

[18] David Shambaugh, "China and Japan Towards the 21st Century – Rivals for Pre-eminence or Complex Interdependence," in *China and Japan, History, Trends and Prospects*, ed. Christopher Howe (New York: Oxford University Press, 1996), 93.

[19] Yoichi Funabashi, "Considering China's Peaceful Rise," *Japan Echo*, 31-5 (2004).

[20] David Shambaugh, "China and Japan Towards the 21st Century – Rivals for Pre-eminence or Complex Interdependence," in *China and Japan, History, Trends and Prospects*, ed. Christopher Howe (New York: Oxford University Press, 1996), p. 93.

apologized sufficiently for its terrible actions in China and would like to move beyond history. Some Japanese as well feel that China uses history as a card to deflect nationalistic feelings away from other domestic problems. President Jiang Zemin's visit to Japan in 1998 for Japan heightened these perceptions. The visit was not well received due to Jiang's repeated public statements concerning the history issue between the two nations and demands concerning the joint declaration. Specifically, the Japanese government refused Chinese demands to include an official apology in the joint declaration concerning past Japanese actions in WWII as well as an affirmation of Japanese non involvement if a contingency occurred involving Taiwan.

Japan also resents China interference in what Japan feels are domestic problems, such as, the visits to Yasukuni Shrine and the revision of the textbooks. A local Japanese politician said China and Japan have different perspectives concerning the war dead. If the war dead did something wrong, China feels that it can never be forgiven. Japan supports the opposite view.[21] This kind of perceptual gap contributes to the intransigence on both sides concerning the ever present history problem.

China, on the other hand, has not forgotten the past, calling for Japanese actions not just words concerning historical disputes. Although the Chinese government gave up its claim to compensation when it normalized relations with Japan in 1972, private claims, China feels, should still be addressed, such as, those from comfort women; relatives of victims of chemical and gas warfare; and forced laborers. In addition, China feels that Japan must sincerely reflect on and apologize for its past atrocities against the PRC. China asserts, for example, that although feelings of remorse or recognition of Japanese aggressive actions during World War II have been made by prime ministers, the emperor, and other political figures, these statements have been negated by visits to the Yasukuni Shrine, distorted textbooks and an increase in war museums in Japan glorifying the past.[22]

Although Japanese culture is influenced by Chinese traditions, there is an emotional wall that separates both peoples. Part of this wall is based on stereotypes; another part is embedded in the Japanese insider-outsider mentality; and yet another part is related to past and modern history. Both Chinese and Japanese suffer historically from superiority and inferiority complexes. In addition, as national pride grows respectively, separation between politics and economics will become more mutually difficult. These emotional walls, national pride and the lack of appropriate Japanese response concerning historical problems in Chinese eyes makes it easier for the political coldness between both nations to spill over into their area of economic interactions. It also clouds mutual perceptions and further undermines Sino-Japanese relations, an important pillar for regional stability and prosperity.

In the following analysis, I examine, whether Sino-Japanese competition for political influence in Asia can further fuel the previously discussed misperceptions and threat perceptions, fostering a climate conducive to conflict in N.E. Asia.

---

[21] Interview with Mr. Shingu Matsuhiko, Fukuoka Prefectural Assemblyman, Liberal Democratic politician, Fukuoka, Japan, January 1, 2005.

[22] Zhixin Wang and Guanyi Wu, Hannichi Kanjoo ka Soretomo Tai Nichi Kenokan Ka – Nihon gawa tono Ronsoo, Hatashite – Dare no Mondai nano ka? (Saitama, Japan: Nihon Kyohosha, 2005), 60-81.

SINO-JAPANESE COMPETITION FOR POLITICAL INFLUENCE IN ASIA

Part of a nation's "power depends in considerable measure on what other nations think it is or even on what it thinks other nations think it is."[23] The asymmetry concerning China's and Japan's respective political influence in Asia itself does not constitute an immediate threat for a constructive Sino-Japanese relationship. Rather, how this asymmetry is perceived by both nations causes problems. Rising nationalism and overconfidence concerning respective political influence can also fuel further tensions between China and Japan.

China's Rising Political Influence

More now than ever, China's political influence is playing a greater role in the Asian region. There are many factors behind this. The period post 9/11 has allowed the U.S. and China to cooperate on fighting anti-terrorism, the North Korean problem and other transnational issues. With the end of the cold war in general, China increased international participation allows China to counter U.S. dominance and Japanese influence in the region. It also 'ensures recognition of China's major power status.'[24]

China's political influence is rising not only because of its participation in these kinds of mechanisms but also because of its growing economic capabilities. Although the idea of a China threat has not disappeared, its neighbors increasingly see China too as a source of trade, FDI and technology transfer opportunities. The fact that China not Japan is becoming more of the hub for Asian integration also adds to the image of China's rising political influence. Sino-Japanese competition for political influence in Asia is evident in both countries' public statements and actions. Specifically, in 2002, China concluded, the Framework Agreement on Comprehensive Economic Cooperation with ASEAN. Soon afterwards, Japan followed with the Tokyo Declaration for the Dynamic and Enduring Japan-ASEAN Partnership in the New Millennium. In addition, ASEAN+3 plans to create an East Asian community. Although neither Japan nor China would be designated as the leaders of such a community, their predominance and rivalry for ASEAN markets can not be ignored.

As China tries to project an image of a peaceful power, seeking economic development, modernization, regionalization, strong homeland defense, and a multi-polar order, it should be able to build up political capital in the region. Unfortunately, this peaceful image is not shared universally by either the U.S. or other nations in Asia. If key actors in the region, like Japan, still harbor misperceptions about China's intentions in acquiring political influence, this kind of situation could also be conducive to further regional tensions.

---

[23] John Stoessinger, "The Anatomy of the Nation-State Nature of Power," in *Perspectives on World Politics-A Reader*, ed. Richard Little and Michael Smith (Routledge, London and New York, 1991), 27.
[24] Joseph Y. S. Cheng and Wankun Zhang, "Patterns and Dynamics of China's International Strategic Behaviour," *Journal of Contemporary China* (2002): 239.

Japan's Greater Political Role

In the post cold war, Japan has worked to change its image as a small political power. Consequently, more conservative Japanese administrations in the nineties and into the millennium are working towards turning Japan into a more "normal nation". In line with this vision, the Japanese government has expanded SDF functions not only for homeland security but also for international peace and cooperation. For example, SDF has contributed to peace keeping and or peace building activities in Afghanistan and Iraq. In addition, Japan is reviewing its constitution including Article 9 for future amendment in line with the new global order in the 21st century. Japan too has already become more active in multilateral economic and security from ASEAN Regional Forum [ARF][25] to the six party talks.

Japan is especially susceptible to misperceptions about China's growing political influence because of the growing sense of rivalry between the two powers. At the same time, 'both Japanese and Chinese play down the notion of serious competition between them. Alternatively, some Chinese tend to be dismissive or condescending toward Japan's role when discussing regional issues."[26] In the past, Japan 'has acted as the China Expert" at the G-7 meeting, thus setting a bridge between the West and China.'[27] Japan, however, now worries about a "Super China", challenging its regional role.'[28]

Japan's worst nightmare would be encirclement by China. A strengthening of U.S.-Sino ties, for example, deepen Japanese concern about a potential decline in its regional influence. Consequently, 'Japan is checking China's growing power through, such means as, multilateral approaches to indirectly influence Chinese behavior, CBMs and economic tools like ODA.'[29] To also ensure its own security, Japan is building up political capital in Asia and with the U.S. If Japanese initiatives to build up its political regional influence are misinterpreted by China, this kind of situation is conducive to conflict. At the same time, as Japan perceives that China is passing it up economically and possibly politically and militarily in the future, the potential is there for Japanese misperceptions to increase about China's use of its political influence.

At the moment, there is a kind of symbiotic tension between China and Japan because of their mutual needs. "China's asymmetrical dependence on Japan's technology, market, investment, and loans heightened the volatility of emotional reactions to issues of disagreement, and reinforced China's sensitivity to Japan's regional intentions."[30] On the other hand, 'Japan needs China's support and influence also to increase Japan's political status.[31] Japan increasingly needs Chinese trade and investment opportunities as well to stimulate its economy. China's cooperation and political influence along with that of other regional actors to create peace and prosperity in Asia is also a necessity.

---

[25] "ARF was established in 1994 to address security issues," Bodell, Nenner and Wall, Connie, *Glossary* at *http://first.sipri.org/www/first_glossary.html*
[26] Brad Glosserman, "Japan-China Mind Games," *The Japan Times* (2004): 13.
[27] Deng Yong, "Chinese Relations with Japan: Implications for Asia Pacific Regionalism," *Pacific Affairs* 70 (1997): 6 at *http://www.findarticles.com/p/articles/mi_qa3680/is_199710/ai_n8767518*
[28] Ibid.
[29] Michael J. Green and Benjamin L. Self, "Japan's Changing China Policy: From Commercial Liberalism to Reluctant Realism," *Survival* 38-2 (1996): 50-53.
[30] Ibid.
[31] Deng Yong, "Chinese Relations with Japan: Implications for Asia Pacific Regionalism," *Pacific Affairs* 70 (1997): 7 at *http://ww.findarticles.com/p/articles/mi_ga3680/is_199710.ai_8767518print.*

Nationalism, over Confidence and Political Influence

The growing nationalism in both countries is also another possible trigger for misguided Sino-Japanese perceptions about the nature of their respective asymmetrical political influence. Nationalism and the drive for economic development are the strong glue that holds together a rising China. China is proud of its increasing hard[32] and soft power[33] in such a short space of time. At the same time, it is antagonistic towards Japan for past historical issues and territorial claims. Nationalism, for example, allows the 'Chinese government to maintain its legitimacy and demonstrate resolve abroad.'[34] It also permits the Chinese Communist Party [CCP] to turn attention away from internal economic development problems.

Nationalism as well as a growing Chinese sense of over confidence in its own capabilities could trigger misguided perceptions about Sino-Japanese asymmetrical political influence. For example, 'many Chinese strategic thinkers now see Japan as a declining power due to its stagnant economy and shrinking population. They are confident that in the future, China's expected economic superiority will force Japan to accommodate Beijing, ensuring smooth Sino-Japan relations.'[35] Over confidence could also lead China to misperceive how Japan's perceives China's intentions concerning the future use of its asymmetrical political influence based on its rising hard power.

Nationalism in Japan has grown stronger in the 90s and into the millennium. Japan, however, during the short administration (1994-96) of Prime Minister Tomiichi Murayama, the then head of the Japanese Socialist Party, made some additional progress towards alleviating Sino-Japanese tensions over historical issues. For example, under PM Murayama's, the No War Resolution[36] was brought to the Diet. Although, this resolution was supposed to be a stronger statement about Japanese responsibilities for a war of aggression, it was later watered down due to conservative opposition. In spite of this, Chinese public statements often comment about PM Murayama's positive actions concerning the resolution of historical problems. Concurrently, other Chinese public comments are critical of the rightwing backlash post PM Murayama to the present PM Koizumi administration.

Japanese nationalism too has grown in response to Japan's economic decline and China's rising asymmetrical capabilities including political influence. For example, 'Japanese

---

[32] Hard power is defined as 'economic, military' and soft power – 'political, social and intellectual'. Lijun Sheng, *China's Dilemma The Taiwan Issue* (NewYork: I.B. Taurus 2001): 53.

[33] Soft power is also described as "the ability to get what you want through attraction rather than coercion or payments. It arises from the attractiveness of a country's culture, political ideals, and policies." Joseph Nye Jr., *Soft Power – The Means to Success in World Politics* (New York: Public Affairs, 2004), 5.

[34] Thomas J. Christensen, "Pride, Pressure, and Politics: The Roots of China's Worldview," in *In the Eyes of the Dragon: China Views the World*, ed. Deng Yong and Fei-Ling Wang (Lanham, Maryland: Rowman and Littlefield Publishers, 1999): 250.

[35] Denny Roy, "Stirring Samurai, Disapproving Dragon: Japan's Growing Security Activity and Sino-Japan Relations," (2003): 1 at *http://www.apcss.org/Publications/OcasionalPapers/OPStirringSamurai.Roy.pdf*

[36] Statement by Prime Minister Murayama Tomiichi issued on 8/15/95 (excerpt) "During a certain period in the not too distant period past, Japan following a mistaken national policy, advanced along the road to war, only to ensnare the Japanese people in a fateful crisis and through its colonial rule and aggression, caused tremendous damage and suffering to the people of many countries, particularly to those of Asian nations. I hope that no such mistake be made in the future. I regard in a spirit of humility, these irrefutable facts of history, and express here once again my feelings of deep remorse and state my heartfelt apology." *Japan Times Weekly*, 8/21-27/1995, p. 6 quoted in Caroline Rose, *Sino Japanese Relations Facing the Past: Looking to the Future?* (London and New York: RoutledgeCurzon, 2005), 113.

nationalists due to these changes along with strategic tensions with China also feel that Japan should once more possess military power to rival that of its neighbors.'[37] In addition, Japanese nationalism is venting its anti-Chinese feeling through provocative actions on the Senkaku islands; assertions about the rights of political officials to visit Yasukuni Shrine; antagonistic statements made by politicians concerning World War II atrocities and Japanese war responsibility as well as a more confrontational attitude towards China concerning Chinese submarines and or vessels near or in the Japanese EEZ.

There is an asymmetry concerning about how much nationalism impacts on China and Japanese foreign policy that is hard to quantify here. However, nationalism in Japan is still associated with the excesses of the Japanese military in World War II. The right wing minority in Japan does have influence but Chinese perception of the weight of their influence outweighs the actual reality. Chinese perceptions of Japanese ultra-nationalism may also fail to distinguish clearly between ultra-nationalism and neo-conservatism. For example, while the Koizumi administration carries out some actions which would be approved by ultranationalists, his administration is neoconservative rather than ultranationalist.

Complicating Chinese perceptions and Japanese nationalism are present political sympathies shared by the neo-conservative administrations in both Japan and the U.S. Both governments are very much in sync at the moment about common interests, value and strategic goals. The U.S.-Japan alliance too is often perceived as well by the Chinese as a means to constrain China. The U.S.-Japan's alliance also enhances Japan's political influence in the region. Consequently, Japan often acts as a conduit between the U.S. and other powers who find it difficult to agree with the U.S.

Nationalism in both countries generates pride in one's culture identity, international status and growing capabilities. China and Japan are no exceptions to this trend. In addition, nationalism could foster a lack of political will to address Sino-Japanese problems due to past impasses and an increase in asymmetrical capacities including political influence. If this kind of nationalism also leads to misperceptions about the use of their respective asymmetrical political influence in the region, there is danger of conflict.

Although China and Japan are working together in the region economically and politically, the potential for enhanced tensions or conflicts caused by mutual misperceptions concerning the use of their respective political influence remains. One challenge for Sino Japanese relations is not to allow misperceptions about their increasing tangible and intangible disparities like political influence in Asia to impede further their cooperation whether inside a future East Asian community or the larger Asia Pacific Rim. In the last part of this paper, I examine how both powers can work towards a constructive relationship in the new millennium.

Towards a Constructive Asymmetry

In spite of ongoing tensions including misperceptions and or threat perceptions between China and Japan, conflict is not inevitable. Both powers can work towards a constructive relationship in the new millennium. Conclusion of historical animosities and U.S. leverage are key to this positive outcome. In addition, Brantly Womack suggests four other measures for the possible amelioration of conflicts in a dyadic relationship; namely, 1) "rhetoric which

---

[37] Eugene A. Matthews, "Japan New Nationalism," *Foreign Affairs* (2003): 81.

articulates the vital interest of both sides; 2) converting issue areas to low politics through routinization and institutionalization; 3) ritual diplomacy and 4) precedent."[38]

Reconciliation of Historical Animosities

It is easy for China and Japan to get locked into certain patterns of interaction. Of course, it does not help that part of this friction is due to differences concerning interpretations of history and Japan's aggressions against China in the 19th and 20th centuries. These issues have created a wall between both countries which is difficult to remove for several reasons. This wall in turn fuels a negative atmosphere conducive to mutual misperceptions regarding future intentions and capabilities. In addition, a lack of trust, sufficient political will, growing national pride and new post Cold War dynamics impede reconciliation.

Now that the cold war has ended; Sino-American relations are friendlier post 9/11; China is rising and Japan is deepening ties with the U.S., political will on both sides to reconcile over the past is weak. As China's rises, it will become easier for China to use political friction to create a thicker wedge between China and Japan, especially, if the friction is linked to domestic discontent and or nationalism.

According to Dr. Richard Solomon, President of the U.S. Institute of Peace, reconciliation is a process that must proceed through four phases: truth, memorialization, compensation and accountability,"[39] In the case of China and Japan, this process has yet to be effectively carried out. Mutual animosities were never really resolved and walls were never really broken down. Reconciliation over historical issues can only serve to strengthen the foundation of Sino-Japanese relations in the new millennium. One Chinese scholar stated, "History is an objective reality. It will not change its form or vanish into thin air even if China no longer mentions it or Japan refuses to acknowledge it. The point is it is not a historical dispute with one side asking for apology and the other side refusing to do so. Rather, it enshrines hope of both sides for a common bright future."[40]

If there is sufficient political will and increasing trust, constructive dialogue can lead the parties concerned down the road toward reconciliation. Reconciliation has to be an ongoing process involving central, local governments and grassroots efforts. Otherwise, it is too easy for misperceptions to flourish and dialogue to become politically skewed and fueled by nationalistic forces. In addition, external and domestic factors are also making it difficult for both governments to foster the right atmosphere for reconciliation. Globalization has brought a wider dissemination, for example, of the Internet and mobile phones to China, making it difficult for the government to control the nature of its people's discontent including anti-Japanese sentiments. 'The CCP in order to maintain its legitimacy as well must increasingly reflect the will of the people rather than just imposing the government's will on the people.'[41] Both China and Japan, while balancing delicately domestic concerns, must also engage in

---

[38] Brantly Womack, "Asymmetry and Systemic Misperception: China, Vietnam and Cambodia during the 1970s,"*Journal of Strategic Studies* (2003): 104-106.

[39] Yoichi Funakoshi, "Conclusion," in *Reconciliation in the Asia Pacific* (Washington D.C.: U.S. Institute of Peace, 2003) p. 176.

[40] Zhongwei, Lu, " Sino-Japanese Relations Understanding and Promoting," *Contemporary International Relations.* China Institute of Contemporary International Relations, Beijing, Vol. 13, No. 11, (2003): 9.

[41] Interview with Mr. Tang Yin, Urban Research Center, Fukuoka, Japan, May 25, 3005.

diplomatic performances that satisfy their local constituencies. At the same time, however, these performances aggravate bilateral tensions.

Routinization and Institutionalization

Related to building a constructive relationship between China and Japan, Brantly Womack's suggestion for the amelioration of conflicts in a dyadic relationship, namely, "converting issue areas to low politics through routinization and institutionalization" applies especially to the reconciliation of Sino-Japanese historical animosities. With this in mind, various kinds of cultural, academic, sports and people-to-people exchanges between China and Japan continue to play an important role and be expanded. Some specific examples of already existing exchanges include the Japan-China Youth Friendship Exchange; the Japan, China, Republic of Korea Lecture Tour in Japan; the Japan China and Republic of Korea Young Leaders Program or the new 21st Century Committee for Japan China Friendship.[42] In addition, in 2002, the 30th anniversary of the normalization of Sino-Japanese relations, a Japan-China Cultural Friendship Goodwill Delegation of 10,000 visited China and 5,000 China nationals visited Japan on goodwill visits, Both governments respectively declared 2002 China Year in Japan and Japan Year in China. In addition, there are presently 'more than 70,000 Chinese students in Japan, more than 3,000 Japanese students in China and 220 sister city relationships.'[43] Both China and Japan too have relaxed some visa restrictions towards the others' nationals. And 'in 2003, 2.25 million Japanese visited China and in 2002, some 452,000 Chinese visited Japan.'[44]

Besides these kinds of exchanges, in addition to the new Japan-China Committee for New Friendship in the 21st century, a Track II initiative, I also propose that an official committee for reconciliation or a Track I initiative between both governments be started for better relations. Both kinds of efforts are needed to resolve lingering historical conflicts. One positive step in this direction includes an accord, agreed to under the previous 21st Century Committee for Japan-China Friendship, to "initiate joint history research involving experts from both sides."[45] Third party dialogue/conference initiatives like those of the Mansfield Foundation, the Pacific Forum CSIS, the Asia Foundation, the U.S. Institute of Peace and the Tokyo Foundation as well as the Korea, China and Japan Three Countries Gakujutsu Minkan Dantai could also help both China and Japan move towards reconciliation.

---

[42] In October of 2003, the New 21st Century Committee for Japan-China Friendship, a bilateral advisory board with members from academia, business and media was launched to make recommendations on the bilateral relations to both governments, aimed at extensive exchanges." This new committee replaces a previous 21st Century Committee for Japan-China Friendship. Ministry of Foreign Affairs of Japan, Meeting between PM Junichiro Koizumi and President Jiang Zemin of the PRC on the occasion of APEC Summit Meeting on Shanghai at *http://www.mofa.go.jp/policy/economy/apec/2001/china.html*

[43] Brad Glosserman, "Japan and China Mind Games," *The Japan Times* (2004):13.

[44] Ibid.

[45] "Friendship Panel Calls for Japan-China Cooperation on Terror," *Japan Policy and Politics* (2001) at *http://www.findarticles.com/p/articles/mi_mOXPQ/is_2001_Dec_24/ai_83370891*

Beyond Rhetoric

Brantly Womack also stresses "rhetoric which articulates the vital interest of both sides" as a way to reduce conflicts in a dyadic relationship. Both China and Japan need to move beyond their present rhetoric and emphasize reconciliation. However, how much of a role does China or Japan allow history to play in the present dynamics of the Sino-Japan relationship? It appears China more and Japan less. However, both sides, having recognized these differences, need to forward to the next stage of their reconciliation. A "future oriented" Sino-Japanese relationship must address issues not just mutually important to both powers but also those issues which are more important for one side versus the other. The political will to deal with the former is easier than the latter. However, the latter is just as important as it can lead to a breakthrough for a Sino-Japanese constructive relationship in the new millennium.

Just how difficult a lack of political will makes going beyond the rhetoric in Sino-Japanese relations is exemplified by the discussion surrounding "New Thought." "New Thought," a minority philosophy first postulated in a *Strategy and Management Journal* article in 2002 by Ma Licheng, a senior official and commentator of the *People's Daily*, gave both Chinese and Japanese public and private sectors food for thought. Other important representatives of "New Thought" include Professor Shi Yinhong of Renmin University of China in Beijing and Fu Shookei (phonetic) of China's Japan Institute.

> "In Argument of New Thinking Toward Japan," Fu promoted five principles for new thinking – 'national interest as the highest principle vs. emotionalism in consideration of policy; economic interests should be placed at the core of China's national interests; global and regional peace and stability are pre-requisites for China's economic success; CCP has the responsibility to develop the leading ideas for policy toward Japan; and successful development of bilateral relations requires cooperation of both countries.'[46]

Shi Yinhong's tenets are: '1) be satisfied with the degree of regret and apology Japan has officially shown so far for its aggressive war against China, leave this historical issue well enough alone and avoid disputing over it for a relatively long period of time; 2) increase China's business with Japan and decrease it with the E.U. and the U.S.; 3) inwardly watch Japan's military expansion, outwardly follow a tolerant enough policy towards this situation; stop exaggerating about Japan's possibility of becoming a military superpower; 4) welcome Japan's participation in the important issues of the region and even positively request this participation. In this way, Japan would be sure that China sees Japan as a future political power in East Asia; and 5) treat Japan equally as a candidate for the UNSC; do not impose any conditions.'[47]

Although each makes some different points, there are similarities in their positions, especially that of Ma Licheng and Professor Shi Yinhong, such as, downplaying historical animosities, recognition of Japan's superpower status and working together in an East Asian community.[48] Specifically, Ma Licheng advocated 'removing the history problem from public

---

[46] Quoted in James J. Przystup, "Japan-China Relations Bridges to the Future, Reflections on the Past," *Comparative Connections* (2003) at *http://www.csis.org/pacfor/cc/0303Qjapan_china.html*

[47] These tenets, which were originally published in "Nichuu Sekkin to Gaikoo Kakumei" *Strategy and Management Journal* (2003). They are then quoted in Xide Jin and Zhibo Lin, *Nichuu Shin Shikoo to wa Nani ka – Ma Licheng-Shi Yinhong Ronbun e no Hihan* (Saitama, Japan: Nihon Kyoohoosha, 2003), 13, 19.

[48] Ibid.

announcements; balancing strategic demands and economic necessity, while watching Japan's military power internally; taking a generous stance towards Japan, creating an atmosphere of trust; treating Japan as a superpower; working together for prosperity and stability in East Asia through multilateral mechanisms and not making special conditions for Japan to join the UNSC.'[49] His ideas, which were criticized as being 'overly optimistic, one sided, appeasing the Japanese and downplaying the significance of the extent of Japanese past aggression towards Chinese victims,' were basically rejected by the mainstream in China.[50] At the same time, the Japanese mass media discussed them widely.

Whether or not "New Thought" is seen as leaning too much in favor of the Japanese, there is a Chinese perception that the China government did use this discussion as a lever to create a more positive atmosphere for Sino-Japanese relations concerning reconciliation over the past. Moreover, 'China sees that Japan did not maximize this opportunity. President Hu Jintao and Wen Jiabao did refrain from publicly criticizing Koizumi's visits to Yasukuni. And the PRC tried to limit the scope of a growing resentment among ordinary Chinese toward Japan on various issues. However, the Japanese Prime Minister continued his visits to Yasukuni; the Japanese press celebrated new thinking as a vindication of the Japanese stance in bilateral disputes; and from right wing opinion magazine to semi-official circles, the China threat is increasingly equated to that of North Korea.'[51]

Ritual Diplomacy

The third mechanism or ritual diplomacy, as suggested by Brantly Womack, is also important for building a Sino-Japanese relationship. Although the relationship between the two powers runs hot and cold, the lines of communication still remain open at various levels – high ranking ministry officials, leader summits and parliamentarian visits. Grassroots and student exchanges continue in spite of up and down tensions. If China and Japan can break the current impasse over historical issues, mutual state visits by Prime Minister Koizumi and President Hu Jintao will also enhance the mechanism of ritual diplomacy, leading again hopefully to a more constructive relationship between these two Asian powers.

Setting Precedents

Brantly Womack's fourth mechanism or "setting precedents" is also key to the amelioration of conflicts in a dyadic relationship. CBMs, in this sense, can help temper Sino-Japanese misperceptions concerning asymmetrical disparities and reduce situations conducive to conflict. Especially important is that the CBMs convince the other side that asymmetrical capacities will be used only for defensive not offensive purposes.

China in general tends to be cautious about CBMs and sees them as another way for others to contain the PRC. However, China has already engaged in various military and non-

---

[49] Xide Jin and Zhibo Lin, *Nichuu Shin Shikoo to wa Nani ka – Ma Licheng-Shi Yinhong Ronbun e no Hihan* (Saitama,Japan: Nihon Kyoohoosha, 2003), 35-64.
[50] Ibid.
[51] Ibid.

military CBMs with other powers, organizations or mechanisms in the region. These CBMs include the releasing of Chinese defense white papers; signing the Treaty of Amity and Cooperation in Southeast; Asia; the carrying out of negotiations on arms reductions with Russia, Kazakhstan, Kyrgyzstan and Tajikistan as well as agreeing to the Action Strategy on Trilateral Cooperation among the People's Republic of China, Japan and the Republic of Korea. These CBMs, which help foster overall security and stability in Asia, also benefit the Sino-Japanese relationship. Some specific Sino-Japanese CBMs include establishing a hot line agreement; mutually waiving visas for short term visits; and holding the Japan-China Security dialogues which involve defense and foreign ministry officials as well as security related cooperation through ASEAN+3.

China, Japan and the Republic of Korea officially committed themselves in 2003 to the 'intensification of security dialogues and the extension of exchanges among defense and military officials in East Asia and the strengthening of cooperation in the fields of disarmament and non-proliferation as well as the realization of a nuclear free Korean peninsula.'[52] However, additional CBMs between China and other regional actors including Japan are not only needed but are also conducive to a more constructive regional order.

U.S. Leverage

As U.S. foreign policy continues to influence heavily Japanese foreign policy choices, consideration of U.S. leverage concerning Sino-Japanese relations is also essential. Both Japan and China as well "regard their relationship with each other as second in importance only to the U.S."[53] Although China and Japan's respective relationships with the U.S. are both different and asymmetrical, each relationship is essential for the growth and stability of the Asia Pacific Rim. To Japan, the U.S. is a top trading partner, sole ally and its protector in the event of a contingency in the region. Japan, along with the U.S., shares many common values and goals concerning regional stability, prosperity and human values. Alternatively, the U.S. is China's number one strategic rival and trading partner. At the same time, China has yet to really become America's "constructive strategic partner".

While the U.S. and Japan remain wary of China's geopolitical strategies, China recognizes there is a perceptual gap between how others perceive its rise and China perceives itself. China, however, sees its rise as something natural and emphasizes its need for an effective military force for homeland defense and protection against future foreign domination. China further asserts it harbors no ambitions to become a global military power but instead seeks peace in the Asia Pacific Rim. In line with this thinking, China has 'formed various partnerships, for example, with the U.S., Japan, ASEAN, Russia, France and Germany.' [54] It is also supportive of an East Asia multilateral security framework which would also involve the U.S. and Japan.

For the promotion of regional security and prosperity, the U.S. also needs a constructive Sino-Japanese relationship. Through the U.S.-Japan-China Trilateral Summits, the U.S. has a

---

[52] Joint Declaration on the Promotion of Tripartite Cooperation among the People's Republic of China, Japan and the Republic of Korea, Bali, Indonesia at *http://www.aseansec.org/15284.htm*
[53] Quansheng Zhao, "China and Major Power Relations in E. Asia," *Journal of Contemporary China* (2001): 666.
[54] Avery Goldstein, "The Diplomatic Face of China's Grand Strategy: A Rising Power's Emerging Choice," *The China Quarterly* (2001): 846, 863.

chance to dialogue with both Japan and China in a minilateral framework. During the six party talks, the U.S. is also working with not only Japan and China but also Russia and South Korea to handle the North Korean problem. These kinds of mechanisms are important not only for all three countries' national interests but also for a stable regional order. At the same time, the U.S. must be careful that its own strategic ambiguities, for example, concerning Taiwan or geopolitical plans for the Korean peninsula, do not further fuel Sino-Japanese misperceptions.

CONCLUSION

Presently, the relationship between China and Japan is like two frosty mirrors. It is hard to see clearly the images reflected in them, leading to distorted perceptions of each side's tangible and intangible asymmetries. The Sino-Japanese competition for political influence in Asia, based on tensions during 1995-2005, does fuel mutual misperceptions and or threat perceptions conducive to conflict in N.E. Asia. This potential for conflict, however, can be ameliorated through various mechanisms for a constructive relationship in the new millennium. Specifically, these keys include overcoming historical animosities, "routinization and institutionalization," moving beyond the rhetoric, engaging in "ritual diplomacy", "setting precedents" and benefitting from U.S. leverage. Beyond these measures, both China and Japan's real political commitment to the realization of a future oriented relationship is, without a doubt, essential for a constructive Sino-Japanese relationship in the new millennium. It is also imperative for a prosperous and stable regional order in Asia.

In: China in Focus Economic, Political and Educational Issues   ISBN 1-60021-543-8
Editor: Ernest P. Nolan, pp. 17-28   © 2007 Nova Science Publishers, Inc.

Chapter 2

PEACEFUL RISE: CHINA'S 'POLICY OF ASSURANCE'

Jia Qingguo

School of International Studies of Peking University, China

One of the most important challenges facing China since the mid-1990s is how to address the rising foreign concerns over its increased international presence. Confronted with China's rapid economic development and growing international influence, some critics have begun to revive discussions concerning historical disorders and wars associated with the growth of great power (Bernstein & Munro, 1997; Kristof, 1993; *Economist*, 1992). Others have come up with a worrying image of a communist power, backed by virtually unlimited economic potential, challenging the western way of life (Chanda, 1996: 20).[1] Still others working on strictly technical issues have predicted the potentially disastrous impact that a modernising China would have on the world's supplies of food, energy, minerals and other resources, as well as on the globe's ecological balance (Brown, 1994).

The implication of these differing perspectives is, however, the same: if China represents a threat, they suggest, the world needs to do something about it. Subsequently, a variety of suggestions have been made to address the 'problem'. Some commentators, for example, have called for the introduction of a broad containment policy (Krauthammer, 1995). A narrower approach has also been suggested, such as the strengthening of the US-Japanese military alliance (Bernstein & Munro, 1997: 31-32). Others have advocated stricter regulations to control the international transfers of military technologies (Cox Report, 1999).[2] In addition to these geopolitical containment strategies, attention has also been drawn to the need to liberalise and democratise China. The ultimate hope is that these measures would make China's increasing stature less threatening (*Economist*, 1996: 12). Some have embraced a push for a tougher American stance on the question of Taiwan as a way of stymying China (Friedman, 1997: 31-32; *Far Eastern Economic Review*, 1992: 3). On the other hand, somewhat less confrontational approaches have included exerting greater pressure on China to spend more of its resources on environmental protection, and inducing the country to

---

[1] According Nayan Chanda of the Far Eastern Economic Review, the French military was opposed to the proposed sale of a French aircraft carrier to China for ideological reasons.
[2] See the Cox Report recommendations (Select Committee, United States House of Representatives, 1999).

adhere more closely to international standards of behaviour deemed more desirable by the critics.[3]

Confronted with such a broad array of critical perspectives, the Chinese government has realised that it must respond if it wishes to continue to exist in a peaceful international environment. Accordingly, it has gone to some lengths to alleviate international concerns over its emergence as a global power. *Inter alia*, it has worked to reassure the outside world that it harbours no sinister ambitions, working instead to reinforce perceptions that China's destiny is tied to, and compatible with, those of other countries. Moreover, China has encouraged the view that its development as a rapidly emerging international power presents not just challenges, but, more importantly, opportunities for others. However, rhetoric not being enough to provide this comprehensive reassurance, the Chinese government has introduced numerous specific measures to back up its professed position. Taken as a whole, the Chinese government's approach constitutes what I would term a 'policy of assurance'.

This paper describes and analyses China's 'policy of assurance' by first of all outlining the central features of this policy. It then seeks to explore the major factors shaping it. Finally, this paper speculates as to its future possible development. In doing so, it seeks to engender a more balanced understanding of China's foreign policy.

THE POLICY OF ASSURANCE

A policy of assurance needs to satisfy at least three requirements if it is to work. First, the party doing the assuring needs to clarify its general policy objectives. Second, the party doing the assuring must address the specific concerns and fears of the party that is to be reassured. Finally, it is important that such a process allows the latter to believe that it is not in the former's interests to betray its own commitments. This is, it can be argued, exactly what the Chinese government has been seeking to achieve in recent years.

Clarifying Policy Objectives

The Chinese government has repeatedly stressed that peace and development constitute China's most important foreign policy objectives. In his report to the Sixteenth National Representative Congress of the Chinese Communist Party, Jiang Zemin, the then Secretary General of the Chinese Communist Party (CCP) Central Committee, stated that the goal of China's foreign policy is to maintain world peace and promote common development (Jiang, 2002: 47). Jiang's successor, Hu Jintao, in his speech to the opening ceremony of the 2004 annual conference of the *Bo'ao Forum for Asia*, stated that: 'The very purpose of China's foreign policy is to maintain world peace and promote common development' (Hu, 2004a). Shortly after this, in an address to mark the fiftieth anniversary of the formulation of the Five

---

[3] An editorial of the Economist argued that the US should abandon efforts to link China's most favoured nation status with China's human rights record and arms sales behaviour and that it is more fruitful to do business with China while trying to promote change in China's human rights situation and arms sales behaviour consistently but quietly (1993: 16). In another editorial, the Economist argued that 'the best hope of getting rid of dictatorship in Beijing is the West's continued economic engagement' (1996: 12).

Principles of Peaceful Coexistence,[4] Premier Wen Jiabao also stressed the importance China attaches to peace in the conduct of its foreign relations (Wen, 2004a).

In addition to peace and development, the Chinese government has stated that it wants to see the evolution of a harmonious world that tolerates diversity and provides benefits to all countries, while maintaining full regard for national sovereignty. Indeed, according to Premier Wen Jiabao, national sovereignty is the essence of national independence, constituting the collective manifestation, and reliable protection, of national interests. He has pointed out that, despite growing interdependence between states in the age of globalisation, national sovereignty remains an important and useful international institution. No state, he observes, has the right to impose its will on other states; the practice of showing disrespect for other states' sovereignty in international relations simply will not work (Wen, 2004a).

Beyond the more mechanical aspects of national sovereignty, according to the Chinese government, the international community should also recognise, and show respect for, the reality of cultural and political diversity in the world. Diversity of civilisations in the world, according to Premier Wen, is a basic feature of human society. It is also an important driving force for world progress. The numerous differences in historical tradition, religion, culture, social system, values and levels of development, he argues, are what make the world colourful and fascinating. Countries should recognise and accept such a reality. They should show greater tolerance and respect for diversity, and, he concludes, should learn to live in peace despite the differences between and among them (Wen, 2004a).

Moreover, to the Chinese government, the international economic system needs to be reformed to benefit all countries, especially the poorer and less developed ones. A major challenge to the international community, it argues, is to provide a favourable international environment for the poorer countries to catch up with the richer ones, thereby arresting the trend of further polarisation. To meet such a challenge, the international community should strive to respect poorer countries' perspectives, allowing them to pursue development in accordance to their own needs and conditions (Wen, 2004a). At the same time, developed nations should also do as much as possible to help poorer states in their efforts to develop. As Chinese Foreign Minister Tang Jiaxuan put it, the developing countries sustain greater difficulties in the age of globalisation, and the developed states 'ought to lend them a helping hand in such areas as finance, trade, technology transfer and development aid and make good on their debt relief promises' (Tang, 2002). In the eyes of the Chinese government, helping the poorer countries to develop not only benefits the latter, but also the developed countries themselves. Thus, in Tang's words: 'Assisting the developing countries today is to invest in the common destiny of all human beings' (Tang, 2002).

China has often stated that multilateralism is the right path for coping with the world's problems. According to former Vice-Premier Qian Qichen, the international community 'should opt for multilateralism and give full play to the important role of the UN. Our world is one big family. Naturally, family affairs should be handled by all its members through consultations' (Qian, 2004). In areas of multilateral cooperation, the Chinese government believes that the United Nations has an especially important role to play. Qian has observed that the United Nations is

---

[4] Mutual respect for sovereignty and territorial integrity; mutual non-aggression; non-interference in each others' internal affairs; equality and mutual benefit; peaceful coexistence.

the core of the collective security mechanism and the best venue for multilateral interchanges.... [Therefore, it] should continue to play its important role in international affairs. Facts have proved that no major international issues can be tackled by just one or two countries or a group of countries laying down the law. (Qian, 2004)

In stressing the need for multilateral cooperation, China sees this as not only an important condition for peace, but also an important requirement for development. As Chinese Foreign Minister Tang put it in 2002:

It would not be in the interest of a sound world economy if the laws of the marketplace were given a free rein to dominate globalization. The international community needs to reform the current rules in the world economy, strengthen guidance and management of the globalization process, take account of fairness and reduce risks while seeking efficiency, and steer globalization in an 'all-win' direction of coexistence. (Tang, 2002)

Whether in a multilateral or bilateral setting, the Chinese government believes that dialogue and negotiation is the preferred approach to dealing with international problems. Chinese Premier Wen reiterated this when arguing that it was time to abandon the old Cold War mentality and develop a new way of thinking on the basis of mutual trust, mutual benefit, equality and cooperation. The international community should seek security through dialogue and stability through cooperation. It should work together to fight against terrorism, the proliferation of weapons, drug smuggling and other forms of transnational crime. It should also join hands in dealing with such global problems as AIDS and ecological degradation (Wen, 2004a).

Finally, China has reaffirmed in a number of ways the firm position that it will not seek hegemony,[5] even when it becomes a global power. In his speech at the second annual meeting of the *Bo'ao Forum*, Premier Wen Jiabao announced that the world should rest assured that a dynamic, strong and prosperous China will be dedicated to world peace and development, and will never seek to gain hegemony (Wen, 2003).

Addressing Specific Concerns

In addition to clarifying its broad foreign policy objectives, the Chinese government has also tried to address the specific concerns of the outside world, and to do so on a whole range of issues. On the question of terrorism, the Chinese government has repeatedly stated that it is opposed to any resort to terrorism as a means of attaining political goals, and has called for international cooperation in the war against terrorism. At the Opening Session of the Asia Europe Meeting (ASEM) Seminar on Anti-Terrorism on 22 September 2003, China's Assistant Foreign Minister Shen Guofang argued that: 'As a victim of terrorism, China has firmly supported and actively participated in the international campaign against terrorism while pushing for the leading role of the UN in this regard'. China, he concluded, 'has

---

[5] In the Chinese vocabulary, hegemony is translated as baquan. It means the power to manipulate and control on the basis of power capabilities. It is often understood in negative terms, as opposed to power gained by virtue and example.

earnestly implemented the relevant Security Council resolutions and acceded to most counter-terrorism conventions':

> [It] has advocated vigorous regional anti-terrorism cooperation and conducted fruitful bilateral cooperation with countries concerned.... [It] has also stepped up within our competent departments the crackdown on terrorism, including measures in legislation, aviation, finance, customs and other fields with a view to preventing terrorist incidents. (Shen, 2003)

On the question of arms control and non-proliferation, the Chinese government has repeatedly stated that it is committed to participating in any international efforts undertaken in these areas. According to Vice-Foreign Minister Zhang Yesui, the Chinese government is firmly opposed to the proliferation of weapons of mass destruction and their means of delivery, pointing out that China has already set up a complete system of laws and regulations on export control. This, he concludes,

> cover[s] various kinds of sensitive technologies and items in nuclear, biological, chemical and missile fields, employed universally-practiced export control measures including the end user/use certificate, licensing system, control list and catch-all, and introduced clear-cut punishment measures against acts in breach of the relevant laws and regulations. (Tang, 2002)

As a result of these efforts, China's non-proliferation export control practice is 'basically in line with such mechanisms as MTCR [missile technology control regime] and NSG [nuclear suppliers group] and the practice of the US' (Zhang, 2004). According to government sources, China will 'complete further improvement on its export management mechanisms for biological and chemical dual-use items' in the days to come. Moreover, it 'supports the international community in taking effective measures to prevent the dangerous trend of weaponization in outer space' (Tang, 2002).

With regard to regional security mechanisms, China has voiced its full support to efforts at institutionalising regional security cooperation. For example, it has endorsed the 10+3 Cooperation Mechanism between ASEAN and China, Japan and the Republic of Korea (South Korea). It commended the mechanism for respecting 'the diversity of national conditions and the unevenness in the level of economic development of various countries' (Zhu, 2001a). China also stressed the importance of furthering 'such principles as mutual benefit, incremental progress and stressing practical results' (Zhu, 2001a). Finally, it gave 'full consideration to the interests of all parties, the small and medium-sized countries in particular, which makes it unique among regional cooperation mechanisms in the world' (Zhu, 2001a).

On the question of human rights, the Chinese government has made clear its intention to improve its human rights situation and engage in international efforts to promote human rights on a basis of equality and mutual respect. According to Vice-Foreign Minister Wang Guangya, human beings are 'the most precious among all things on earth.... To promote their development and protect all their due rights is not only the common pursuit of mankind, but also the symbol for the evolving progress of human civilization' (Wang, 2002).

The Chinese government acknowledges that China's human rights situation is by no means perfect and, in the words of Wang, it still has 'a long way to go before human rights and fundamental freedoms are fully realized' (Wang, 2002). Accordingly, the Chinese government will be 'firmly and unswervingly' committed to such a goal. The government points out that China stands ready to strengthen dialogues and exchanges with all countries, the Office of the UN High Commissioner for Human Rights (UNHCHR) and other international organisations, but to do so on the basis of equality, mutual respect, 'a positive and open attitude, [and] with a view to learning from each other and making common progress' (Wang, 2002).

On the question of international economic relations, the Chinese government has advocated 'a global partnership geared to development' (Tang, 2002). In his speech at the General Debate of the 57th Session of the United Nations General Assembly on 13 September 2002, Chinese Foreign Minister Tang Jiaxuan observed that governments, international organisations, transnational corporations, and non-governmental groups are all 'parties to the cause of development and should work together for the implementation of the UN's millennium development goals. Between the South and the North, the aid recipient countries and international aid institutions, there should be a partnership characterized by mutual benefit, equality and cooperation' (Tang, 2002).

In response to international concerns over China's rapidly growing economic influence, Chinese authorities have argued that while China's economic development may appear as a challenge to the outside world, it also offers fresh and expanding opportunities. At the Fifth China-ASEAN Summit on 6 November 2001, Former Premier Zhu Rongji reassured Southeast Asian neighbours that China's accession to the World Trade Organization (WTO) would 'provide other countries ... with [a] better environment for investment and more business opportunities' (Zhu, 2001b). Elsewhere, Wen Jiabao argued in a similar vein by stating that 'China's growth will provide enormous business opportunities for all countries and regions of the world' (Wen, 2004b). Hu Jintao, too, has observed: 'A more prosperous China is destined to offer more business opportunities to the rest of the world', adding: 'China's WTO accession has resulted in further improvement in its investment environment' (Hu, 2004b). Indeed, Hu has promised that China would:

> keep its market open by reducing access restrictions, improving our laws and regulations on foreign investment and making more services and trade available to foreign investors,... creat[ing] new ways of attracting foreign investment, and push for greater reform in government administrative system by building a predictable and more transparent management system for sectors open to foreign investment..... [At the same time it would] protect still more effectively the intellectual property rights of overseas investors and their enterprises in China and provide a better environment and more favorable terms to both foreign investment in China and China's foreign trade and economic cooperation with the other countries. (Hu, 2004b)

Concerning the issue of environmental protection, China has stated that it attaches great importance to this, and has repeatedly expressed its determination to do more in this area in future. At the World Summit on Sustainable Development on 3 September 2002, Premier Zhu said: 'We in China will, as always, energetically participate in international environment cooperation and work with all other countries in protecting the global environment and realizing sustainable development throughout the world' (Zhu, 2002).

China also has a number of more immediate localised concerns, but ones which potentially have considerable implications for the region and, indeed, for the world as a whole. One of these is the Korean nuclear crisis. In this, the Chinese government has repeatedly stated that it is opposed to nuclearisation of the Korean Peninsula and urges for peaceful resolution of the crisis. Premier Wen has stated that China advocates a nuclear-free Peninsula and a peaceful solution of the Democratic People's Republic of Korea (DPRK) nuclear issue with diplomatic means, to maintain peace and stability of the Peninsula (Permanent Mission of the PRC to the UN, 2003).

The other relates to the problem of Taiwan and reunification. The Chinese government has made it clear that even though the Taiwan problem is a domestic issue, it will take into account other countries' concerns and interests and make greater efforts to seek a peaceful resolution. In his visit to the US, Premier Wen told President Bush that China would make the greatest efforts with utmost sincerity to achieve the peaceful reunification of the motherland (Permanent Mission of the PRC to the UN, 2003). In addition to this, Chinese leaders have made numerous comments to this effect on various occasions.

Words and Deeds

The Chinese government understands that its efforts to formulate, clarify and disseminate increasingly sophisticated policies are not enough in themselves sufficient to allay the concerns and fears of the outside world. It needs to follow these up with concrete actions. Accordingly, it has adopted a series of measures to back up its rhetoric. To begin with, China has assumed many legally binding international responsibilities by subscribing to international agreements and covenants. On the question of arms control and non-proliferation, for example, it is a party of:

- Protocol for the Prohibition of the Use in War of Asphyxiating, Poisonous or Other Gases, and of Bacteriological Methods of Warfare
- Convention on Prohibition or Restriction on the Use of Certain Conventional Weapons Which May Be Deemed to Be Excessively Injurious or to Have Indiscriminate Effects
- Antarctic Treaty
- Treaty on Principles Governing the Activities of States in the Exploration and Use of Outer Space
- Convention on the Prohibition of the Development, Production and Stockpiling of Bacteriological (Biological) and Toxin Weapons and on Their Destruction
- Treaty on the Prohibition of the Emplacement of Nuclear Weapons and Other Weapons of Mass Destruction on the Seabed and the Ocean Floor and in the Subsoil Thereof
- Treaty on the Non-Proliferation of Nuclear Weapons
- Convention on the Prohibition of the Development, Production, Stockpiling and Use of Chemical Weapons and on Their Destruction (Information Office of the State Council of the PRC, 1995).

This is also the case on other issues such as environment, human rights and trade.

Second, China has increased its levels of support for multilateral cooperation, both at regional and global levels. In recent years, it has increased markedly its financial contribution to the UN, as well as its participation in various UN peacekeeping operations.[6] It has also played an active role in regional security mechanisms, including official dialogues such as the ASEAN Regional Forum and many second-track security dialogues such as the Shanghai Cooperation Organization (SCO), Conference on Interaction and Confidence-Building Measures in Asia (CICA), Council on Security Cooperation in the Asia-Pacific Region (CSCAP), Northeast Asia Cooperation Dialogue (NEACD). It has attached much importance to playing such a role (Informational Office of the State Council of the PRC, 2002).

Third, China made significant concessions to join the World Trade Organization (WTO) and has made substantial efforts to fulfil its commitments, despite domestic political resistance to some of the dimensions of its membership of this body. It has *inter alia* repealed, revised or enacted more than a thousand laws, regulations and other administrative measures in its efforts to comply WTO requirements (United States Trade Representative, 2004: 3). It has lowered its trade tariffs, reduced thresholds for foreign investment in previously restricted sectors, and given access to foreign presence in financial, legal and other sectors that had previously been closed to foreign involvement. Furthermore, it has actively promoted the establishment of free economic areas with ASEAN countries, and free trade agreements with Australia and other countries.

Fourth, China has made significant efforts to improve security relations with its neighbours. It has concluded border agreements with a number of countries with which it shares borders, including Russia, Kazakhstan, Tajikistan, Kyrgyzstan and Vietnam. It has also stepped up negotiations over borders with India, a country with which it has had tense relations for some time. China has also advocated peaceful resolution of the disputes over maritime borders between itself and other countries in the region, such as disputes with Vietnam, the Philippines, Malaysia and Brunei over the ownership of the Spratley Islands in the South China Sea, and disputes with Japan over Diaoyu Island and the East China Sea. And it is a principal founding member of the Shanghai Cooperation Organization and has tried to work together with Russia and Kazakhstan, Tajikistan, Kyrgyzstan and Uzbekistan to promote broad spheres of cooperation between these states, such as joint efforts to fight against terrorism, separatism and extremism, as well as maintaining regional stability and promoting economic relations among member states.

Finally, China has tried to promote peaceful settlement of the Korean nuclear crisis. Ever since the recent round of tension over the alleged North Korean nuclear program escalated, the Chinese government has tried to bring the concerned parties together and push for a peaceful settlement of the problem. It conducted shuttle diplomacy between Washington, Pyongyang, Seoul, Moscow and other capitals. Furthermore, it has successively hosted a three-party dialogue and several rounds of six party talks.

---

[6] 'China's representative said his country's assessment for 2004-2006 would increase by 35.18 per cent over the last period.... Not only had China fulfilled its financial obligations to the Organization, but as a permanent member of the Security Council it had also assumed additional financial obligations towards peacekeeping' (UN Press Release GA/AB/3576, 2003).

INTERESTS, PRIORITIES AND PERCEPTIONS: AN EXPLANATION

In describing the dimensions of China's 'policy of assurance', one finds that three factors play an especially important role in shaping the latter: (1) China's interests and priorities; (2) China's growing stake in peace and prosperity of the world; and (3) evolution in China's view of its relations with the rest of the world.

China's Interests and Priorities

China's interests and priorities have made the adoption of the 'policy of assurance' not just a choice, but a necessity. As a developing country undergoing drastic social, political and economic transformations, China is confronted by numerous domestic challenges, ranging from uneven economic development, to the poor management of state-owned enterprises; from growing social inequality, to a worsening ecological environment; and from official corruption, to human rights abuses. Some of its main priorities have been, as discussed earlier, to find ways to devote both effort and resources to the business of dealing with these complex challenges. In order to succeed in these areas, and in the process transform China into a modern, humane and harmonious state, the Chinese government needs all the time, energy and resources it can muster. For these reasons alone, it badly needs the perpetuation of a peaceful, stable international environment.

However, the growing international uneasiness and fear about the rise of China represents a potential problem. If left unaddressed, this unease and fear is likely to spread, and lend itself to manipulation by forces hostile to China.[7] This could lead to an elaboration of defensive, and perhaps even the projection of aggressive, policies by foreign governments against China. The unfolding of such policy lines would tend to undermine China's international environment. To avoid this, the Chinese government must continue to do all in its power to ease the fears of the international community.

China's Political and Economic Integration with the Outside World

In the same way that China's interests and priorities have made the adoption of the 'policy of assurance' necessary, China's political and economic integration into the outside world has helped to define the ways in which it reassures the outside world. Following China's rapprochement with the United States in the early 1970s, China established diplomatic relations with most countries in the world and became an active member of most important international governmental organisations. In the process, and especially after the launching of the Open Policy in 1979, China's economic relations with the outside world have increased rapidly. The ever-deepening political and economic linkages between China and the outside world have provided China with enhanced channels via which it can express its views, defend its legitimate interests, and promote the reform of the existing international order. With time, China has also developed the expertise and experience necessary to take

---

[7] Such as the so-called 'Blue Team', a group of people inside and outside the official establishment in Washington who believe that China is a threat and the US should devote its resources to contain China (Branegan, 2001).

advantage of the opportunities afforded by its membership in a variety of international institutions. This has allowed it to defend and facilitate its interests and aspirations. The latter have included efforts to reform existing rules and formulate new rules for proper international behaviour. Growing economic relations between China and other countries have given China an ever-larger stake in international stability and prosperity. This has in great measure—and most usefully—reduced the distrust and hostility China harboured towards aspects of the international order, and has in the process provided China with an enhanced sense of identity.

All this has, in turn, done much to change the nature of China's relations with the outside world. It has enabled China to reassure the outside world. The task at hand, however, is to prevent these gains from being reversed or tarnished by growing suspicions and fears of what China might do with its enhanced place in the world.

Evolution in China's View of its Relations with the Outside World

China's changing perceptions of its relations with the outside world has, it has been argued above, enhanced the way it can reassure the outside world. As China's interactions with the rest of the world have increased, China's view of international relations has undergone three important changes: (1) from viewing international relations in ideological (that is, Marxist or communist) terms to viewing them in more conventional terms; (2) from viewing international relations as a zero-sum game to a positive-sum game; and (3) from a position of suspicion and hostility toward the international system, to one with which China identifies. These attitudinal changes have, in turn, led to China's conceptualisation of its relations with the outside world, and its redefinition of the objectives of its foreign policy in a way that is reassuring to the international community.

In sum, China's interests and priorities, China's integration with the outside world and China's changing perceptions of its relations with the outside world, have made it necessary for China to take the previously discussed measures to assure the outside world of its benign intentions, but in so doing has also helped to shape positively the way in which China engages in the sphere of international cooperation.

PROSPECTS

Will the Chinese government adhere to the 'policy of assurance' discussed in this essay? Analysis of the factors shaping this policy shows that it is likely. To begin with, at least for the foreseeable future, China will continue to face considerable—and pressing—problems at home, so the goal of maintaining a peaceful international environment is likely to remain its key foreign policy objective. Second, as China's integration with the outside world deepens, its identification with the existing international system is likely to grow stronger. This will in turn continue to shape the way it reassures the outside world of its intent and sense of responsibility. Finally, short of drastic changes in China's relations with the outside world, China is likely to continue to view these in a non-zero sum way, aligning its interests to, and advocating policies largely consistent with, those of the international community.

REFERENCES

Bernstein, Richard and Ross H. Munro (1997) 'The Coming Conflict With America'. *Foreign Affairs*, March/April.

Branegan, J. (2001) 'The Hardliners: A 'Blue Team' Blocks China'. *Time*, 16 April.

Brown, Lester (1994) 'Who Will Feed China?' *World Watch*, 7(5).

Chanda, Nayan (1996) 'No Cash-Carrier: France May Be Buckling on Chinese Arms Embargo'. *Far Eastern Economic Review*, 10 October.

Cox Report (1999) Select Committee, United States House of Representatives, *U.S. National Security and Military/Commercial Concerns with the People's Republic of China*, Chapter 11, Washington: U.S. Government Printing Office.

Economist (1992) 'The Titan Stirs: The Chinese Economy'. 28 November: 3-18.

———— (1993) 'Gripped By China'. 27 November.

———— (1996) 'Changing China'. 23 March.

Far Eastern Economic Review (1992) 'A New China'. 29 October.

Friedman, Edward (1997) 'Chinese Nationalism, Taiwan Autonomy and the Prospects of a Larger War'. *Journal of Contemporary China*, March.

Hu, Jintao (2004a) *China's Development is an Opportunity for Asia*, 27 April. *http://www.chinataiwan.org/web/webportal/W5023952/A2175.html*

———— (2004b) *Advancing Win-Win Cooperation for Sustainable Development: Speech by President Hu Jintao of China At the APEC CEO Summit*, 19 November, *http://www.fmprc.gov.cn/eng/wjdt/zyjh/t172475.htm*

Information Office of the State Council of the PRC (1995) *China: Arms Control and Disarmament*, November, http://www.china.org.cn/e-white/army/a-7.htm

———— (2002) *China's National Defense in 2002*, Beijing, December, *http://www.china.org.cn/e-white/20021209/VI.htm#1*

Jiang, Zemin (2002) *Quanmian jianshe xiaokang shehui: kaichuang zhongguo tese shehuizhuyi shiye xin jumian*, Beijing: Renmin Publishing House.

Krauthammer, Charles (1995) 'Why Must We Contain China?' *Times*, 31 July.

Kristof, Nicholas D. (1993) 'The Rise of China'. *Foreign Affairs*, November/December.

Permanent Mission of the PRC to the UN, *Premier Wen Jiabao Holds Talks with the US President Bush*, 10 December 2003, *http://www.china-un.org/eng/xw/t56088.htm*

Qian, Qichen (2004) *Multilateralism, the Way to Respond to Threats and Challenges*, Statement by H.E. Mr. Qian Qichen, Former Vice-Premier of China at the New Delhi Conference, 2 July, *http://www.fmprc.gov.cn/eng/wjdt/zyjh/t142393.htm*

Shen, Guofang (2003) Speech by H. E. Mr. Shen Guofang, Assistant Foreign Minister of China, at the Opening Session of ASEM Seminar on Anti-Terrorism, 22 September, *http://www.fmprc.gov.cn/eng/wjdt/zyjh/t26278.htm*

Tang, Jiaxuan (2002) Statement by H.E. Tang Jiaxuan, Minister of Foreign Affairs of the People's Republic of China, and Head of the Chinese Delegation, at the General Debate of the 57th Session of the United Nations General Assembly, 13 September, *http://www.fmprc.gov.cn/eng/wjdt/zyjh/t25092.htm*

UN Press Release GA/AB/3576 (2003) *Importance of Timely, Full Payment of UN Contributions, 'Capacity to Pay' Principle Reaffirmed, as Fifth Committee Takes Up*

Scale of Assessments, Fifty-eight General Assembly Meeting- Fifth Meeting (AM), 14 October, *http://www.un.org/News/Press/docs/2003/gaab3576.doc.htm*

United States Trade Representative (2004) *2004 Report to Congress on China's WTO Compliance, http://www.cecc.gov/pages/virtualAcad/commercial/USTR.china.2004.pdf? PHPSESSID=fdbf190484029bff1b8d5fb0881d1c2db*

Wang, Guangya (2002) *Make Joint Efforts Towards a Healthy Development of the Cause of Human Rights*, Statement at the 58th Session of the United Nations Commission on Human Rights, Geneva, 2 April, *http://www.fmprc.gov.cn/eng/wjdt/zyjh/t25072.htm*

Wen, Jiabao (2003) *Yong bu chengba de zhongguo jiang wei yazhou zhenxing zuochu xin gongxian* (*The China That Never Seeks Hegemony Will Make New Contributions to the Rise of Asia*), 2 November, *http://finance.sina.com.cn/g/20031102/1129501516.shtml*

———— (2004a) *Hongyang wu xiang yuanze: cujin heping fazhan* (*Uphold Five Principles and Promote Peace and Development*), 28 June, *http://www.fmprc.gov.cn/chn /wjdt/zyjh/t140781.htm*

———— (2004b) *Strengthening Partnership Through Increased Dialogue and Cooperation: Speech at the Fifth Asia-Europe Meeting*, 9 October, *http://www.fmprc.gov.cn/eng /wjdt/zyjh/t164329.htm*

Zhang, Yesui (2004) *Speech by Vice Foreign Minister Zhang Yesui at the Fifth China-US Conference on Arms Control, Disarmament and Non-Proliferation*, 20 July, *http://www.fmprc.gov.cn/eng/wjdt/zyjh/t143538.htm*

Zhu, Rongji (2002) 'Steadfastly Take the Road of Sustainable Development'. Speech by H.E. Mr. Zhu Rongji, Premier of the State Council of the People's Republic of China, at the World Summit on Sustainable Development, 3 September, *http://www.fmprc.gov.cn/eng /wjdt/zyjh/t25091.htm*

———— (2001a) *Premier Zhu Rongji Attended the 5th Leaders' Meeting between the Association of Southeast Asian Nations (ASEAN) and China, Japan and the Republic of Korea and Issued A Speech*, 5 November, http://www.fmprc.gov.cn/eng/wjdt /zyjh/t25045.htm

———— (2001b) 'Working Together to Create a New Phase of China-ASEAN Cooperation'. Address by Premier Zhu Rongji at 5th China-ASEAN Summit, 6 November, *http://www.fmprc.gov.cn/eng/wjdt/zyjh/t25046.htm*

In: China in Focus Economic, Political and Educational Issues
Editor: Ernest P. Nolan, pp. 29-46

ISBN 1-60021-543-8
© 2007 Nova Science Publishers, Inc.

Chapter 3

WHY DOES CHINA SUCCEED IN ATTRACTING AND UTILIZING FOREIGN DIRECT INVESTMENT?

*Kevin H. Zhang**

Department of Economics, Illinois State University
Normal, IL, USA

ABSTRACT

China has emerged as the most dynamic FDI-host country, and the contributions of FDI to the Chinese economy have burgeoned in ways that no one anticipated. Although considerable studies on the role of FDI in Chinese economy have appeared in recent years, a systematic treatment of the issue is still limited. This study first identifies several features of FDI in China, such as the export-oriented FDI strategy and the massive predominance of FDI from Hong Kong. After providing an analytical framework about determinants of FDI, its economic impact, and host countries' bargaining power, the paper explores factors behind China's success in attracting FDI and utilizing it to foster economic growth. These factors include China's huge country-size, effective FDI strategies, overseas Chinese investors, and a strong central government.

Keywords: Foreign direct investment (FDI), Economic growth, and FDI policy
JEL Code: F21, F23, and O53.

China has emerged as the most dynamic host country of foreign direct investment (FDI). In the two decades since economic reforms were initiated in 1978, China has become the largest recipient of FDI in the developing world and globally the second largest (next to only the US) since 1993.[1] FDI flows were over $37 billion in 1995 alone, constituting 35% of total FDI into all developing countries in that year. By the end of 2001, the cumulated FDI received in China reached as much as $393 billion (SSB, 2002).

---

* Phone: (309) 438-8928, Fax: (309) 438-5228, Email: khzhang@ilstu.edu
[1] It is estimated based on the data of the first eight months in 2002 that China would be the largest recipient of FDI in the world in 2002 with $50 billion of inflows (UNCTAD, 2002).

The contributions of inward FDI to the Chinese economy have burgeoned in ways that no one anticipated. The important role of FDI in Chinese economy might be suggested from the following indications. FDI inflows in 1995 constituted 26% of gross fixed capital formation. The foreign-invested firms employed 18 millions Chinese by the end of 1996, constituting 18% of total non-agricultural labor force (UNCTAD, 1999). In 1997, 19% of total gross industrial output was produced by the foreign affiliates. By 2001 half of China's exports is created by foreign-invested firms (SSB, 2002).

China's liberalized policy toward FDI inflows to promote exports - in many respects - is similar to strategies pursued by other developing countries as they move away from restricting foreign capital toward more open, externally oriented development strategies. China's real distinctions are its huge country size, massive overseas Chinese, and its strong government. Thus China's FDI boom and the rapid growth of GDP at annual rate of 9.5% in 1978-2001 raise a host of interesting questions. What in hell attracts multinational corporations to China? How does China take its advantage in promoting economic growth through FDI? How does FDI affect the Chinese economy, and is it really as great as it appears? What FDI strategy should China take after its access to the World Trade Organization (WTO) in December 2001? This paper addresses these questions; based on the premise that understanding China's success in promoting growth through FDI requires attention on China's comparative advantages and disadvantages from the international perspectives.

The study has interesting policy implications to developing countries as well as China. Unlike the widely accepted view of the export-led growth, the position on the FDI-growth nexus has been extremely divergent. In addition to capital formation, export promotion, and employment expansion, the spillover efficiency and technology transfer are emphasized as key contributions of FDI to host economies in recent theoretical studies. But no countries except China have been found to be successful in fostering growth through FDI. FDI is more important in the Chinese economy than in most other developing countries in terms of its magnitude and its role in generating exports. Is China's experience unique? Or may China's experiences suggest some lessons for other developing countries?

The basic message of the paper is as follows. (a) China's achievement in attracting and utilizing FDI is real, but it faces severe challenges due to its accession to the World Trade Organization in the near future. (b) What most attract foreign investors are China's huge market, liberal FDI regime, and cheap resources (labor, land, and raw materials). More important, Hong Kong and Taiwan (HKT) and overseas Chinese investors contribute in a large part to the FDI boom. (c) The gains from FDI concentrate on expanding exports and spillovers effects (in diffusing technology and stimulating reforms toward market systems), in addition to formatting capital, augmenting employment, and training labor force. (d) The overall success in utilizing FDI is a result of China's effective FDI strategy, strong government, and contributive HKT investments, in addition to China's growing bargaining power due to outstanding performance in economic growth.

The rest of the paper begins with stylized facts of FDI in China, which highlight important characteristics of multinational firms in China. The second section provides an analytical framework of FDI location determinations, the potential gains and costs from FDI, and the bargaining power of host governments. Section three explores factors that determine the FDI boom and its contributions to Chinese economy. The last section discusses challenges China will face in the new setup of the WTO and summarizes conclusions.

1. FDI IN CHINA: 1979-2002

Several major characteristics of FDI in China may be identified as follows.

(1) FDI Boom in the 1990s

Table 1 shows annual flows and cumulative amount of FDI over 1979-2002. The most impressive character of the time trend is the sharp FDI rise in the 1990s in contrast with the moderate growth in the 1980s. Although a surge of interest among foreign investors in China emerged after 1979, large FDI inflows did not occur in the initial period because of the poor infrastructure and the lack of experience in dealing with foreign investors. The period of 1984-91 saw a steady growth and relatively large amount, due in part to the extension of the special economic zones from four to another fourteen cities in 1984, and FDI incentives introduced in 1986.

Table 1. FDI Flows in China and China's Position in Developing Countries and in the World: 1979-99 (in Millions of US Dollars and Percentages)

Year	FDI Flows (millions of US$)	Accumulated FDI (millions of US$)	Share of FDI Flows in Developing Countries (%)	Share of FDI Flows in the World (%)
1979-83	1802	1802	11.48	3.88
1984	1258	3060	7.67	2.33
1985	1661	4721	13.31	3.26
1986	1874	6595	15.15	2.46
1987	2314	8909	15.75	1.89
1988	3194	12103	14.33	2.12
1989	3392	15495	12.92	1.78
1990	3487	18982	11.64	1.74
1991	4366	23348	10.72	2.83
1992	11007	34355	22.51	6.61
1993	27515	61870	34.91	12.59
1994	33767	95637	33.37	13.93
1995	37521	133158	35.32	11.40
1996	41725	174883	30.83	12.49
1997	45257	220140	26.23	10.83
1998	45463	265603	27.40	7.06
1999	40319	305922	19.42	4.66
2000	40715	346637	16.95	3.20
2001	46846	393483	20.82	6.16
2002	50000	443483	25.00	12.00

Notes: The shares of FDI flows in developing countries and in the world in 1983 are calculated based on the accumulated FDI in China over 1979-83. The figures in 2002 are estimated based on FDI flows in the first eight months of 2002

Sources: *China Statistics Yearbook 2002* (SSB, 2002), *International Financial Statistics Yearbook* (IMF, various years from 1979 to 2001), and *World Investment Report* (UNCTAD, various years from 1992-2002)

In 1992 China seemed to reach its critical threshold of attracting FDI on a large scale. The single-year FDI flow in 1993 ($26 billion) exceeded the cumulative flows ($23 billion) of thirteen years (1979-91). FDI fell in 1999 and 2000 due to the Asian financial crisis, but soon recovered in 2001. The estimated FDI flows in 2002 are no less than $500 billion as China became more open to FDI after entry of WTO in 2001. The cumulative FDI flows would thus exceed $440 billion at the end of 2002.[2]

China's FDI boom seems not merely a part of the global expansion of multinationals. Table 1 shows China's position in the world as well as all developing countries during the period 1979-2002. China's FDI as shares in both developing countries and the world experience a significant rise over time, particularly in the 1990s, though slight falls in the late 1990s. This fact suggests that location factors play a critical role in China's FDI boom, and China indeed has unique advantages over other potential host countries in attracting foreign investors (Zhang, 2001b and 2001c).

(2) Export-Oriented FDI Strategy

China's opening to FDI was symbolized by the promulgation of the "Chinese-Foreign Joint Venture Law" on July 1 of 1979. While permitting entry of foreign firms, the law did not create a legal framework that allows some currency convertibility and reduces red tape. In 1986, new provisions including preferential tax policies were established to encourage foreign investment. However, FDI was invited exclusively for exports except offshore oil exploration and the real estate sector. Under such an export-promotion FDI regime, many export-processing and export-assembling plants (mainly from Hong Kong and Taiwan) were established in the special economic zones, the open coastal cities, and the economic and technological development zones.[3] At the same time, the foreign investors that aim at domestic markets encountered many difficulties and their investment had been relatively small (Zhang, 2000b).[4]

The "export-promotion" FDI regime did not change much until 1992, when China began to open gradually its domestic market to multinational firms in certain sectors, including telecommunication, transportation, banking, and insurance. The gradual shift from the "export-promotion" to the "technology-promotion" FDI regime was largely due to pressures from the U.S. and West European countries that had increasing trade deficits with China due to China's export boom through FDI. Moreover, China realized that technology transfers from industrial countries might be possible only as the market-oriented FDI is allowed.

---

[2] FDI rose in the early 1990s in part because of the "round-trip" capital of Chinese origin, which is carried by subsidiaries based in Hong Kong but owned by Chinese central or local governments to take advantage of preferential treatments under the name of foreign capital. While no accurate figures for this type of FDI are available, it is estimated that they are not large relative to total FDI from Hong Kong (UNCTAD, 1996).

[3] This strategy was motivated by the success of the export-led-growth strategy adopted in Japan and the four tigers (Hong Kong, Korea, Singapore, and Taiwan). FDI has been regarded as a powerful engine of exports, although FDI was also expected to make contribution in capital formation and technology transfers (Zhang and Song, 2000).

[4] A major difficulty facing foreign investors, for example, was how to reconvert their investment and repatriate their earnings. Firms with exported-oriented FDI are able directly to earn foreign exchange and have been most successful in avoiding serious foreign exchange deficits. However, firms with market-oriented FDI are unable to earn sufficient foreign exchange to cover their foreign exchange obligation, including distribution of profits to investors.

(3) Hong Kong and Overseas Chinese as a Dominant FDI Source

Considering that over 90% of global FDI originates from industrial countries (UNCTAD, 1996 and 2002), it is striking that the majority of FDI in China did not come from industrial countries, but was received from Hong Kong and the overseas Chinese in Asia, which control large part of economic activities in Indonesia, Malaysia, Singapore, and Thailand.[5] Table 2 shows to 15 origins of FDI into China in the period 1979-99. FDI sources of Asian developing economies include Hong Kong (ranked as the first), Taiwan (4th), Singapore (5th), South Korea (7th), Macao (10th), and Thailand (14th), which account for 71% of the FDI flows in China. With the share of 19%, the United States (2nd), Japan (3rd), and European Union together played a minor role.[6] The unique pattern of FDI sources is a result of China's export-oriented strategy and special links of Hong Kong, Taiwan, overseas Chinese in Asia with China in culture and history (Zhang, 2003).

(4) Distinctive Features of FDI Projects: Technology, Sectors, and Project Size

The predominant share of the FDI from Asian developing economies raises the question about their competitive edge in the world markets for investment, because Hong Kong and Asian developing-country firms appear to lack ownership advantages such as advanced proprietary technology and established brand names. It seems that the competitive edge of Hong Kong, Taiwan, and Singapore rests primarily on managerial and marketing advantages in making and selling light consumer goods such as textiles, garments, toys, light electronics, which are their main export products (USCBC, 1991; Zhang, 2000b). Overall, their investment is small by international standards (see Table 2), and specializes in labor-intensive, low technology activities. Their products tend to be undifferentiated and sold mainly on the basis of price rather than distinct design or performance characteristics (Wells, 1993).

---

[5] Although Hong Kong was returned to China on July 1, 1997 from the UK, its capital flows into China are still viewed as "foreign" investment under the policy of "one country and two systems." It should be noted that a part of the reported Hong Kong FDI is actually either Western industrial countries' investment through their subsidiaries based in Hong Kong, or Taiwanese investment under the name of Hong Kong for political reasons. The latter was especially true before 1992 when Taiwanese government permitted officially FDI into China. Moreover, in the early 1990s a small part of the reported Hong Kong FDI was carried out by subsidiaries located in Hong Kong but owned by Chinese central or local governments to take advantage of preferential treatment under the name of FDI (UNCTAD, 1996).

[6] The FDI from the U.S., Japan, and West Europe are the dominant sources for many developing countries. In comparison with other host countries, Wei (1995) found that China attracted less FDI from major investing countries in terms of both flows and stock measurements. He pointed out, for example, that Chinese hosting of US investment falls short of its "potential" by almost 89%.

Table 2. Top 15 Investors in China by Realized FDI: 1979-1999

Sources	Rank	Realized FDI		Contracted FDI		Projects of FDI	
		Amount	Share	Amount	Share (%)	Number	Share
Hong Kong	1	154794	50.32	310957	50.67	184824	54.12
USA	2	25648	8.34	52610	8.57	28702	8.40
Japan	3	24886	8.09	35134	5.72	18769	5.50
Taiwan	4	23863	7.76	43774	7.13	43516	12.74
Singapore	5	14820	4.82	33349	5.43	8500	2.49
Virgin Islands	6	9395	3.05	20405	3.32	2031	0.59
South Korea	7	8837	2.87	16320	2.66	12726	3.73
UK	8	7584	2.47	16141	2.63	2554	0.75
Germany	9	4811	1.56	9335	1.52	2128	0.62
Macao	10	3636	1.18	9309	1.52	6418	1.88
France	11	3582	1.16	5113	0.83	1583	0.46
Netherlands	12	2201	0.72	4070	0.66	722	0.21
Canada	13	2049	0.67	7065	1.15	4351	1.27
Malaysia	14	2002	0.65	4547	0.74	1913	0.56
Australia	15	1804	0.59	5796	0.94	3864	1.13
Others		17716	5.76	39792	6.48	18937	5.54
Total		307631	100.00	613717	100.00	341538	100.00

Notes: Amount of realized and contracted FDI is in millions of US dollars. Investing economies are ordered by realized FDI

Sources: Computed from *Statistics on FDI in China* (MOFETEC, 2000)

(5) Uneven Regional Distribution within China

While FDI is located in every corner of China, it tends to be highly concentrated in southern coastal provinces and major metropolitan cities, which account for about 86% of total FDI in China (Table 3).

In particular, the top three provinces (Guangdong, Jiangsu, and Fujian) attracted half of the total FDI in China. The uneven regional distribution of FDI in China is a result of a variety of factors, including the FDI policies and regional differences in investment environments, particularly the "hometown connection" of Asian investors. The destinations of the investments from Asian developing economies reflect ethnic factors, and the "Chinese connection" factor is pervasive. Most overseas Chinese originally come from coastal areas (Guangdong and Fujian Provinces in particular) that have received a huge share (67%) of total Asian FDI (Zhang, 2001b). The Western investors concern themselves primarily with market access. Metropolitan cities (such as Beijing, Tianjin, and Shanghai) and coastal areas were the heavily favored sites relative to inland regions (Zhang, 2000b; Hou and Zhang, 2001). Table 3 also indicates the rising share of FDI in inland areas over time, since the favorable policies toward FDI were extended from coastal to the inland regions.

Table 3. Regional Distribution of FDI within China: 1979-99

Provinces	1979-1999		1986-1991		1992-1997	
	Amount	Share (%)	Amount	Share (%)	Amount	Share (%)
Coastal Areas	26314613	85.54	14618	92.00	174079	87.47
Guangdong	8691119	28.25	6596	41.53	55016	27.64
Jiangsu	3730497	12.13	640	4.03	24007	12.06
Fujian	3007847	9.78	1506	9.48	20316	10.21
Shanghai	2517965	8.19	1448	9.11	18254	9.17
Shandong	1813791	5.90	544	3.42	13369	6.72
Beijing	1271475	4.13	1438	9.05	7010	3.52
Tianjin	1210860	3.94	380	2.39	7972	4.02
Others	4071059	13.23	2066	12.99	28135	14.14
Inland Areas	4448458	14.46	1269	8.00	24935	12.53
Total	30763071	100.00	15887	100.00	199014	100.00

Notes: Amount of realized and contracted FDI is in millions of US dollars. The coastal areas consist of 12 provinces. The others in coastal areas include Tianjin, Hebei, Liaoning, Shandong, Zhejiang, Hainan, and Guangxi. The inland areas include 18 provinces as follows: Jinlin, Heilongjiang, Inner Mongolia, Shanxi, Anhui, Jianxi, Henan, Hubei, Hunan, Sichuan, Guizhou, Yunan, Tibet, Shaanxi, Gansu, Qinghai, Ningxia, and Xingjiang

Sources: Computed from *Statistics on FDI in China* (MOFETEC, 2000). Data for 1986-1997 are taken from *China Regional Economy* (SSB, 1996) and *China Statistical Yearbook* (SSB, 1997 and 1998)

2. AN ANALYTICAL FRAMEWORK

(1) Location Determinants of FDI

Based on multinational firms' motives, technology, and production structure, it is convenient to distinguish between vertical (export-oriented) and horizontal (market-oriented) FDI. The vertical FDI, motivated by foreign cheap labor, fragments the production process across countries by production stages based on labor intensities, while horizontal FDI that are induced by foreign market access build plants in multiple countries to serve local markets (Markusen et al., 1996, Zhang, 2000a). In general, the vertical multinationals involve standardized technologies and locate abroad at least one stage of production in which unskilled labor is used intensively. The vertical FDI thus is more likely to be attracted to host countries with low wages relative to source countries. Trade costs (tariffs and transportation costs) would reduce investment to the extent that a subsidiary of the vertical multinationals in the host country would import equipment or intermediate products from its parent country (Zhang and Markusen, 1999). Due to its "footloose" feature, this type of FDI is also attracted to countries that offer favorable incentives such as tax holiday.

The horizontal multinational builds up similar production facilities abroad for scale economies to gain an access to foreign markets. To compete with local producers, the horizontal multinationals must possess certain superior technology that is not grasped by a host country. The host market size is expected to play a key role in attracting this type of FDI because the larger market size offers greater opportunities to realize effectively economies of scale (Markusen, 1984). As a country's market grows to a critical threshold level, foreign firms would start investing and increase sharply their investment. Since this type of FDI involves advanced technology, it generally has higher requirements for human capital and infrastructure in the host country. The substitute relationship between the horizontal FDI and exports for a multinational to serve the foreign market implies that import restrictions in the market might induce more horizontal FDI (the "tariff jumping" hypothesis).

(2) Economic Impact of FDI on Host countries

Few areas in the economics of development arouse so much controversy and are subject to such varying interpretations as the issue of the benefits and costs of FDI. Theoretically, one point of view suggests that inward FDI is likely to detrimental to the host economic growth because, for example, (a) FDI might lower domestic savings and investment and lead to shrinking of indigenous industries; (b) FDI may reduce a host country's welfare when multinational firms manipulate market power and transfer pricing; (c) FDI may create enclave economies within a host country, widen income gap, and bias the host economy toward an inappropriate technology and product mix.[7] At the other extreme, one could argue that FDI is likely to be an engine of host economic growth. The arguments on which this point of view is based include, beside others, that (a) inward FDI may enhance capital formation and employment augmentation; (b) FDI may promote manufacturing exports; (c) By its very nature, FDI may bring into host economies special resources such as management know-how, skilled labor access to international production networks and established brand names; and more important, (d) FDI may results in technology transfers and spillover effects.[8]. The arguments both for and against FDI are still far from being settled theoretically and empirically, and may never be as they ultimately reflect important differences in value judgments and political perceptions about desirable development strategies.

(3) Bargaining Power of Host-Country Governments

Studies of host country attempts to influence and control FDI suggest that such the control may depend on its bargaining power and the possibilities for increasing it. A country's ability to bargain with multinationals, in turn, depends in large part on attributes of the industries with FDI and the nature of the host country. Three aspects of industrial structure may be crucial in determining the bargaining power of a host country: (a) the extent of competition in the industry; (b) the changeableness of the technology; and (c) the importance

---

[7] For more discussions of the issue, see surveys by Helleiner (1989) and Caves (1996).
[8] It has been recognized that the positive externality or spillover effects of FDI in host economies may be more critical than its direct impact mentioned above (UNCTAD, 1992). The spillover efficiency occurs when advanced technologies and managerial skills embodied in FDI are transmitted to domestic plants simply because of the presence of multinational firms. The technology and productivity of local firms may improve as FDI creates backward and forward linkages and foreign firms provide technical assistance to their local suppliers and customers. The competitive pressure exerted by the foreign affiliates may also force local firms to operate more efficiently and introduce new technologies earlier than what would otherwise have been the case.

of marketing and product differentiation (Moran, 1985). Bargaining power for the host country is high relative to the multinational corporations (MNC) if competition is high, if technology is stable, and if marketing is of little importance. The nature of the host country has large influences on its bargaining power as well. Large market, strong government, If a developing country is large and is seen as an important market for the multinational, if it would be costly for the multinational to relocate and if the government is well informed about the multinational's costs, then the country's bargaining position will be relatively strong. It may be able to get away with relatively high taxes on the MNC's profits and tight regulation of its behavior (e.g. its employment practices and its care for the environment). If, however, the country is economically weak and the MNC is footloose, then the deal it can negotiate is unlikely to be very favorable.

Underlying standard bargaining models for FDI is the view that FDI is not a zero-sum proposition. Rather, despite the myriad potential conflicts between partners, there is a range of conditions within which the interests of a host country and a foreign investor may converge to generate an outcome that makes each side better off.

3. WHY CHINA SUCCEEDS IN ATTRACTING AND UTILIZING FDI?

3.1. Factors behind China's FDI Boom

Many observers view China's success in attracting FDI as a puzzle by noting its obvious disadvantages relative to other host countries (Kamath, 1990; Lardy, 1994; Perkins, 1994): (a) China had little legal security so that property rights were not well-defined; (b) China's currency was not convertible so that foreign investors have no insured sources of hard-currency earnings; (c) Corruption in China has been severe and growing so that foreign investors incur additional costs. These negative influences, however, have been offset by China's huge market, large FDI flows from HKT and other overseas Chinese, and the liberalized FDI regime.

(1)Huge Markets

The prospect that China would open what foreign investors had long believed to be its huge potential domestic market made China a highly desirable location for new investment, and hence was an extremely strong positive lure for multinationals.[9] The "market of one billion" was the primary reason why most foreign investors were interested in China, although investors from Hong Kong and other Asian developing economies were also attracted by the Chinese cheap labor. It is the lure of one billion customers that can offset many worries.

The advantage of market size has been enhanced by China's rapid economic growth in last twenty years. China's real GDP grew at average annual rate of 9.5 in 1978-2001, the highest in the world in that period. The size of market measured by GDP rose by a factor of almost 7, and per capital GDP by a factor of near 5 (SSB, 2002).

---

[9] There are many empirical studies in which the impact of the market size on FDI flows into China are significantly positive (for example, Wei, 1995a; Zhang, 2000b, 2001b, and 2001c).

(2) Large FDI from HKT and Overseas Chinese Diaspora

China has a special asset of overseas Chinese, particularly Hong Kong and Taiwan (HKT). The unique fact that most FDI in China did not came from developed but developing countries is obviously related to large amount of overseas Chinese diaspora, particularly HKT and Singapore. This can perhaps be explained by "Chinese connections" which refer to the special link of overseas Chinese with their homeland such that they would like to identify themselves as part of China in spirit and be willing to devote their effort to make contributions to China's modernization. The Chinese connections are based on the facts that overseas Chinese share the same language, culture, and family tradition; and that they also have relatives, friends, and former business ties on China. Therefore the connections make overseas Chinese much easier to negotiate and operate joint ventures in China relative to investors elsewhere.[10]

By the end of 1998, there were more than 227,000 registered foreign enterprises established in China, among them are 165,000 projects invested by overseas Chinese, composing of over 73% of the total number (MOFTEC, 2000). In a world of business that is familiar to overseas Chinese, Westerns often fell lost. The diaspora speaks the right languages, and they are relatively untroubled by the absence of a legal and accounting framework or reliable market research.

(3) Liberal FDI Regime and Incentive Policies

China has been systematically liberalized its FDI regime since 1979. The attitude of Chinese government toward multinationals is far more liberal than most other developing counties, especially those in East Asia such as Japan, South Korea, and Taiwan.[11] In the early 1990s China developed one of the most liberal FDI environments among the developing countries (Lardy, 1994). Many sectors such as power generation, transportation, port development, oil exploration and exploitation, and services were opened up to foreign investors. Liberalization of foreign participation in property development led to particularly significant FDI flows directed toward the development of residential housing, retail complexes and other projects.

China also offered impressive package of incentive policies. In the 1990s, some of the special provisions to attract FDI that were only available in the special economic zones have been made much more widely available. For example, special tax concessions, liberalized land leasing and other inducements were made available in a growing number of open coastal cities, economic development areas and high technology development zones.[12]

---

[10] Chinese have a long history of overseas-immigration, and almost in every country in the world is there Chinese. According to the *Overseas Chinese Economic Yearbook* by Committee of Overseas Chinese (Taiwan) (1991), the total overseas Chinese were roughly 36 million, most of them (80%) live in Hong Kong and six Southeast Asian countries (Indonesia, Thailand, Malaysia, Singapore, and Burma). Over 3 million overseas Chinese reside in North America, including 2 million in the US. Overseas Chinese, except those living mainland China but including Taiwan and Hong Kong, are estimated to possess assets as much as US$1500 to 2000 billion (*The Economist*, May 30, 1994).

[11] FDI regimes in Japan, South Korea, and Taiwan have been more restrictive than in China in both comparative development stages and even to this day. For example, foreign ownership in Japan was limited to a maximum of 49% of any joint venture, and FDI explicitly was not allowed to be presence in a large number of industries. Wholly foreign-owned firms were not permitted to operate until 1973 (Lardy, 1994).

[12] The positive effects of liberal FDI regime and incentive policies on FDI flows into China have been supported empirically (for example, Zhang, 2000b, 2001b, and 2001c).

While the market size, overseas Chinese, and the FDI regime play a critical role in the FDI boom, the contributions of other factors may not be ignored. These factors include China's cheap resources (labor, land, and raw materials), improving infrastructure conditions, and the overall expanding of multinationals in developing world in the 1990s.

3.2. Factors behind China's Success in Using FDI

The positive impact of FDI on China's economic growth has been recognized in both policy and academic circles (Wei, 1995; Zhang, 1999, 2001a, and 2001d). Table 4 presents some indications of the importance and contributions of FDI to Chinese economy. FDI stock as a ratio of GDP rose dramatically from 6% in 1991 to 33% in 1998. With large amount of foreign capital inflows, FDI has become an increasingly important source of capital formation. The ratio of FDI flows to gross domestic investment increased from 4% in 1991 to 15% in 1997. While the share of industrial output by foreign affiliates in total industrial output grew from 5% in 1991 to 18.6% in 1997, the total industrial output grew at average rate of 20% in the same period (SSB, 1998). FDI also has reduced significantly China's unemployment pressure and made a significant contribution to government revenues. By the end of 1998, 18 million Chinese were employed in around 145,000 foreign affiliates in China, comprising 11% of total manufactured employment. Tax contributions from foreign affiliates rose largely with FDI flows, and its share in total tax revenue of China increased from 4% in 1992 to 13% in 1997 (SSB, 1998).

The most important contributions of FDI to Chinese economy perhaps are its role in export expansion and its spillover effects on China's market-oriented reforms. The contribution of foreign affiliates to China's exports concentrates on augmenting export volume as well as upgrading export structure (Zhang and Song, 2000). As indicated in Table 5, while China's exports totaled $18 billion with 47% in manufactured goods in 1980, the corresponding numbers in 1999 were $195 billion and 87%. Exports by foreign affiliates in China rose 48% annually in 1980-99, and the value of their exports in 2001 (mainly manufacturing goods) were $131 billion, comprising 49% of China's total exports in that year.

FDI has brought extra gains to China in facilitating its transition toward a market system that started in the late 1970s, which in turn enhanced the income growth (Zhang, 2001d). These gains include stimulating the move towards marketization by introducing a market-oriented institutional framework; contributing to changes in the ownership structure towards privatization by promoting competition and facilitating the reform of state-owned-enterprises; and facilitating the integration of China into the world economy.

Table 4. The Importance of FDI in China

Items	1991	1992	1993	1994	1995	1996	1997	1998
FDI flows (billions of US dollars)	4.4	11.2	27.5	33.8	35.8	40.8	45.3	45.5
FDI stock as a ratio of GDP (%)	5.6	7.1	10.2	17.6	18.8	24.7	29.4	32.6
FDI flows as a ratio of gross domestic investment (%)	3.9	7.4	12.7	17.3	15.1	17.0	14.8	n.a.
Exports by foreign affiliates (billions of US dollars)	12.1	17.4	25.2	34.7	46.9	61.5	75.0	88.6
Share of exports by foreign affiliates in total exports (%)	17.0	20.4	27.5	28.7	31.3	41.0	41.0	44.1
Share of industrial output by foreign affiliates in total industrial output (%)	5.0	6.0	9.0	9.5	11.7	12.2	12.7	14.9
Number of employees in foreign affiliates (millions)	4.8	6.0	10.0	14.0	16.0	17.0	17.5	18.0
Tax contributions from foreign affiliates as share of total tax revenue (%)	n.a.	4.1	n.a.	n.a.	10.0	n.a.	13.2	n.a.

Sources: Computed from *China Statistics Yearbook* by SSB (various years), *World Investment Report* (UNCTAD, 1998 and 1999), and *China Foreign Economic Statistics Yearbook* by SSB (various years)

Table 5. Role of Foreign Invested Enterprises (FIEs) in China's Export 1980-2000

Year	Total Exports	Exports by FIEs	Share of Exports by FIEs in Total Exports (%)
1980	18119	8.2	0.05
1981	22007	32.4	0.15
1982	22321	52.9	0.24
1983	22226	330.4	1.49
1984	26139	68.9	0.26
1985	27350	296.7	1.08
1986	30942	582.0	1.88
1987	39437	1208.1	3.06
1988	47516	2456.4	5.17
1989	52538	4913.2	9.35
1990	62091	7813.7	12.58
1991	71910	12047.3	16.77
1992	84940	17356.2	20.43
1993	90970	25237.2	27.51
1994	121047	34712.9	28.69
1995	148797	46875.9	31.51
1996	151050	61506.4	40.72
1997	182790	74899.9	40.98
1998	183760	80961.9	44.06
1999	194791	88630.0	45.50
2000	249203	119441.2	47.93
2001	266160	131030.6	49.23
2002	300000	156000.0	52.00

Note: Amount of exports is in millions of US dollars. The figure for 2002 are estimated. *Sources*: Computed from *China Statistical Yearbook 2002* (SSB, 2002) and *China Foreign Economic Statistical Yearbook 2000* (SSB, 2000)

(1) Effective FDI Strategy

An effective FDI strategy should consist of two elements: creating attractive locations for foreign investors, and capturing benefits from FDI and avoiding unnecessary costs. The first element has been proved to be effective due to the fact of the FDI boom. The second element, which influences or controls multinational corporate activities such that the host country welfare is maximized, should be able to generate jobs, expand exports, secure resources, penetrate markets, and create technology. To implement of the effective strategy, China singled out two categories of foreign-invested enterprises (FIEs) and offered incentive packages to them. The two-type FIEs are export-oriented ones and technologically-advanced ones. The first type is defined as one whose products are mainly destined for exports (usually 70% of the output value and which enjoys a foreign-exchange balance (or surplus) after deducting from its foreign exchange revenue foreign exchange expenditure and foreign currency remitted abroad. A technologically-advanced FIE refers to one in which the foreign investor provides advanced technology for the development of new products, product upgrading and renewal, in order to increase exports or substitute for imports. Incentives offered to the two-type FIEs include lower corporate taxation rates, prolonged tax holidays, exemption from paying part of the state subsidies that their employees receive, lower site fees, priority supplies of water, electricity, transport and communication facilities, and priority access to bank loans.

China's demands thus clustered around performance requirements in two areas: (a) pressuring the multinationals to produce more value-added domestically, provide more local content in their finished product, and expand the linkages into the indigenous economy; and (b) pushing the multinationals to use their worldwide marketing networks to export more products and components out of China. China is likely to have to do more than merely take competition among potential foreign investors for granted. Rather, whether through public or through private efforts, China may play an active role in stimulating rivalries within the sectors in which foreign investors are seeking investment.

(2) Contributions of FDI from Hong Kong and Taiwan (HKT)

HKT investors have several unique attributes that give them a competitive edge over Western multinationals and contribute to the overall development process in China. The Western multinationals, driven by the strategies of their parent, tend to focus their efforts on technological invocation and marketing rather than on cost minimization or the adaptation of production processes and product lines to Chinese markets. As a result, there is a niche for HKT investors who offer investment projects suited for efficient, small-scale manufacture and for less expensive, labor-intensive technology.

HKT multinationals possess an advantage over their Western counterparts in most small-scale manufacturing industries because they are generally small themselves and the capacity utilization of their plants in host countries is much higher. HKT multinationals are more competitive in the adaptation of Western technology to the needs of Chinese markets. The have demonstrated an ability to scale down Western technology to fit China's requirements, which is an important know-how to indigenous firms. Relative to Western multinationals, lower overhead enables HKT multinationals to offer less expensive products in China's more price-sensitive markets. In addition, the operations of HKT multinationals are more flexible in responding to China's needs.

There are other advantages to Chinese government from dealing with HKT multinationals. The fact that HKT subsidiaries are more independent from their parent than are their Western counterparts often means more host government control over the project and less conflict with investors. HKT multinationals thus have extra appeal because a major source of contention – trying to make the global strategy of the company mesh with the economic priorities of the host country – is less prominent. And because their capital resources are relatively less, HKT firms are more likely to seek out local partners and more likely to obtain inputs locally without the need for a push from the government.

The benefits of HKT investments are therefore various: they present more opportunity for local control, their technology is more labor intensive and consistent with China's comparative advantages, their focus is primarily on cost reduction and price competitiveness, majority of output is exported, and the overall expense to the local economy is less.[1]

(3) Strong Governments

China has a tradition of centralized government in the history. A strong and centralized government contributes to the ability of the state leaders to formulate development policies and to push for successful implementation of those policies. Mass political stability, which is easily maintained under a strong government relative to a weak government, is expected to contribute host bargaining power before FDI is made by increasing investor certainty. Since the Chinese economy has been under market-oriented reforms, the strong government shapes the willingness of the elite to undertake economic development policies, as well as their willingness to use FDI as a policy tool. The implementation of such reforms and the open-door policy must be backed by a strong government with a competent bureaucracy and financial autonomy. If a government is unable to implement regulation of FDI, it opens the way for corruption and unrealistic expectation about its capacity. China's competent government indeed lends credibility to its bargains and thus contributes to a stable investment environment. That stability is attractive to foreign investors, so it adds to the China's bargain leverage and allows China to implement its own development strategy more smoothly.

Several elements of a socialist form may be hypothesized to contribute to the strong government and therefore to contribute the bargaining power to control FDI and multinational corporate behavior. China's socialist political and economic structures strengthen the government's bargaining position in negotiating foreign contracts and overseeing operations. The government's monopoly over joint venture approvals has potential to allow it to determine the range of terms for FDI contracts. The central government also is positioned to supervise individual bargaining sessions at the firm level; and the state organs and personnel subject to central supervision could control the negotiating process. Since majority of FDI projects are formed as joint ventures with state-owned enterprises, the government has the opportunity to directly foster its own ends and control the role of foreign capital in China's development. Socialist planning mechanisms also offers ready organizations and personnel to determine the role and function of FDI in Chinese economy through well-positioned line ministries, finance bureaus, and party bureaucracies. For example, although Chinn did not explicitly inhibit foreign affiliates from selling their products locally in the 1980s, the

---

[1] There are, however, some disadvantages in comparison to Western multinationals. HKT investors are less likely to provide China with a continuing stream of technology that could result in product innovation or increased productivity. Moreover, HKT subsidiaries also tend to pay lower wages to local workers.

monopoly power of Chinese foreign currency authority over foreign exchange transactions and of China's state economic bureaucracy over domestic marketing allowed the government to regulate marketing by foreign-invested firms.

It is noted that government participation in joint ventures and the existence of planning mechanism are also associated with developing capitalist economies (such as Japan, South Korea, and Taiwan), particularly in strategic sectors. What is different in China, however, is that the state routinely pervades and sanctioned to pervade most aspects of the economy, including multinational corporate activities. What is also potentially unique in China is the existence of a will or interest, supported by ideology, to enact economic policies strong enough to control FDI.

In sum, the strong government allows China to take an active role in pursuing the obsolescing bargain. Well-designed and implemented regional and industrial FDI strategies have been used for China to capture benefits and avoid unnecessary costs from foreign investments.

There is some other strength that contributes to China's success in utilizing FDI. The growing market size due rapid economic growth in the last two decades, for example, perhaps the greatest strength China used in bargaining with foreign investors, particularly in industries in which international competition to enter the huge market is fierce. The strength specially provides China with the ability to utilize competition among the multinationals to play one off against another for better terms.

4. CONCLUDING REMARKS: SUMMARY AND CHALLENGES

China has achieved significant economic growth success through attracting and utilizing FDI. What most attract foreign investors are China's huge market, liberal FDI regime and incentive policies, and cheap resources (labor, land, and raw materials). More importantly, investors from HKT and overseas Chinese contribute in a large part to the FDI boom. The gains from FDI concentrate on export expansions and spillovers effects of diffusing technology and stimulating reforms toward market systems, in addition to capital formation, job creations, and human capital development. The overall success in utilizing FDI is a result of China's effective FDI strategy, dominant FDI from HKT, and strong government.

While the success is impressive, the challenges China faces in using FDI to enhance growth are severe, particularly under China's accession to the World Trade Organization in the near future. China's FDI regime and relevant policies have to adjust to be consistent with the rule of the WTO, resulting in growing share of FDI made by multintiaonls corporations (MNCs) in West (the U.S., Western Europe, and Japan). Two central characteristics of West MNCs are their large size and the fact that their worldwide operations and activities tend to be centrally controlled by parent companies. Many MNCs have annual sales volumes in excess of the GDP of the developing nations in which they operate.[2] Enormous size confers great bargaining power on MNCs relative to developing host countries. This power is greatly

---

[2] For example, as the largest MNC in 1994, General Motors had sales revenues in excess of the GDP of Turkey and Denmark. In fact, its gross sales exceeded the GDP of all but seven developing countries (China, India, Brazil, Indonesia, Mexico, Argentina, and South Korea). The five largest MNCs had combined revenues ($871.4) in excess of the GDP of all 48 least developed countries combined by a factor of 11 (UNCTAD, 1995).

strengthened by their predominantly oligopolistic positions in worldwide product markets. This situation gives MNCs the ability to manipulate prices and profits, to collude with other firms in determining areas of control, and generally to restrict the entry of potential competition by dominating new technologies, special skills, and, through product differentiation and advertising.

Advanced technology and management skills that China very much wants are frequently found in industries in which oligopolistic MNCs dominate. In many of these industries China has few alternatives, and hence its ability to bargain with any one MNC is limited. Moreover, MNC have considerably more experiences bargaining with host governments than China has bargaining with the West MNCs even after China's open-up for twenty years.

In many aspects of interests, conflicts exist between China and MNCs. For example, China may desire large investment with export orientation, but MNCs may prefer small investment aiming to domestic market; China wants high-technology and high value-added projects, which may be opposite to what MNCs are willing to offer; MNCs desire wholly-owned affiliates, rather than Chinese majority joint venture structure which is enjoyed by China. While China's commitments to the entry of the WTO (such as in liberalized ownership structures and opening up more sectors including services) may help attract more FDI flows from West MNCs, the benefits China can draw from the investment depend on changes in China's bargaining power relative to MNCs. China may develop a regulatory system to manage and control MNC behavior under the TWO frameworks. Several aspects may be questioned to make sure the national welfare maximized.

The net impact of FDI on Chinese economy in the future will depend largely on how China balances between technology transfers and domestic market protection. China may take advantage of its large country-size in forming its strategy to shape MNC activities. In particular, China may adopt well-defined measures of investment promotion to choose right FDI projects; to design realistic domestic-content requirements to upgrade domestic industries; and to set up optimal export-performance requirements to create advanced comparative advantages in global markets.

REFERENCES

Caves, Richard (1996), *Multinational Enterprises and Economic Analysis*, the 2nd edition, Cambridge, MA: Cambridge University Press.

Helleiner, G. (1989), "Transnational corporations and direct foreign investment," in H. Chenery and T. N. Srinivasan, ed, *Handbook of Development Economics*, Elsevier Science Publishers B.V., 1441-1480.

International Monetary Fund (IMF) (1979-2001), *International Financial Statistics Yearbook* (various yearsfrom 1979-2001), Washington D.C., IMF.

Hou, Jack and Kevin H. Zhang (2001), "A Location Analysis of Taiwanese Manufacturing Branch-Plants in China," *International Journal of Business*, 6 (2), 53-66.

Kamath, S. J. (1990), "Foreign direct investment in a centrally planned developing economy: The Chinese case," *Economic Development and Cultural Changes*, 39 (1), 107-130.

Lardy, Nicholas R., 1994, *China in the World Economy*, Washington, DC: Institute for International Economics.

Lardy, Nicholas R. (1995) "The role of foreign trade and investment in China's economic transformation," *The China Quarterly*, 144: 1065-1082.

Markusen, James R (1984), "Multinationals, multi-plant economies, and the gains from trade." *Journal of International Economics*, 16, 205-225.

Markusen, James, Anthony Venables, Denise Konan, and Kevin Zhang (1996), "A United treatment of horizontal direct investment, vertical direct investment, and the pattern of trade in goods and services". *NBER Working Paper* No. 5696.

Ministry of Foreign Trade and Economic Cooperation (MOFTEC) of China (2000), *Statistics on FDI in China*, Beijing: MOFERT Press.

Moran, Theodore H. (1985), *Multinational Corporations: The Political Economy of Foreign Direct Investment*, Lexington: Lexington Books.

Perkins, Dwight (1994), "Completing China's move to the market," *Journal of Economic Perspectives*, 8 (2), 23-46.

State Statistical Bureau (SSB) (1992-2002), China Statistical Yearbook (1992-1999), China Statistics Press, Beijing, China.

United Nations Conference on Trade and Development (UNCTAD) (1991-2002), *World Investment Report* (various years, 1991-2002), New York: United Nations.

U.S.-China Business Council (USCBC) (1990), *Special Report on US Investment in China*, The China Business Forum, Washington, D.C., 1990.

Wei, Shang-Jin (1995), "Attracting foreign direct investment: has China reached its potential?" *China Economic Review*, 6 (2), 187-200.

Wells, Louis T. Jr. (1993), "Mobile exporters: new foreign investors in East Asia." in K. A. Froot, ed. *Foreign Direct Investment*. Chicago: The University of Chicago Press.

Wheeler, David and Ashoka Mody (1992), "International investment location decisions: the case of US firms", *Journal of International Economics*, 33, 57-76.

Zhang, Kevin H. (1999), "How Does FDI Interact with Economic growth in a Large Developing Country? The Case of China," *Economic Systems*, 23(4), 291-303.

Zhang, Kevin H. (2000a), "Human Capital, Country Size, and North-South Manufacturing Multinational Enterprises," *Economia Internazionale/ International Economics*, 53 (2), May 2000, 237-260.

Zhang, Kevin H. (2000b), "Why is US Direct Investment in China so Small?" Contemporary Economic Policy, 18 (1), 82-94.

Zhang, Kevin H. (2001a), "Roads to Prosperity: Assessing the Impact of FDI on Economic Growth in China," *Economia Internazionale / International Economics,* 54 (1), 113-125.

Zhang, Kevin H. (2001b), "What Explains the Boom of Foreign Direct Investment in China," *Economia Internazionale / International Economics*, 54 (2), 1-24.

Zhang, Kevin H. (2001c), "What Attracts Multinational Corporations to Developing Countries? Evidence from China," *Contemporary Economic Policy,* 19 (3), 336-346.

Zhang, Kevin H. (2001d), "How Does FDI Affect Economic Growth in China?" *Economics of Transition*, 9 (3), 679-693.

Zhang, Kevin H. (2003), "Why does China receive so much FDI from Hong Kong and Taiwan?" *China Economic Review*, forthcoming.

Zhang, Kevin H. and James Markusen (1999), "Vertical Multinationals and Host-Country Characteristics", *Journal of Development Economics*, 59, 233-252.

Zhang, Kevin H. and Shunfeng Song (2000), "Promoting Exports: The Role of Inward FDI in China," *China Economic Review*, 11 (4), 385-396.

In: China in Focus Economic, Political and Educational Issues
Editor: Ernest P. Nolan, pp. 47-65

ISBN 1-60021-543-8
© 2007 Nova Science Publishers, Inc.

Chapter 4

THE CHALLENGE OF REMOVING ADMINISTRATIVE BARRIERS TO FDI IN CHINA

*Yong Li** and Shukun Tang*

School of Business, University of Science and Technology of China
Hefei, Anhui, 230026 P. R. of China

ABSTRACT

This paper presents a picture of administrative barriers to foreign direct investment (FDI) in China –its current situation, manifestations, causes, damaging effect and related measures to curb it. China is in a transition from a closed economy to an open market economy. Administrative barriers to FDI in China is reflected largely in investment restriction, non-transparent and inaccessible FDI rule and regulation, as well as bureaucratic interference in terms of the distortion of FDI operation behavior and the preclusion of market competition. They have become a pressing issue facing foreign investors in making decision to invest in china. China has made great effort to develop a regulation framework on incentive FDI, but this framework currently appears weak and powerless in the face of the administrative barriers. However, the construction of a complete legal framework for FDI and rebuild the government administrative system will be undoubtedly helpful in removing excessive administrative barriers.

* Yong Li: Current address: 86 Foster Street, New Haven, CT 06511 U.S.A. Telephone: 1-203-772-4202; E-mail: yylilei@hotmail.com

INTRODUCTION

China has benefited from its foreign direct investment (FDI) boom in 1990s, which has been accompanied by high GDP growth. For a long-term prospect, it is indispensable that China has a sustainable growth of FDI inflows. Unfortunately, FDI inflows have declined in the last few years. More precisely, FDI went from a peak of 45.46 U.S. $billion in 1998, to 41.73 U.S. $billion in 2001, when foreign investors withdrew or reduced their investment in China. The most important factor for blocking inward FDI is its high administrative barriers. What was enough for attracting FDI before 1998 will not be enough when the competition for FDI has increased, and most developing countries in Asia have already liberalized FDI regimes and economies at large, during the last years. The situation is aggravated by structural changes or economic recessions in some of the larger home countries of FDI, notably Japan, Korea and Hong Kong. Economic turmoil in these countries has decreased the supply of FDI in South East Asia. Removing excessive administrative barriers have become a pressing issue facing China in order to keep the trend of attracting FDI. The purpose of this paper is to present a picture of administrative barriers to FDI in China –its current situation, manifestations, causes, damaging effect and related measures to curb it. The main argument put forward, is that it is essential for China to remove excess administrative barriers in order to build a favorable investment climate for FDI, and any such remove will have to rely on some crucial factors, such as good legal institutions and an effective administrative mechanism.

BACKGROUND

1. China's FDI Regime Liberalization Program

Attitudes and policies toward FDI in China have undergone a marked change, from hostility and distrust in the 1960s to passive acceptance since the 1970s, and then to active encouragement since mid-1980s. Several considerations lie behind these changing perceptions. The first is the increasing preference for the non-debt-creating forms of capital finance over commercial bank borrowing due to the debt crisis of the early 1980s. The second is the growing awareness of FDI's benefits as exemplified by the positive role played by FDI in Chinese economy.

Although the promulgation of the 1979 "Law on Chinese-Foreign Equity Joint Ventures" together with the establishment of the four special economic zones formally signaled the adoption of the "open-door" policy by the central government, only in 1986 and 1987 was serious attention given to providing investment incentives. The "Provisions for the Encouragement of Foreign Investment" were promulgated in October 1986 and their implementing regulations announced over the next year. These measures addressed some of the problems, and improved the investment climate both by adding new incentives and by reducing past uncertainties.

In order to make foreign investment further meet the national industrial development direction and avoid blind investment, in June 1995, China formulated and published "Temporary Provisions for Direction of Foreign Investment" and "Master List for Foreign

Investment Industries", announcing the industrial policies of attracting foreign investment in the form of regulations, and lightened the transparency of policies. The Provisions and List divide industrial items into four kinds including the encouraged, the permitted, the restricted, and the forbidden, making investors clear at first sight.

According to the development of China's economy, in December 1997, the government revised the "Master List for Foreign Investment Industries". The revised List encourages foreign investors to set up export enterprises and has put the permitted items 100 per cent of whose products are for export into the encouraged items. During period of "the Ninth Five-year-scheme" (1995-2000), Chinese government depresses customs in a large scope so as to further open the market. The average duty level has been depressed from 35.6% in 1995 down to the current 16.7%. The range of depressed tariff is 53%. The scope of import license management commodity was decreased from 53 classifications in 1992 down to the existing 35. In addition, the import commodity classifications checked and ratified used for management by government are further decreased to 13 at the moment.

The Chinese government promulgated new policy measures to encourage foreign investment in 1999, in order to get adapted to the new challenges imposed by scientific and technological breakthroughs and the rapid changes of knowledge economy and, to act in line with the overall arrangement for China's economic development strategic objective and industrial restructuring. The core of these new policies is: First, to further push forward the opening-up in the service sector gradually. Second, to encourage the establishment of RandD centers and investment in high-tech enterprises by foreign investors. Thirdly, to promote the technological innovation for existing enterprises with foreign investment. Fourthly, to encourage foreign investors to invest in central and western China. In order to achieve these goals, a series of new preferential treatments, which include the exemption or reduction of import duties, income tax holiday, decentralization of the approval power, improving of the legal system and so on, were unveiled to further perfect the investment environment and create even better conditions for foreign investment enterprises (FIEs) in their competitiveness improvement.

China's recent revisions to its regulatory regime governing foreign investment is the "Regulations Guiding the Direction of Foreign Investment" (Guiding Regulations) and the "Catalogue Guiding Foreign Investment in Industry" (Catalogue), both were enacted on April 1, 2002. They broaden the scope of foreign investment opportunities and ease approval requirements for a number of industries, particularly those in manufacturing. The new regime, brought about largely as a result of the country's December 2001 World Trader Organization (WTO) entry and national plans for economic development, outlines which foreign investment projects can be approved by local or central authorities, which projects enjoy preferential tax treatment, and which projects are off-limits to foreign investment. China has already put in place an FDI regulation framework that is relatively mature and liberal by international standards.

Over the last two decades China's FDI inflows has undergone fundamental changes. The main indicators of these changes are:

(1) With the exception of those sectors relating to national security, scarce resources, natural resources, and a few others thought unsuited to competition (such as civil aviation, express mail service, electric publication and water processing), an attract FDI mechanism has been established in a majority of sectors, By the end of 2001,

China has accumulatively approved the establishment of more than 411,495 foreign-invested enterprises with a total contractual foreign capital of US$69.76 billion and over US$41.73 billion of actually paid-in foreign investment, with a total output accounting for about 25% of GDP, tax takes account 19.01%, export 50.1%, and employees 23 million (China Daily, May 9, 2002). FDI has generated large and significant spillover effects in that it raises both the level and growth rate of productivity of non-recipient firms, and the domestic (previous state-owned) enterprises are the main beneficiaries (Liu 2000).

(2) Using natural resources, a vast market potential, and a wide pool of cheap labor, and preferential policies, numerous foreign companies have achieved great economic benefit. As indicated in table 1, in 1999 the provinces in which foreign-funded industrial enterprises got highest efficiency in terms of productivity were Shanxi (116,553 Yuan/person-year), Jilin (108,825), and Hubei (102,992).

(3) With the government's gradual open domestic market, FIEs have begun to acquire various autonomous rights in their business operations. Ownership restrictions, rate of return restrictions have been loosen since 1996, following China's admission to WTO, they will be further freed from administrative dependencies.

CHINESE FDI PATTERN

1. FDI's Time Trend

The most impressive feature of the time trend is the sharp FDI boom in 1990s in contrast with steady but small amount of inflows in the 1980s and slightly slow down in recent years (Table 2). Literatures (Lardy 1995, Zhang 2001) attributed the FDI boom to a further liberalization of China's FDI regime and the explosive growth of domestic economy, along with the worldwide rise in FDI outflows in the first half of the 1990s and China's political stability. After its peak year 1998, Actual foreign investment in China in 1999 was US$40.32bn, 11.3 per cent less than the total in 1998, and contracted foreign investment was US$41.24bn, 18.9 per cent less.

Investment from Hong Kong and Macau fell by 6.2 per cent, from the rest of Asia by 10.3 per cent, from the US by 10.2 per cent and from the EU by 33.4 per cent (China Economic Review, 2001, September). Although there is a little rise again (2.3% year to year increase) in 2001, China cannot expect a higher FDI growth unless further steps are taken to open more sectors and improve the climate for foreign investors. We argue that weaknesses in China's legislation and complex bureaucratic procedures are significant deterrents to FDI, according to our analysis below.

Table 1. Main Indicators on Economics Benefit of Foreign-Funded Industrial Enterprises by Region (1999)

Region	Ratio of Value Added to Gross Industrial Output Value (%)	Ratio of Total Assets to Industrial Output Value (%)	Assets-Liability Ratio (%)	Annual of Turnover Circulating Funds (times/year)	Ratio of Profits to Cost (%)	Productivity (yuan/ person-year)	Proportion of Products Sold (%)
National Total	25.59	7.93	57.73	1.69	4.39	61260.23	97.18
Beijing	27.88	7.87	61.41	1.50	3.91	85611.93	97.94
Tianjin	18.28	8.68	53.52	1.77	5.81	63351.14	99.85
Hebei	27.33	7.67	63.59	1.56	3.41	56360.63	96.87
Shanxi	30.22	3.89	63.02	1.19	-1.83	40804.65	92.35
Inner Mongolia	32.56	8.93	53.44	0.83	7.38	42001.01	106.87
Liaoning	25.18	7.30	54.10	1.72	4.25	62905.76	99.20
Jilin	32.23	12.06	61.42	1.78	6.27	108825.53	98.25
Heilongjiang	31.29	5.25	71.29	1.02	1.15	62524.18	94.81
Shanghai	25.73	9.31	51.52	1.52	6.12	96270.37	97.84
Jiangsu	24.50	7.95	58.53	1.97	3.91	69637.61	96.97
Zhejiang	23.83	9.24	57.85	1.73	5.40	49201.90	96.01
Anhui	26.82	7.53	60.37	1.69	2.07	54824.16	96.14
Fujian	27.34	7.48	55.01	1.87	4.16	51172.46	95.41
Jiangxi	23.21	7.80	63.56	1.46	3.64	37417.41	96.02
Shandong	26.60	9.00	63.14	2.00	4.91	49067.15	96.38
Henan	32.53	8.49	55.26	1.29	5.71	71095.91	96.45
Hubei	34.58	8.76	70.05	1.51	5.77	102992.86	98.05
Hunan	28.98	11.82	51.79	1.64	8.37	52172.28	95.79
Guangdong	24.87	6.76	59.97	1.79	3.34	51930.26	97.03
Guangxi	29.19	5.75	52.00	1.38	1.70	51536.85	94.98
Hainan	27.95	5.89	55.17	0.74	3.89	70980.18	95.52
Chongqing	27.50	6.55	48.43	1.29	1.45	76275.47	100.09

Table 1. (Continued)

Region	Ratio of Value Added to Gross Industrial Output Value (%)	Ratio of Total Assets to Industrial Output Value (%)	Assets-Liability Ratio (%)	Annual of Turnover Circulating Funds (times/year)	Ratio of Profits to Cost (%)	Productivity (yuan/ person-year)	Proportion of Products Sold (%)
Sichuan	31.86	6.33	58.12	1.28	2.99	66943.48	94.81
Guizhou	27.81	0.90	61.63	0.73	-6.16	27617.45	96.26
Yunnan	34.61	8.22	49.08	1.23	10.37	85163.04	95.79
Tibet	39.28	0.31	13.45	0.70	2.19	4080.21	87.92
Shaanxi	28.09	12.39	56.49	1.37	12.26	116553.06	96.08
Gansu	26.61	7.55	62.71	1.15	4.32	42132.17	99.24
Qinghai	23.52	3.71	60.48	1.26	1.20	60286.65	92.97
Ningxia	33.47	8.11	58.86	0.95	3.21	44178.54	95.75
Xinjiang	32.39	8.20	61.39	1.21	7.83	72531.14	97.96

Data: http://www.allchinadata.com/english/industrial%20economy.htm (2002)

2. FDI's Origins

As table 2 shown, among all FDIs, Asian direct investment (ADI) was the dominant source of Chinese FDI activity, particularly Hong Kong direct investment (HKDI) constituted over one half of China's inward FDI in almost every single year since 1979, which are otherwise not significant international investors. Even after the government strengthened the project's examination and approval to enhance the FDI's quality from September, 1999, in 2001, HKDI still constituted 36%, While U.S. direct investment constituted 8.02%, Japan 8.2%, and European 7.9% (the US-China Business Council). A well accepted reason for this structure is ADI which primarily is export oriented, has been encouraged by China's cheap labor and incentive policies toward this type of FDI; the Western investors has been induced essentially by China's potentially huge market and trade barriers, the amount of Western FDI flows has been limited largely due to China's restrictive policy toward the market-oriented FDI. Table 3 suggests that relative to the Asian developing economies, industrial countries have places less emphasis on export-oriented light industries and textile projects in China. Though the share of ADI in these two groups is as high as 44%, that for the Western FDI is only 26%, the ADI is concentrated on labor-intensive and relatively low-technology goods (such as garments, toys, shoes, and consumer electronics) aimed at the international market. Their products tend to be undifferentiated and sold mainly on the basis of price rather than distinct design or performance characteristics. In contrast, FDI from developed countries (the US, Japan, and western Europe) aim their investments much more to china's domestic market in capital-intensive goods such as machinery, chemicals, health care products, and services.

Table 2. FDI Flows to China, by Time Trend and Origin, 1979-2001

Year	FDI (US$ bn)	Percent change of flow from previous year (%)	FDI Distribution by Source (%)		
			Asia	Western	Others
1979-1982	1.17				
1983	0.64	81.9			
1984	1.26	98.3			
1985	1.66	32.2	67	27	6
1986	1.87	12.7	74	23	3
1987	2.31	23.4	84	14	3
1988	3.19	38.1	82	12	6
1989	3.39	6.2	77	14	9
1990	3.48	2.8	84	16	0
1991	4.37	25.3	82	13	5
1992	11.01	152.1	90	8	3
1993	27.52	150.3	87	11	3
1994	33.77	22.7	84	13	3
1995	37.52	11.0	82	15	4
1996	41.73	11.2	80	15	5
1997	45.26	8.9	68	16	16
1998	45.46	0.42	69	18	13
1999	40.32	-11.3	59	21	20
2000	40.77	1.1	57	22	21
2001	41.73	2.3	59	24	17

Data: Computed based on data from International Trade (various issues) by MOFTEC for 1992-2001, and from China Statistical Yearbook (various issues) by SSB for other years

Note: All numbers of FDI flows and stock are realized investment in current values

Table 3. FDI Sector Distribution in China in 2000, by Sources of FDI, Scale and Projects

Sector	Asian FDI			Western FDI			Total		
	No.	%	Average scale (US$ Million)	No.	%	Average scale	No.	%	Average scale
Agriculture	36	1.82	1.30	71	6.72	1.38	107	3.53	1.35
Building materials	96	4.86	1.51	56	5.30	2.32	152	5.02	1.81
Chemicals	152	7.68	1.92	87	8.24	1.02	239	7.91	1.59
Electronics	145	7.33	1.35	119	11.3	1.47	264	8.71	1.41
Energy	4	0.20	2.66	29	2.74	2.57	33	1.08	2.58
Food	101	5.11	0.75	84	7.95	1.94	185	6.10	1.29
Heavy industry	131	6.63	2.14	108	10.2	2.42	239	7.90	2.27
Light industry	570	28.8	1.87	173	16.4	2.09	743	24.5	1.92
Medical	34	1.72	2.26	69	6.53	2.22	95	3.13	2.42
Packaging	66	3.34	0.89	17	1.61	2.17	83	2.73	1.15
Printing	14	0.71	0.81	12	1.14	1.77	26	0.88	1.25
Property development	61	3.09	2.38	27	2.56	2.97	86	2.85	2.62
Services	73	3.69	0.75	35	3.31	1.49	108	3.57	0.99
Textiles	358	19.5	0.79	101	9.56	1.34	459	15.2	0.95
Transportation	94	4.76	1.35	54	5.11	2.57	148	4.90	1.79
Miscellaneous	46	2.33	1.28	14	1.33	1.42	60	1.97	1.31
Total	1,977	100	1.48	1,056	100	2.26	3,033	100	1.62

Data: Special Report on Foreign Direct Investment in China by the China Industry-Business Council (2001)

Notes: Western FDI denotes FDI from all developed countries. Asian FDI is the FDI from all developing economies

Another plausible explanation is cultural similarity. Hong Kong and Taiwan's ethnic with China is an unique ownership: both share the same language and culture, which enables investors to conduct negotiations and operations much easier. Western investors who have a tendency to make business practice hurry, impersonal, shallow, and focus on the short-term bottom line can not endure Chinese executives who view business deals too personal, too time wasting, and too inefficiency.

3. FDI's Sectoral Distribution

The sectoral distribution of FDI is complicated and varies greatly from sector to sector. Most FIEs are small scale, especially Asian FIEs, only average 1.48US$ million per project (table 3). Studies show that there is very little technological content in FDI investment, at least regarding hardware transfer. The level of technology transferred through FDI is only 2 years ahead of current Chinese technological capabilities. However, the gap between Chinese and foreign technology levels is approximately 20 years (Sheng 1999).

According to FDI theory, small firms do not invest abroad, due to the many costs involved in overseas transactions. But small project, not large project was favored by foreign investors in China, the possible explanation is small projects were less stringently regulated which reduced their investment cost more than what their overseas transaction could bring in. Large market-oriented projects took higher administrative barriers which increased their investment cost more than what their low wages could saved.

Despite their small size, most FIEs in certain sectors such as home appliances, automobiles, chemicals and machine building engage processing trade as shown in table 4, the net trade effect was persistently and substantially negative. FIE has not been expected to be a net foreign exchange earner. The main reason is the increasing ratio of processing trade in the total trade.

Encouraged by China's cheap labor and incentive policies toward export-oriented, more importantly to avoid administrative barriers, more and more FDI take the form of export processing, where raw materials, components or unfinished goods are imported into the country for final assembly and re-export. According to reports of Ministry of Foreign Trade and Economic Cooperation (MOFTEC), in 1985, General trade exports took on 87% of the total export, processing trade only took on 13%, the two ratios were 51% and 47% in 1992, 48% and 50% in 1995, and 41% and 56% in 1997, respectively. It is predicted that import still has an increasing trend.

There are two undesirable consequences of this processing trade for FDI recipient country. First, low labor cost would no longer be an advantage for domestic firms to gain more profit, when exports and imports were both controlled by FIEs or their subsidiaries because they had special competence, and could run them better, or simply because they had cash and the locals did not. Domestic exporter had to depend on FIEs' R and D, product design, brand and international market network. This situation depressed the development of domestic firms. Second, the increased import substitute decreased the demand for domestic intermediate-product industries, which in turn reduced the pulling effect of export to economic growth. So, the export processing would lead to slow growth of total foreign trade, thus weakened the positive effect of foreign trade on the economy as a whole.

Table 4. 1986-1999 External Trade of FIEs (10 thousands US$ and %)

Year	Export		Imports		Export and import	
	Value	As percent of national total (%)	Value	As percent of national total (%)	Value	As percent of national total (%)
Average-1985-90	33.96	5.23	65.51	10.98	99.47	8.28
Average-1991-95	272.47	24.32	402.01	37.70	674.48	30.86
1996	615.06	40.71	756.04	54.45	1371.10	47.29
1997	749.00	41.00	777.20	54.59	1526.20	46.95
1998	809.62	44.06	767.17	54.73	1576.79	48.68
1999	886.28	45.47	858.84	51.83	1831.33	50.78
2000	1194.00	47.90	1591.56	70.70	2785.56	58.73
2001	1271.47	49.56	1789.27	71.09	3060.74	60.79
Average-1985-2001	651.48	29.69	745.48	42.41	1409.28	36.26

Data: calculated according to China statistical yearbook (2000) and various issues of Foreign Investment Statistics

4. FDI's Regional Distribution

The unevenness of the distribution of FDI inflows by province is well known. As table 5 shows, inflows to the ten (eastern) provinces which each took more than 5 per cent of cumulated FDI inflows in 1985-2000, accounted for 86.35 per cent of the total inflows in the same period. These ten provinces (the three municipalities of Beijing, Tianjin, and Shanghai plus the six eastern provinces of Liaoning, Jiangsu, Zhejiang, Fujian, Shandong, Guangdong and the island of Hainan), moreover, accounted for only 42.46 per cent of China's population in 2000.

Even though the government deliberately introduced incentives to invest in west regions. For example, offer super-national treatment of foreign investors in a variety of ways (e.g., benefits of reduced or exempted taxes that are not available to other regions' FIEs). Both in terms of the overall shares and on the per capital basis, the inequality between the East and the West has been enlarged. Besides, we may also note that all the major recipient provinces/ cities of FDI are located in the East. In terms of the share in the total national cumulative actual investment, the four biggest recipient provinces/cities are Guangdong, Jiangsu, Fujian, and shanghai, in descending order. The reason for this concentration are multiple. Provinces with much better industries and human capital bases as well as the infrastructure attract more multinational enterprises. The recent literature, e.g. Dollar, et, al (2001) also demonstrated that administrative procedures-and the costs and delays associated with them-can significantly influence the location of multinational firms and their resulting productivity. Compared with West province, the investment climate in east area generally have held a permanent dominant position as self-authorized operators and have easy market access to other firms. Their low administrative barriers, such as hardly suffering from work stoppages or other turbulences can reduce greatly investment cost and increase investment profit.

Table 5. Foreign Direct Investment Inflows by Region (Millions $)

Year	Eastern Provinces Value	% of total	Central Provinces Value	% of total	Western Provinces Value	% of total	Eastern Western
1985-89	10,417.9	87.78	823.1	6.93	627.9	5.29	9,790
1990	2,974.10	93.86	122.60	3.87	71.71	2.26	2,902.39
1991	3,888.49	94.28	168.46	4.08	67.61	1.64	3,820.88
1992	6,715.50	59.32	4,397.88	38.85	207.59	1.83	6,507.91
1993	23,887.99	87.37	2,427.99	8.88	1,025.76	3.75	22,862.23
1994	25,872.40	86.47	2,612.69	8.73	1,434.91	4.79	24,437.49
1995	31,669.39	87.38	3,429.36	9.46	1,144.74	3.16	30,524.65
1996	36,859.58	88.03	3,985.92	9.52	1,024.21	2.45	35,835.37
1997	34,782.30	84.58	4,787.65	11.64	1,554.14	3.78	33,228.16
1998	39,490.12	87.21	4,420.22	9.76	1,373.55	3.03	38,116.57
1999	35,049.74	87.77	3,747.41	9.38	1,137.67	2.85	33,912.07
2000	35,675.49	88.12	3,585.72	8.85	1,221.72	3.01	34,453.77
2001	36,397.56	87.22	4,189.31	10.04	1,145.13	2.74	35,252.43
1985-2001	287,283	86.35	34,509	10.37	10,891.5	3.27	276,391.5
Population (Million)	535.97	42.46	439.40	34.81	286.91	22.73	249.06

Data: Computed based on data from International Trade (various issues) by MOFTEC for 1992-2001, and from China Statistical Yearbook (various issues) by SSB for other years

Note: All numbers of FDI flows and stock are realized investment in current values

The distribution of the 500 largest foreign-funded enterprises (FIEs) (in terms of sales value in 1999) is even more skewed. The top 500 FIEs were mainly engaged in electronics; machine-making; food-processing; textiles and clothing and automobiles and more than half of them (257) were funded with capital from Hong Kong and Macau. Of the rest, Japan accounted for 66 and the USA for 50. The top 500 were distributed among 24 provinces and municipalities, 91 per cent of them along the coast (China Economic News, 2000, 12.9).

MANIFESTATIONS OF ADMINISTRATIVE BARRIERS

Administrative barriers exist in all countries. Indeed, it is legitimate for governments to control or even screen for some activities and investors who are going to install on their territory. Authorities have generally advanced arguments such as security, protection of the environment, health protection, and quality control. But the excessive administrative barriers which lie in fundamental factors such as the legal system, the political regime, trade and financial openness, and public wages hinder necessary FDI inflows. A country where it takes excessive time and costs to accomplish all the procedures necessary to establish and operate a business will see its potential investors lose money and decide to locate elsewhere or cancel their investment projects. The problem tends to be more serious in China because of the incomplete regulation framework and because of unnecessary bureaucratic interference. Major Chinese barriers of concern include:

1. Investment Restrictions

1.1. Ownership Restriction

Although the number of projects in the encouraged category has increased from 186 to 263 while the number of restricted projects has been reduced from 112 to 75. The new Catalogue brought no significant breakthrough other than the existing commitments contained in the WTO Protocol; moreover, while the total number of encouraged projects may have increased and the number of restricted areas is fewer, some of the key industries and big ticket items, such as construction and operation of power grids, and futures, are still off-limits to foreign investors. Here are percentages of permitted foreign ownership of businesses in several "restricted" sectors of China's economy:

1. Advertising agencies: Will rise from current 49 percent limit to 100 percent by 2005.
2. Banking and financial services: Local currency transactions with Chinese enterprises starting 2003. With Chinese individuals, starting 2006. Financial companies can offer auto financing.
3. Insurance: Non-life insurers, from less than 51 percent now to 100 percent by 2003. Life insurers, limit will remain at less than 50 percent, though AIA has offered life and non-life insurance through a wholly owned subsidiary since 1992. Brokerages, from less than 50 percent now to 100 percent by 2006.
4. Securities and mutual funds: Prohibited till 2004, when up to one-third or more will be permitted. Mutual fund companies, to 49 percent by 2004.
5. Telecom: Paging services, to 50 percent by 2003; mobile voice and data, 49 percent by 2004 and 100 percent by 2006; international and domestic long distance, 49 percent by 2007.
6. Wholesale and retail: 50 percent as of 2002, rising to 100 percent by 2004, except for chain retailers, which cannot be majority-owned by foreigners. Chains cannot have more than 30 stores (Source: Mike View partner-Asia business group, Ernst and Young LLP).

1.2. Rate of Return Restrictions

Although not officially documented, there is general agreement that beginning in 1993, the State planning Commission, which must approve all projects costing more than $30 million, stopped approving all FDI projects with projected rates of return in excess of a limit, for example, fifteen percent for power project, (World Electric Power Industry, 1996). Though regulations on rates of return to FDI in power sector are not uncommon in developing countries, the Chinese government's de facto cap was set at an unusually low level given the risks involved. In other Asian countries, rates of return in excess of twenty percent are the norm (Blackman 1997).

The de facto cap on rate of return had several impacts. First, many foreign investors lost interest completely. And second, a bias was created in favor of small-scale projects costing less than $30 million that do not need the approval of the state Planning Commission. It is not uncommon for foreign investors to split relatively large projects into several "phase" to by-pass the state regulatory agencies.

1.3. Operating Rights restriction

Chinese officials pressure foreign investors to agree to contract provisions which stipulate technology transfers, exporting a certain share of production, and commitments on local content. China restricts the number and types of entities in China that are allowed to import products into China, and foreign companies are not permitted to directly engage in trade in China.

1.4. Distribution Rights Restriction

Most foreign companies are prohibited from selling their products directly to Chinese consumers.

2. Non-Transparent and Inaccessible FDI Rules and Regulations

While China has enacted legislation to facilitate foreign investment in general, the country lacks of an adequate rule-based legal and regulatory environment for investment FDI. Among problems disappointed foreign investors are:

1. There are too much uncertainty, as interpretation and enforcement of rules-from registering a new company, to acquiring land, to paying taxes-change rapidly and depend on which government official is doing the interpreting or enforcing.
2. The country lacks a specific law governing the specific sectors to serve as a basis for operating business. For example, the telecom sector is currently guided only by a few fragmented administrative rules and regulations. Several drafts of a telecom law have been prepared, but bureaucratic inertia and irreconcilable interests have stymied the process. Without a national law with an overarching set of regulations, procedures, and enforcement mechanism, the legality of foreign investment projects remain unclear, thus most foreign investors interested in China's post-WTO telecom market are wary of this lack of protection, and many are holding off on future investment until the investment environment improves.
3. It is not easy to get access to the content of the laws and regulations that apply to business operations. The dissemination of legal information in China is so underdeveloped, so unsystematic that it is often difficult simply to find the applicable law. Even when the relevant rule can be found, provisions are often so broad and sketchy that it is difficulty to be certain of correct interpretation. There is also no systematic compilation of case-law precedents that would aid in the interpretation of statutes and regulations. There is also the vexing problem of the so-called "neibu" or internal agency rules.
4. Until now, minority shareholders rights have not been understood by Chinese officials, or addressed fully and consistently in Chinese law.

3. Bureaucratic Interference

Most of the complaints by foreign-investors is unnecessary bureaucratic interference on their firm's decision-making process, and subordinates' appointment and dismiss, unexpected labor, health and safety inspections, etc. The party's pervasive influence is in every branch of government. According to a survey of firms around the world by the world bank (1997), on a 1-7 scale where 7 indicating the highest level of regulatory burden, China received a rating of 4.58 (In comparison, Singapore's bureaucratic burden received a score of 2.08). The viability of foreign firms in China depends critically on their ability to enforce business contracts in an environment in which contract law is still in its infancy. Though legal uncertainties affect operating contracts for production, input and sale, they are perhaps most daunting for so-called "power purchase contracts". The mechanism that foreign private investors seem to have relied upon in lieu of improvement in the investment environment is to create incentives for various level governments to uphold their contracts by including them as partner in joint ventures. But this strategy promotes rent seeking and vertical integration that limits competition.

Given the advantage of teaming up with strategically chosen Chinese partners to mitigate financial and operational risk, the joint corporations (JCs) has been a main vehicle for FDI, it has been reported recently that more than half of JCs in China are failing to make a profit (Henley et. al. 1999). Of the three main kinds of foreign direct investment, table 6 shows the number of JC decreased considerably during 1990s, declining from 72.9 percent of the total value of projects signed in 1992 to 60 percent in 2000. The decreasing popularity of this form of foreign direct investment testifies, inter alia, to a losing confidence which investors feel about establishing a presence in China.

Table 6. FDI by Type of Investment, 1992 and 2000

	1992			2000		
	No of Projects	Value ($m)	% of total	No of Projects	Value ($m)	% of total
Joint venture	34,354	29,128.5	50.1	7,050	15,827.3	39.9
Co-operative venture	5,711	13,255.5	22.8	1,656	8,233.7	20.8
WFO	8,692	15,696.2	27.0	8,201	15,544.8	39.3
Total	48,764	58,123.5	100	16,907	39,605.8	100

Data: From China Statistical Yearbook by SSB, 1994 and 2001

High administrative barriers made the other vehicles of foreign investment, such as Joint-stock companies and limited-liability companies, are less prevalent. Wei (1999) offered a striking sample calculation: if China is able to reduce red tape and corruption to a level comparable to Singapore, a double FDI increase could be expected.

4. Foreign Exchange Control

After the January 1994 reform prohibited the settling of transactions in foreign currency and eliminated the swap centers,, now foreign firms must use a network of foreign exchange banks. These provide foreign exchange subject to the annual approval of the State Administration of Exchange Control (SAEC). FDI firms are no longer guaranteed by the government that sufficient foreign exchange will be available to them. Because the Chinese currency is not yet fully convertible, foreign joint ventures have to take a risk that their foreign exchange needs cannot be met by purchasing it at banks.

CAUSES OF EXCESSIVE ADMINISTRATIVE BARRIERS

As already noted, administrative barriers in China mainly arises from incomplete regulation framework and bureaucratic interference. China's economy remains an unbalanced mixture of imperfect markets with noncompetitive enterprises and markets where market systems and the forces of competition are gradually emerging. Its administrative system remains politics. China's major problem in achieving perfect investment climate is the immaturity of government policy, mainly reflected in the following ways:

1. Current Chinese FDI policy is vague regarding the administrative of foreign investor's entry and operation, the project's examination and approval are implemented by government politics, and obtaining a operation licence to some extend depends on officials' willingness not on clear criteria. They held monopoly status when their authority cannot be supervised, and once they became profit-oriented, tended to seek profits far higher than normal.
2. Unequal treatment, due to unfavorable policy reasons, makes it impossible for some FIEs to compete with an equality of opportunity to succeed. Export-oriented FDI policy made Western investors who are aim at China's potential vast market frustrated in 1990s, but current hi-tech-oriented FDI policy ignoring local capabilities and economic fundamentals also let them disappointed.
3. In the process of transition and without a sound supervisory system, officials of various level governments tend to take a short-term view and pursue local protectionism policy against foreign investors.

An absence of institutional independence from political control and the uniform enforcement of national regulations present a serious obstacle to the establishment of an good investment climate. For example:

1. The government's multiple roles as social and economic manager, owner of state assets, and business operator, have remained basically unchanged.
2. Government regulatory bodies do not have enough control over local level sectors. Control, if any, stays at the administrative levels, without legislative and regulatory support.

3. For the administrative mechanism to play its role in securing the FDI entry and operation, the competitive process must be allowed, and encouraged, to work. Problems arising in the transition of the open market in China have to be addressed through the reform of FDI regime. The unique situation in China is a problem of the institution, not one caused by the institution. Distortions of administrative mechanisms caused by the administrative economy over the years can be observed everywhere. It will take time to remove them, and to build up a universal appreciation in China of the sound institution structure.

THE DAMAGING EFFECTS OF EXCESSIVE ADMINISTRATIVE BARRIERS

Excessive administrative barriers represent an abuse of power by government, driven by the vested interests of a department or a locality, and manifested in local blockades, departmental barriers, sector monopolies, and collaboration between the bureaucracy and businesses. FDI can damage indigenous industries' development are deeply rooted in some aspects of China's economic life, are extremely powerful, and directly affect the development of an open, competitive economy and hinder it integrate into international market. Among the damaging effects are:

1. Harm to the enthusiasm of foreign-investors. Excessive administrative barriers discourage foreign investors show no current signs of abatement. Most foreign companies are hesitant to say the least, regarding the formation of new venture. For example, two of the largest chemical multinational corporations, E.I. du Pout de Numours and Co. and the Dow Chemical Co. have tended to adopt a more cautious approach, no more investment in China in 2002 because of concern about profitability and administrative risk. Disillusioned from their idealism and tired of the bureaucratic red tape and regulatory hassles involved in investing in China, many investors who are developing an Internet business have exited the Chinese market (Gigalaw.com).

2. Lead to inadequate investment. This, together with declining employment and depressed consumer demand, are major issues facing China's economy. Take the power sector as an example, according to China's Ministry of Electric Power, between 1995-2010, China's power sector need an average investment of 15.8 billion $ per year in order to meet the growing demand for electricity. Of the funding needed between 1995-2000 China expected to be able to finance 30 percent (about 4,740 million per year) with foreign resources. Only one third was realized in 1998, the most ideal FDI inflows year for power industry. As for construction industry, during 1999 the value of contracted (as opposed to realized) FDI fell by 124 per cent; it fell by another 120 per cent, to $916.9 million in 2000 (China Statistical yearbook, 2001).

3. Reduce FDI's leading effect on economic growth. Although development experiences in many industrial and developing countries indicate that FDI can lead to desirable outcomes such as positive spillovers for the local economy in terms of

growth and productivity. Li (2002) demonstrate the experience of China suggests that Policies biased against FDI in an attempt to protect national industrial and export-orientation have undermined FDI's contribution to national economic development, according to the analysis in this paper. On one hand, domestic enterprises (DEs)-FIEs segmentation made it impossible for economy to benefit from productivity improvement via technology transfer and spillover, which can be obtained through the introduction of capital-intensive technology that can be emulated by domestic firms, the training of workers and managers who may transfer their skills elsewhere. On the other hand, export oriented FDI, which has been encouraged by China's cheap labor and incentive policies toward this type of FDI, concentrated on labor-intensive and some simple capital-intensive manufacturing activities. Processing trade has been taken as its first choice. The increased import has lead to a reduction in China's favorable balance of trade, thus weaken the pulling effect of foreign trade on the economy as a whole.

4. Breed corruption. State propaganda decries corruption, yet China has been called one of, if not the most corrupt nations in Asia. With a few officials abusing their power in public administration to get money, FDI has become a hotbed of corruption, from high-level officials who demand "partnership" in companies that look like they will be profitable ventures-to the lowest level customs or expertise official. The problem in China is that besides published regulations agencies often issue internal (neibu) unpublished rules, which are inaccessible to outsiders and which at times are the real rules under which the agency operates. To find out the content of these rules would require many visits to an agency and even then would often not result in disclosure. This practice leaves too much power in the hands of agency bureaucrats, forms a main source breeding corruption. There is a sentence "relative connection is very important to do business in China". Jeffrey McChesney, vice president of process excellence for corporate services with Atlas Air Inc., the world's third-largest air cargo carrier based in White Plains (Harrison), acknowledged Atlas Air has spent the past five years developing relationships with Chinese officials in hopes of tapping into China's air cargo market, especially as it looks to grow through foreign investment in the next few years. Corruption not only causes reduced inward foreign direct investment due to higher sales expenses in the invested country, but also reduces incentives for the foreign-invested company to re-invest in the host country. This can result in the flight of the foreign-invested company to another country for their investments.

CONCLUSIONS AND FUTURE MEASURES TO CURB EXCESSIVE ADMINISTRATIVE BARRIERS

China is in a transition from a closed economy to an open market economy. Administrative Barriers to foreign direct investment in China is reflected largely in investment restriction, non-transparent and inaccessible FDI rule and regulation, as well as bureaucratic interference in terms of the distortion of FDI operation behavior and the preclusion of market competition. They have become a pressing issue facing foreign investors in making decision to invest in china. China has made great effort to develop a regulation framework on incentive FDI, but this framework currently appears weak and powerless in the face of the administrative barriers. In order to maintain China's inward FDI trend, the aims of the measures to be taken against excessive administrative barriers are:

1. To complete a legal framework on FDI entry and operation. Reform and liberalizing of the FDI regime should be carried out within this legal framework. With China's accession to the WTO and the need for international integration, it is all the more important and urgent to develop legislation governing FDI entry and operation. The purpose of the existing laws relating to FDI (such as Guiding Regulations and Catalogue) is to ensure the safety of national industries rather than regulating the behavior of FIEs in these sectors. It is necessary to review, revise and improve the existing laws and regulations which are helpful to form excessive administrative barriers and the introduction of effective competition, and to speed up the formulation of a systematic compilation of case-law precedents that would aid in the interpretation of statutes and regulations.

2. To rebuild the government administrative system and exercise effective supervision. Removing excessive administrative barriers should be carried out simultaneously with a change in the role of the government. An effective government supervisory institution and system should be established, so as to ensure the development of rationalizing administrative procedures: to reduce bureaucratic red tape, simplify approval procedures, eliminating unnecessary forms, signatures, and documents. Establishing virtual network or on-line registration linking together agencies and, thus, facilitating the relations not only between investors and government's officials but also within the public administration.

3. To develop institutional mechanisms that limit default contracts. In its current state, Chinese contract law may not be sufficient to eliminate default risk. But it might be possible to structure rules that would at least provide some certainty about the legal process that would ensue upon default and about what remedies could reasonably be expected.

4. To deepen state-owned enterprise reform and the adjustment of ownership structures and to improve competition within sectors. Existing monopolistic sectors should carry out reforms and get ready for competition. The discriminatory policy against FIEs needs to be changed. Competition among state, private and foreign investors should be encouraged through the promotion of foreign investment, breaking up monopolies, and the establishment of a modern corporate system.

5. Last but not least, administrative barriers reflect more profound characteristics of a country. Administrative reforms must be incorporated in broader reforms, such as trade and financial liberalization, corruption and public sector reforms. the reform of the devolved and localized character of the investment regime, especially in the realm of taxation and the foreign exchange regime. Smash the high degree of local government autonomy, develop a united open market in China. Build a good operation environment for FDI enterprises. Reduce interference by party and local government officials in FDI's operation.

REFERENCES

Blackman, A., and X. Wu, (1997) "Climate Impacts of Foreign Direct Investment in the Chinese Power Sector: Barriers and Opportunities" *http://www.rff.org/reports/1997.htm*

Anonymous, (2001) "The institutional and policy environment for investment in Russia" *Financial Market Trends*, Paris, Issue 79, Page 137.

D. Dollar et al., (2002) "Investment Climate and Firm Productivity: India 2000-01 " *World Bank, mimeo. http://econ.worldbank.org/staff/mhallward.*

Djankov, S. La Porta, F. Lopez De Silanes, A. Shleifer, (2002) "The Regulation of Entry" *Quarterly Journal of Economics*, February, Volume 9, Page 19.

Epstein, G. (1996) "Economic beat: Risk measures prove to be excellent forecasters of the rise and fall of markets abroad" *Barron's*, Chicopee, Mar 11, Volume 76, Issue 11, Page 48.

Henley, J., C. Kirkpatrick and G. Wilde. (1999) "Foreign Direct Investment (FDI) in China: Recent Trends and Current Policy Issues" *Public Policy and management Working Paper* No. 7.

http://idpm.man.ac.uk/wp/ppm/ppm_wp07abs.htm.

Lardy, N. (1995) "The Role of Foreign Trade and Investment in China's Economic Transformation" *China Quarterly*, 144, 1065-82.

Li, Y. (forthcoming) "How Beneficial is Foreign Direct Investment for China's Economic Growth?" *Open Economic Review.*

Lui, Z. (2000) "Foreign Direct Investment and Technology Spillover: Some Evidence from China" *http://faculty.Washington.edu/karyiu/confer.*

Wei, S. J. (1999) "Can China and India Double Their Inward Foreign Direct Investment? " *NBER Working Paper*, No. 2399.

Y. Huang, (2000) **"Why is Foreign Direct Investment Too Much of a Good Thing for China?"**

http://www.fas.harvard.edu/~asiactr/mas/summaries/MAS_021100.html.

Zhang, K. H. (2001) "What Attracts Foreign Multinational Corporations to China? " *Contemporary Economic Policy*, Vol. 19, No. 3, July, P336-346.

In: China in Focus Economic, Political and Educational Issues
Editor: Ernest P. Nolan, pp. 67-80

ISBN 1-60021-543-8
© 2007 Nova Science Publishers, Inc.

Chapter 5

CHINESE CIVIL ORGANIZATIONS LEADING THE WAY TO DEMOCRACY?

Chunlong Lu[*]

International Studies, Graduate Program in International Studies,
Old Dominion University

ABSTRACT

This study mainly draws upon Robert Putnam (1993)'s framework, which focuses the effect of civil organization on civic culture, to evaluate the impacts of China's civil organizations on its democratic transition. The result indicates that: 1) there is a positive relation between civil organizational engagement and social trust, however such relation is not strong and significant; 2) participation in all types of civil organizations tends to decrease parochial culture of familism and have a weak relation with one's desire for authority; 3) all types of civil organization participation have a highly significant positive relationship with political discussion but a weak positive relation with one's political interest. These findings support the semi-civil society model of Chinese civil organizations. Chinese civil organizations are still far from developing. When more Chinese people are more active in civil participation, measured by the percentage of membership in more than 2 civil organizations, and when more public interest organizations emerge, the impacts of China's civil organizations on its civic culture will be more positive, and the implication for democratic transitions will be more significant.

I. INTRODUCTION

Democratization theorists have recognized the relations between civil society and democracy. With economic development, civil society will emerge and limit the tyranny of state power, and even become a foundation for democratic transitions. The recent South

[*] Present Address: 1069 W. 41st Street, Apt#2, Norfolk, VA 23508. Email: chunlonglu@hotmail.com. Tel: 757 683 6130 (O)

Korea and Taiwan experiences have demonstrated the linear model between economic development, civil society and democratization (Diamond 1999).

China's economy has experienced rapid growth since 1978. During the process of economic development, the number of China's civil organizations (*Minjian Zuzhi*) has increased. In the year between 1979 and 1992, the number of national civil organizations rises sevenfold (averaging 48% a year), and the averaging increase of provincial civil organizations has developed even faster (Pei 1998). In the end of 2002, there are 13,3340 civil organizations in China. Some scholars equate these civil organizations with civil society. Therefore, it is expected that these civil organizations will work as driving factors for China's democratic transition (White 1993, Johnson 2003). On the other hand, more and more literature emphasizes that these civil organizations are initiated and controlled by Chinese party-state and questions the autonomy of these civil organizations (Dickson 2003, Goodman 1999, Pearson 1997, Unger and Chan 1995, 1996). Therefore, it is argued that these civil organizations cannot be equal with civil society and cannot play an active role in promoting democracy in China.

This study mainly draws upon Robert Putnam (1993)'s framework, which focuses the effect of civil organizations on civic culture, to evaluate the impacts of China's civil organizations on its democratic transition. Extensive civil organizational participation is believed to generate a cluster of civic attributes, which are the underlying values for developing democracy. The basic research question of this study is that, "Will China's civil organizations generate the same civic attributes as their Western counterparts have done?"

This study is based on the scientifically sampled national survey of public opinion in China, the World Values Survey (WVS) 1995. WVS 1995 China Survey replicates the core questionnaire of the international WVS project and provides the feasibility of cross-national comparison. WVS 1995 China Survey inquires about family and social relations, membership and participation in civil organizations, and democratic values. This study will mainly rely on WVS 1995 China Survey to achieve three objectives: first, describing Chinese participation in civil organizations; second, exploring the impacts of Chinese civil participation on their cultural values; thirdly, elaborating their implication for China's democratic changes.

II. THEORIES OF CIVIL SOCIETY

The relations between civil society and democracy have been a salient topic for democracy literature (Diamond 1994, 1999, Putnam 1993, Schmitter 1997). A vibrant civil society is believed to serve the development, deepening, and consolidation of democracy (Diamond 1999). Scholars like Larry Diamond believe that a vibrant civil society is crucial both in producing democratic transitions and in deepening, consolidating democracy. Scholars like Philippe Schmitter admit that civil society plays an important role in democratic consolidation, but disagree with the relation between civil society and democratic transitions (Schmitter 1997). A third school of thought stresses the impacts of civil society on building social capital and cultivating democratic attitudes (Putnam 1993).

Diamond establishes linkage both between civil society and democratic transition and between civil society and democratic consolidation. According to Diamond (1999), civil society is "the realm of social life that is open, voluntary, self-generating, at least partially self-supporting, autonomous from the state, and bound by a legal order or set of shared values" (Diamond 1999: 221). Civil society can promote democracy if they are aimed at achieving democratic values and norms and are actively pursuing such objectives. Diamond identifies five features of democracy-promoting civil society (or democratic civil society): self-government, democratic goals and methods, organizational institutionalization, pluralism without fragmentation, and density (Diamond 1999: 227-233). Diamond concludes, "in a number of prominent cases, civil society has played a crucial role, if not the leading role, in producing a transition to democracy" (Diamond 1999: 235). Diamond identifies ten important functions of civil society playing in promoting democratic development and consolidation: "setting the limit on state power, supplementing the role of political parties, developing democratic attributes, creating channels for interest aggregation and representation, mitigating political conflicts, recruiting and training new political leaders, monitoring elections, disseminating information, supporting economic reform, and strengthening the democratic state" (Diamond 1994: 7-11).

Schmitter (1997) warns against the optimistic view of the role of civil society. He discredits the linkage between civil society and democratic transition by asserting "the existence of civil society is not a prerequisite either for the demise of autocracy or for the transition to democracy, not is it ordinarily sufficient to bring about such a change in regime" (Schmitter 1997: 242). On the other hand, Schmitter acknowledges the role of civil society in the consolidation of democracy by asserting "the presence of a civil society......contributes positively to the consolidation (and, later, to the persistence) of democracy" (Schmitter 1997: 240). Schmitter defines civil society as "a set or system of self-organized intermediary groups that: (1) are relatively independent of both public authorities and private units of production and reproduction, i.e. of firms and families; (2) are capable of deliberating about and taking collective actions in defense/promotion of their interests or passions; (3) but do not seek to replace either state agents or private (re)producers or to accept responsibility for governing the polity as a whole; (4) but do agree to act within pre-established rules of a 'civil,' i.e. mutually respectful, nature" (Schmitter 1997: 240).

Beginning with De Tocqueville, there is a long tradition of political culture research that stresses the beneficial impacts of a vibrant civil society on political culture (Putnam 1993). Civil associations "instill in their members habits of cooperation, solidarity, and public-spiritedness". "Participation in civic organizations inculcates skills of cooperation as well as a sense of shared responsibility for collective endeavors.

Moreover, when individuals belong to 'cross-cutting' groups with diverse goals and members, their attitudes will tend to moderate as a result of group interaction and cross pressures" (Putnam 1993: 89-90). According to Putnam (1993), civil society consists of a set of voluntary organizations and is based on horizontal solidarity of the groups that crosscut vertical ties of kinship and patronage. And such horizontal voluntary associations are capable of generating social capital (i.e., trust, democratic norms and networks). Through the intervening variable of social capital, civil society can influence the effectiveness of democratic governance. In conclusion, for Putnam, a dense associational landscape, high level of social capital and effective democracy are significantly inter-correlated.

Furthermore, the existing literature suggests social trust as the major measure of social capital in a nation. For example, Ronald Inglehart (1997) and Putnam (1993) both use social trust to measure social capital. According to Putnam, 'social capital' means features of social life   networks, norms, and trust   that enable participants to act together more effectively to pursue shared interests" (Jackman and Miller 1998: 49). Inglehart interprets social capital as "a culture of trust and tolerance, in which extensive networks of voluntary associations emerge" (Inglehart 1997: 188).

III. PAST RESEARCH: CHINA'S CIVIL ORGANIZATIONSAND DEMOCRATIZATION

Chinese scholars have adopted all these arguments to analyze Chinese politics and to predict prospective democratization. For example, Gordon White argues that economic development has resulted in the emergence of state-led civil society. Such state-led civil society is expected to be the basis of Chinese democratization in the near future (White 1993). In their *In Search of Civil Society*, White *et al.* (1996) conclude that the balance of power between state and society in contemporary China is shifting gradually in favor of the societal forces. They assert that "the Party/state's coping strategy—a combination of incorporation and repression—has channeled and staunched the rise of organized social forces, but was proving increasingly problematic as the pace of socio-economic change accelerated in the mid-1990s" (White *et al.* 1996: 211). Ian Johnson (2003) optimistically claims that with China's economic development and its people better educated, China's citizens "have started to demand more from their government," and "these sorts of demands have given rise to numerous unofficial—and in many cases illegal—groups outside the government's control: hence, civil society." Such civil groups are "pushing for change" and "China is in a transition from a society of strong governmental control to one where civil society controls more" (Johnson 2003: 553).

On the other hand, many scholars question the applicability of the civil society theory in China. B. Michael Frolic (1997) considers civil society as it is currently theorized to be culturally bound to popular Western narratives of democratic development and prefers to enlarge the category to include what he terms "state-led civil society." This "state-led civil society" is created by Chinese party-state in order to help it govern and to co-opt social forces. Furthermore, a handful of scholars have found that civil society model is not suitable for analyzing Chinese politics, and they assert that state corporatism is more useful in analyzing Chinese politics (Dickson 2003, Goodman 1999, Pearson 1997, Unger and Chan 1995, 1996). Consistent with Schmitter's (1974) definition of state corporatism, all these scholars emphasize Chinese party- state's licensing of intermediary social associations in order to better carry out the party-state goals. Under the structure of state corporatism, Chinese party-state controls, licenses and regulates all of the corporatist associations, and grant them the monopolistic power to represent the relevant sector interests and regulate the activities of relevant sectors. Therefore, China's civil organizations have a dual function: they are designed to give the party-state control over organized interests in society and also to represent their members' interests (Dickson 2003, Pearson 1997).

The debates from the two sides are still far from clarifying the relations between civil society and potential democracy in China. The optimistic scholars emphasize the linear model between economic development, civil organizations, and democratization. The opposite side realizes that Chinese party-state has the will and capabilities to pre-empt the development of Western-style civil society in China. They argue that contemporary Chinese civil organizations are not the automatic result of economic development, but the result of Chinese state corporatist policies. Therefore, such corporatist organizations cannot contribute to China's democracy in the long run; on the contrary, they only strengthen the power of Chinese party-state.

As He Baogang (1997) has suggested the assumption of autonomy and independence is not suited for studying China's civil organizations. The expectation that China's civil organizations will perform the same democratic functions in accordance with Diamond's theory is far from China's real situation. According to He (1997), "Chinese autonomous organizations are neither completely autonomous from the state nor completely dependent on the state. It is the feature of partial autonomy and overlapping with the state that makes Chinese social associations as semi- or quasi-civil society" (He 1997: 7-8). He believes that semi-civil society model is "appropriate, adequate and useful to understand the actual degree of the development of associational life in China and the complexity of the relationship between the state and society" (He 1997: 8). This study adopts He's concept of "semi-civil society" to study China's civil organizations. But when studying the relation between China's semi-civil society and democracy, this study mainly draws upon Putnam's framework, which focuses the effect of civil organizations on civic culture, to evaluate the impacts of China's civil organizations on its democratic transition.

There are two considerations for adopting Putnam's framework in this study: first, Putnam's framework is more appropriate to study the relations between Chinese civil organizations and its democratic potential. Chinese civil organizations are far from performing "real" democratic functions as Diamond or Schmitter claim; second, even though there are some studies about the impacts of Chinese civil organizations on its civic attributes, there is no systemic study about such impacts. Next, this study will examine whether extensive participation in Chinese civil organizations will generate the same social trust as their Western counterparts have done; and then it will examine the impacts of Chinese civil organizations on its political culture.

IV. CIVIL SOCIETY AND SOCIAL TRUST

The political culture literature has identified the relations between social trust and modern democracy (Inglehart 1999). Putnam (1993) argues that social trust can improve the efficiency of society by facilitating coordinating actions (Putnam 1993: 167). After examining the effectiveness of democratic governance across Italian 20 region, Putnam concludes that the performance of democratic governance relies on levels of social trust generated by civic engagement. Inglehart (1997) operationalizes the concept of civic culture by three indicators: (1) interpersonal trust, (2) life satisfaction, and (3) support for revolutionary change, the latter being negatively correlated with the civic culture. His empirical studies show a strong correlation between the number of durable years of democratic institutions and civic culture. Furthermore, Inglehart claims: 1) social trust is a relatively enduring characteristic of given societies and reflects the entire historical heritage of a given society, including economic, political, religious, and other factors; 2) democratic institutions do not necessarily produce social trust (Inglehart 1999). Therefore, if before democratic transition, a given society has accumulated enough social trust, the process of democratic transitions and consolidation will be much smoother.

Chinese society has been characterized with a low level of social trust, since Confucian culture does not encourage social trust at the societal level (Pye 1985).

Pye argues that Chinese traditional culture is family-oriented culture. In traditional Chinese Confucian culture, family relations take precedence over all other social relations (Fukuyama 1995, Pye 1985). Family members have moral obligations to the whole family and children have to respect and obey parents. "Given the strength of intrafamilial bonds within a traditional Chinese society, ties between people unrelated to each other are relatively weak. In other words, in a Chinese society there is a relatively high degree of distrust between people who are not related" (Fukuyama 1995). Pye also concludes that there is a very low level of social trust in Chinese Confucian culture (Pye 1985, 1992). Therefore, traditional Chinese Confucian culture, which possesses the strong familism and consequent reluctance of the Chinese to trust people outside of their kinship groups undermines social trust that is widely linked to democratic politics.

It is important to conduct research to determine whether Chinese civil organizations will generate significant social trust in accordance with Putnam's theory. If Chinese civil organizations can increase social trust significantly, the process of China's potential democratic transitions will be much smoother. According to Putnam, the denser the networks of voluntary associations and organizations, the more likely there will be high levels of social trust. "Networks of associational participation increase the potential costs to a defection in any individual transaction; networks of associational participation foster robust norms of reciprocity; networks of associational participation facilitate communication and improve the inflow of information about the trustworthiness of individuals; networks of associational participation embody past success at collaboration, which can serve as a culturally-defined template for future collaboration" (Putnam 1993: 173-174). Putnam claims that his theory can be dated back from Tocqueville and John Stuart Mill. Furthermore, Putnam makes distinction between horizontally organized associations and vertically organized associations. The horizontally organized associations build norms of generalized reciprocity and interpersonal trust, which are favorable to the durable and effective democracy. On the other hand, the vertically organized associations undermine norms of reciprocity and interpersonal trust, since more powerful members can defect from agreements with less powerful members (Putnam 1993).

The examination between Chinese civil organizations and social trust finds a complex non-linear relationship between the total membership of civil organizations and social trust (Table 1). Social trust is low among those who have only one membership in civil organizations (49.9%). Those who do not have a membership have an even higher (52.2%) level of social trust than those who have only one membership. Such finding supports the hierarchical nature of Chinese civil organizations. The existing literature has suggested that there exists a hierarchically ordered structure from the center downward to the local level in a given civil organization. This structure guarantees that the directives can be transferred from the center downward to the local level (Dickson 2003, Goodman 1999, Pearson 1994, 1997, Unger and Chan 1995, 1996). The hierarchical relationship within Chinese civil organizations therefore undermines norms of reciprocity and interpersonal trust. On other hand, for those whom have more than 2 memberships in civil organizations, the level of interpersonal trust increases significantly (56.1%). The possible explanation is that, with more engagement in civil organization, people can learn the "habit of cooperation and collaboration" and become to appreciate the values of interpersonal trust. However, the percentage of those whom have more than 2 memberships in civil organizations is still very low, 19.0% of the whole population (Table 2).

The existing literature on China's civil organizations has suggested that their autonomy, independence, and functions are not same. Even though some civil associations are under the complete control by Chinese party-state, others enjoy certain level of independence and a capacity to represent their members' interests (Pei 1998, White 1993). This study makes distinctions between three types of civil organizations: cultural, economic and public interest.

Table 1. Crosstab between Civil Organizations and Interpersonal Trust

Interpersonal Trust		Civil Organizations		
		Non-Membership	Membership in 1 Civil Organization	Membership in More than 2 Civil Organizations
Most people can be trusted	Frequency	407	192	157
	Percent	52.2%	49.9%	56.1%
Cannot be too careful	Frequency	373	193	123
	Percent	47.8%	50.1%	43.9%
Total (N)	Frequency	780	385	280
	Percent	100.0%	100.0%	100.0%

Source: World Values Survey 1995: China

Table 2. Membership in Civil Organizations

	Frequency	Percent
Non-Membership	814	54.3
Membership in 1 Civil Organization	400	26.7
Membership in More than 2 Civil Organizations	286	19.0
Total	1500	100.0

Source: World Values Survey 1995: China

Economic civil organizations refer to productive and commercial organizations (Diamond 1994). They include trade unions, associations of private entrepreneurs, and industrial associations (*Hangye Xiehui*) (He 1997). Most of economic civil organizations are typical corporatist associations. Cultural civil organizations refer intellectual, religious and communal organizations (Diamond 1994). They include sport or recreation organization, art, music or educational organizations, and academic organizations (He 1997, White 1993). Most of these organizations have certain level of autonomy and independence, if we compare with economic civil organizations. Public interest civil organizations refer to those autonomous organizations seeking to promote public interest. They are the active and robust part of civil society and play a direct role in promoting public interest. However, they are underdeveloped in China (He 1997, Pei 1997). Only 8.6 % of Chinese people have membership in public interest organizations (Table 3). The most of legally recognized public interest organizations are environmental organizations and charitable organizations. There are also some underground public interest organizations (He 1997, Johnson 2003).

Table 3. Membership in Three Types of Civil Organizations

	Frequency	Percent
Cultural Civil Organizations	296	19.7
Economic Civil Organizations	347	23.1
Public Interest Organizations	129	8.6

Source: World Values Survey 1995: China

Since public interest civil organizations are relatively autonomous and more representative of their member interests, membership in public interest organizations should increase social trust (Johnson 2003). The finding supports such argument (tau-b= 0.014), however, the relationships are very weak and tenuous (Figure 1). This suggests that China's public interest organizations do play some autonomous role in representing their members' interest; however, such autonomous behaviors always meet with government's control. The economic and cultural civil organizations have a negative relation with social trust (tau-b= – 0.030 and – 0.074) (Figure 1). This supports that most of economic and cultural civil organizations are vertically organized corporatist associations. Therefore, economic and cultural civil organizations cannot generate social trust, which is necessary for smooth democratic transitions and consolidation. The overall relations between China's civil organizational participation and social trust are positive however very weak (tau-b = 0.017).

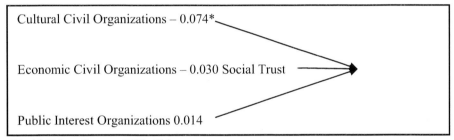

Source: World Values Survey 1995: China
Note: Figures entries are the bi-variable correlations (tau-b) between membership in different types of
    civil organizations and social trust. Coefficients significant at 0.05 level are signified by an asterisk
* The relationship between political interest and civil membership is based on World Values Survey
    1991; other relationships are based on World Values Survey 1995.

Figure 1. The Relationship between Group Membership and Social Trust

Such findings support the cept of "semi-civil society". The overlap between China's civil organizations and Chinese party-state makes the strong positive relations between civil organizational participation and social trust disappear in the Chinese context. On the other hand, the partial autonomy Chinese civil organizations enjoy contributes to the generation of social trust.

V. CIVIL SOCIETY AND AUTHORITY ORIENTATION AND POLITICAL ENGAGEMENT

Chinese traditional political culture has always been regarded as an obstacle to democratic transitions (Huntington 1993, Pye 1985, 1988, 1992). "Classic Chinese Confucianism …… emphasized the group over the individual, authority over liberty, and responsibilities over rights. Confucian societies lacked a tradition of rights against the state; to the extent that individual rights did exist, they were created by the state. Harmony and cooperation were preferred over disagreement and competition. The maintenance of order and respect for hierarchy were central values" (Huntington 1992: 24). Therefore, China's political culture is attributed as "non-democratic or anti-democratic." The nature of China's political culture is authoritarianism and hierarchical and individuals have a strong orientation to defer to authority (Pye 1992). Under this political culture, individuals have little political interest and strong fear of politics. Therefore, two factors inherent in Chinese culture: deference to authority and ignorance of politics are regarded as obstacles to modern democracy.

This study will look at the relations between civil organizational participation and these two core dimensions of China's political culture. Accordingly, this study will answer the following two questions: First, does civil organizational participation will break down Chinese citizen's deference to authority? Second, does civil organizational participation increase Chinese citizen's political engagement?

It is known that Chinese Confucian culture emphasizes respect for authority and social order. Chinese society is a well-ordered society, in which the family is the basic building block (Fukuyama 1995, Pye 1992). Within the family, younger generation is educated to obey and to respect old generation morally. Within the society, individuals are educated to obey and to defer to authority. As Pye insists that, China's traditional cultural basis for legitimacy in China is *filial piety* and family is the primary socializing institutions to inculcate the concept of *filial piety* (Pye 1992). Therefore, Chinese society is a paternalistic society that aims at creating a good society through the leadership of a benevolent state led by the most educated and moral people. The greater good is manifested and overseen by the moral authority of the leadership, reflected in a moralistic father-knows-best paternalism.

The existing literature thus suggests two variables to measure Chinese citizens' authority orientations: one measurement is within family relations and focuses on individual's orientations toward one's parents. The survey question is:

With which of these two statements do you tend to agree?

A. Regardless of what the qualities and faults of one's parents are, one must always love and respect them
B. One does not have the duty to respect and love parents who have not earned it by their behavior and attitudes

1. Tend to agree with statement A
2. Tend to agree with statement B

The second measurement is on social relationships and focuses on individual's desire for authority. The survey question is:
Greater respect for authority

1. Good
2. Do not mind
3. Bad

All types of civil organization participation have a very significantly negative relationship with respect for parents and allegiance toward one's parents (Table 4). The negative relationship between overall memberships in civil organizations and respect for parents and allegiance toward one's parents is surprisingly strong and significant (tau-b= − 0.156). The more civil organizational participation, the less are parochial values of paternalism. Such finding supports development theoriests. Extensive civil participation will break down parochial attitudes and lead to more cosmopolitan views of the world beyond individual families and kinship support systems. The civil participation will indoctrinate communitarian spirit, expose oneself to modern values and learn the good habit of "citizenship". Participation in civil orgnizations could lead to profound cultural changes, reshaping the way children are educated and relate to authority (Diamond 1999).

The relationship between civil organizational participation and desire for authority is complex and non-linear. Economic civil organizations reinforce individual's desire for authority (tau-b= 0.028). Such finding supports corporatist model of Chinese civil organizations. Chinese party-state has created vertically centralized associations in most economic sectors and placed them under strict control, with the purpose of pre-empting any horizontal coalescing of social interests. Most leaders of economic civil association are elected or nominated by Chinese party-state, and the funding of these social associations comes mainly from Chinese party-state, therefore these social associations are highly dependent on Chinese party-state and are rewarded with favorable distribution of social welfares (Dickson 2003, Goodman 1999, Pearson 1994, 1997, Unger and Chan 1995, 1996). As a result, membership in economic civil organizations is not expected to break down individual's orientation of deference to authority. Cultural civil organizational participation has a negative relation with one's desire for authority (Table 4). The possible explanation is that even cultural civil organizations possess characteristics of state corporatism; they enjoy more autonomy and independence than economic civil organizations. Public interest civil organizational membership is expected to decrease one's orientation of deference to authority. The result is that membership in public organizations has a weak positive relation with one's orientation of deference to authority (tau-b= 0.009). The overall relations between memberships in civil organizations and one's desire for authority are negative (tau-b= − 0.017), however, such relations are not very strong and significant. China's civil organizations are still far from working independently, thus, they are far from generating significant favorable orientations.

Chinese traditional political culture is a parochial culture by its nature. Chinese citizens have little knowledge of political affairs and tend to be ignorant and afraid of politics (Pye 1985, 1992). However, modern democracy is based on a participant civic culture, in which the majority of citizens possess certain political efficacy and participate in political affairs (Almond and Verba 1963). toward social authority.

**Table 4. The Relationship between Civil Participation and
Authority Orientations and Political Engagement**

	Authority Orientations		Political Engagement	
	Family	Social	Discussion	Interest
Cultural Civil organizations	-0.157*	-0.041	0.163*	0.042
Economic Civil organizations	-0.081*	0.028	0.155*	-0.024
Public Interest Organizations	-0.060*	0.009	0.065*	0.056
Total Membership	-0.156*	-0.017	0.207*	0.036

Source: World Values Survey 1991, 1995: China

Therefore, the lack of political engagement in Chinese political culture is treated as an obstacle to its search for modern democracy. This study uses two variables to measure Chinese citizens' political engagement: the first one is political discussion, the survey question is:

When you get together with your friends, would you say you discuss political matters frequently, occasionally or never?

1. Frequently
2. Occasionally
3. Never

The second is political interest, the survey question is:
How interested would you say you are in politics?

1. Very interested
2. Somewhat interested
3. Not very interested
4. Not at all interested

Civil organizational participation is believed to increase the political efficacy and skill of democratic citizens that facilitates political engagement. Participation in civil organizations develops a feeling of social efficacy that may spill over to political involvement. The life in civil organizations increases one's democratic attitudes and values and an appreciation of the obligations as well as the rights of democratic citizenship. Furthermore, civil organizational members have access to additional information about political affairs, and this will stimulate an interest in politics (Diamond 1999, Dalton and Ong 2003). These are the causal links between civil organizational participation and political engagement in the western developed countries. This study will study whether such causal relations hold true in the Chinese context.

All types of civil organization participation have a very significantly positive relationship with political discussion (Table 4). The positive relationship between overall memberships in civil organizations and political discussion is surprisingly strong and significant (tau-b=

0.207). The more civil organizational participation, the more it is likely for an individual to discuss politics. Political discussion is a necessary step before considering political action and is regarded as an important dimension of political engagement (Shi 2000). Therefore, such finding is the clear evidence that participation in civil organizations increases political engagement in China.

The relationship between civil organizational participation and political interest is complex and non-linear. Extensive participation in economic organizations decreases one's political interest (Table 4). This supports the corporatist model of Chinese civil organizations. Most economic organizations monopolize the services and benefits in any given sector and make difference between members and non-members (Dickson 2003, Goodman 1999, Pearson 1994, 1997, Unger and Chan 1995, 1996). Organization members have chance to access to services which can only be provided by these organizations. Thus membership comes to be compulsory because otherwise non-members cannot get services. Members in these economic organizations gradually accumulate the feeling that they cannot have any say in political affairs. This kind of feeling dramatically decreases one's political interest. Participation in both cultural and public interest civil organizations increases one's political interest (Table 4). However, such relations are not very strong and significant. There are two possible explanations: First, the autonomy of both cultural and public interest civil organizations always meets with Chinese government's control. These harsh experiences lead to political inefficacy and decline of political interest. Second, members in more autonomous groups can develop low levels of political support of Chinese authoritarian party-state and such low level of political support will lead to decline of interest in politics. The overall relations between memberships in civil organizations and one's political interest are positive (tau-b= 0.036), however, such relations are not very strong and significant.

VI. CONCLUSION

This study has examined the relations between civil organizational participation and social trust and political culture in the Chinese context. Even though Chinese civil organizations cannot work independently like their western counterparts, they do generate some positive impacts on the potential for China's democratic transition through influencing Chinese citizens' cultural orientations. Such findings support the concept of "semi-civil society". The major findings are summarized as follows:

First, there is a positive relation between civil organizational engagement and social trust (tau-b = 0.017); even though such relation is not strong and significant. Due to their corporatist characteristics, participation in both cultural civil organizations and economic organizations tends to decrease social trust. Due to their relative autonomy and "real" representation of their member interests, membership in public interest organizations tends to increase social trust.

Second, participation in all types of civil organizations tends to decrease parochial culture of familism. The possible explanation is that the civil participation will indoctrinate communitarian spirit, expose oneself to modern values and learn the good habit of "citizenship" and thus break down one's respect for parents and allegiance toward family. Membership in civil organizations tends to decrease one's desire for authority; however, such relation is very tenuous. Participation in economic organizations tends to reinforce one's desire for authority. It supports that Chinese civil organizations are far from being independent.

Third, all types of civil organization participation have a highly significant positive relationship with political discussion. On the other hand, membership in civil organizations has a weak positive relation with one's political interest. Such a gap can be explained by the fact that civil organizations are the primary vehicle for exchanging political information, for discussing political events, and for transmitting new political ideas in a non-democratic society. At the same time, civil organizational participation in non-democratic society gradually accumulates the feeling that people cannot have any say in political affairs. Such feeling leads to the sense of political inefficacy and decline of interest in politics.

Chinese civil organizations are still far from developing. 54.3% of Chinese people do not have any membership in any civil organizations (Table 2). The percentage of those who have memberships in more than 2 civil organizations is not high (19.0%). Most of those civil participants are from economic civil organizations and cultural civil organizations. The most active part of civil organizations: public interest organizations are still far from developing. Only 8.6 % of Chinese people have membership in public interest organizations (Table 3). One possible explanation of China's slow growth of civil organizations is its low level of economic development (Pei 1998). With China's continued economic development, with the rise of a vibrant middle class, and with more economic resources controlled by private hands, it is expected that Chinese civil organizations will develop rapidly in the future. When more Chinese people are more active in civil participation, measured by the percentage of membership in more than 2 civil organizations, and when more public interest organizations emerge, the impacts of China's civil organizations on its civic culture will be more positive, and the implication for democratic transitions will be more significant.

REFERENCES

Almond, Gabriel and Sidney Verba. 1963. *The Civic Culture: Political Attitudes and Democracy in Five Nations.* Princeton: Princeton University Press.

Dalton, Russell J. and Nhu-ngoc Ong 2003. "Civil Society and Social Capital in Vietnam," In *Modernization and Social Change in Vietnam,* Munich: Munich Institute for Social Science.

Diamond, Larry. 1994. "Rethinking Civil Society: Toward Democratic Consolidation." *Journal of Democracy,* 5(3): 4-17.

Diamond, Larry. 1999. *Developing Democracy: Toward Consolidation.* Baltimore and London: The Johns Hopkins University Press.

Dickson, Bruce. 2003. *Red Capitalists in China: the Party, Private Entrepreneurs, and Prospects for Political Change.* New York: Cambridge University Press.

Frolic, B. Michael. 1997. "State-Led Civil Society." In *Civil society in China.* eds. Brook, Timothy and B. Michael Frolic, pp. 46-67. Armonk and London: M.E. Sharpe.

Fukuyma, Francis. 1995. "Confucianism and Democracy." *Journal of Democracy,* 6(2): 20-33.

Goodman, David. 1999. "The New Middle Class." In *The Paradox of China's Post-Mao Reforms*. eds. Merle Goldman, Roderick MacFarquhar, pp. 241-261. Cambridge: Harvard University Press.

Huntington, Samuel P. 1992. "Democracy's Third Wave," *Journal of Democracy*, 2: 12-35.

Inglehart Ronald. 1997. *Modernization and Post-modernization: Cultural, Economic, and Political Change in 43 Societies*. Princeton: Princeton University Press.

Inglehart, Ronald. 1999. "Trust, Welling-Being and Democracy." In *Democracy and Trust*, ed. Mark Warren, pp. 88-120. New York and Cambridge: Cambridge University Press.

Jackman, Robert W., Ross A. Miller. 1998. "Social Capital and Politics". *Annual Review of Political Science,* 1(1): 47-73.

Johnson, Ian. 2003. "The Death and Life of China's Civil Society." *Perspectives on Politics*, 1(3): 551-554.

Pearson, Margaret M. 1997. *China's New Business Elite: The Political Consequences of Economic Reform*. University of California Press.

Pei, Minxin. 1998. "Chinese Civic Associations: An Empirical Analysis." *Modern China*, 24(3): 285-318.

Putnam, Robert. 1993. *Making Democracy Work: Civic Traditions in Modern Italy*. Princeton: Princeton University Press.

Pye, Lucian W. 1988. *The Mandarin and the Cadre: China's Political Cultures*. Ann Arbor: Center for Chinese Studies, the University of Michigan.

Pye, Lucian W. 1992. *The Spirit of Chinese Politics*. Cambridge: Harvard University Press.

Pye, Lucian W. and Mary W. Pye. 1985. *Asian Power and Politics: The Cultural Dimensions of Authority*. Cambridge: Harvard University Press.

Schmitter, Philippe. 1974. "Still the Century of Corporatism?" *Review of Politics*, 36: 85-130.

Schmitter, Philippe. 1997. "Civil Society East and West." In *Consolidating the Third Wave Democracies*. eds. Diamond, Larry, Marc F. Plattner, Yun-han Chu, and Hung-mao Tien, pp. 239-262. Baltimore and London: The Johns Hopkins University Press.

Shi, Tianjian. 2000. "Cultural Values and Democracy in the People's Republic of China." *The China Quarterly*, 162: 540-559.

Unger, Jonathan and Anita Chan. 1995. "China, Corporatism, and the East Asian Model." *The Australian Journal of Chinese Affairs,* 33: 29-53.

Unger, Jonathan and Anita Chan. 1996. "Corporatism in China: A Developmental State in an East Asian Context." In *China After Socialism: In the Footsteps of Eastern Europe or East Asia?* eds. Barrett L. McCormick, Jonathan Unger, pp. 95-129. Armonk: M. E. Sharpe.

White, Gordon, Jude Howell, and Shang Xiaoyuan. 1996. *In Search of Civil Society: Market Reform and Social Change in Contemporary China*. Oxford: Clarendon Press.

White, Gordon. 1993. "Prospects for Civil Society in China: A Case Study of Xiaoshan City." *The Australian Journal of Chinese Affairs*, 29: 63-87.

In: China in Focus Economic, Political and Educational Issues
Editor: Ernest P. Nolan, pp. 81-95

ISBN 1-60021-543-8
© 2007 Nova Science Publishers, Inc.

Chapter 6

THE IMPLICATIONS OF THE EXPANSION OF CHINA INTO THE GLOBAL EDUCATIONAL ARENA

Judith M. Lamie
University of Birmingham, Birmingham, United Kingdom

ABSTRACT

There has been a dramatic increase in recent years in the numbers of international students undertaking undergraduate and postgraduate study in the United Kingdom. This has been as a direct result of the huge influx of students coming from the Far East, and in particular from China. This paper presents the findings of an exploratory questionnaire produced in order to reach a better understanding of the needs and expectations of international students in the university community. The paper concludes that this expansion of China into the global educational arena has serious implications for student provision and education both within the United Kingdom and beyond.

INTRODUCTION

China is in a phase of industrial, scientific and commercial expansion which will make it the world's largest economy by the early years of the next century. In order to function efficiently in this role, it needs to bring large numbers of its people to high levels of proficiency in the use of English for a wide variety of functions. (Maley, 1995: 47)

In the United Kingdom (UK), international students are beginning to comprise a significant proportion of the student population in higher education with over 300,000 now attending UK colleges and universities (UKCOSA, 2003). They come from different cultural backgrounds and have different expectations of the teaching and learning process. This has serious implications for international student provision. At the University of Birmingham special courses are run, by the English for International Students Unit, to prepare and support the students, both academically and culturally, for study in Britain. In the past year student numbers for these courses have increased dramatically. The reason for this increase would appear to be the huge influx of students coming from the Far East, in particular from China.

The Chinese education curriculum is, historically, the product of economic and industrial requirements. It can be assumed, therefore, that the recent changes in the importance of English is caused by similar requirements. This paper reports the findings of an exploratory questionnaire produced with the aim of reaching a better understanding of the needs and expectations of international students in the university community and as a result evaluate and improve the English language support provided at Birmingham. The attitudes and opinions of students from the Far East are highlighted. The first section outlines the educational context with reference to both China and the UK. The second introduces the research method and focus. The final section presents the questionnaire results and discusses the findings. The paper concludes that in order to cater for the changes in the international student profile in the UK and the expansion of China into the global educational arena, both subject-based and English language support provision must be re-evaluated. In addition, it suggests that the home nations of the international students must be made aware of the implications of such changes and, if possible, begin initiating courses in these countries to prepare their students for the future.

PART ONE: EDUCATIONAL CONTEXT

1. The Chinese Context

The role and importance of English, and English language teaching, in China first became part of the educational agenda in the early part of the twentieth century (Boyle, 2000). At this stage it was modelled on the system present in Japan. First and foremost, the education process in Japan was intended as a servant to the state. The happiness of the individual, though important, was of secondary importance to the harmony of the state :

> The notion of Japanese dedication to role stems from the Confucian ideology dominant in pre-modern Japan, which de-emphasised the individual as an end in himself or herself, emphasising instead individual responsibilities and obligations. (Shimahara, 1998: 223)

Shimahara continues by observing that changes that have been successfully effected since the inception of the modern system of national education in Japan have done so when the curriculum has had less to do with individual learners' personal, cognitive and imaginative development and more to do with corporate industrial, business and economic requirements. Similar developments have taken place in China.

During the founding of the People's Republic of China, in 1949, English was briefly usurped by Russian, but by 1955 the Ministry of Education became aware that this could potentially damage China's long term goals and English was once again placed on the teaching and learning syllabus. There was to be another period of uncertainty for English during the Cultural Revolution (1966-1976), but by 1978, following a key conference on foreign language teaching held by the Chinese Ministry of Education, English had once again regained prominence. At this time a team from the U.S. International Communication Agency visited five cities, and a number of educational institutions, in China and stated China's reasons for learning English:

> The Chinese view English primarily as a necessary tool which can facilitate access to modem scientific and technological advances, and secondarily as a vehicle to promote commerce and understanding between the People's Republic of China and countries where English is a major language. (Cowan *et al,* 1979: 465)

According to the Report of the English 2000 Conference in Beijing, sponsored by the British Council and the State Education Commission of the People's Republic of China, this is a basic motivation which has not changed. It was at this point in time that the numbers of Chinese students applying for undergraduate and postgraduate courses in the UK significantly increased.

2. THE BRITISH CONTEXT

The British Council, in 2001, stated:

> The efforts of UK universities and colleges to provide more support for overseas students and to create an international campus environment have paid off, new recruitment figures show. (The British Council, 2001: 1)

Nationally the numbers of international students attending UK universities has indeed increased in recent years, with overall numbers in 2002 exceeding those of 2001 by 5.5%. However, universities in the UK have, in reality, been experiencing mixed results, a fact masked by the emergence of strong new international student markets coupled with the falling away of more traditional ones. A decrease in student numbers from a number of previously key markets, such as Spain, Germany, and France, has coincided with large increases from Japan and China, as the statistics on international recruitment reveal:

Country	% change
Spain	-25%
Germany	-17%
France	-13%
Japan	+5%
China	+92%

(UKCOSA, 2003)

This national recruitment situation has been mirrored at the University of Birmingham.

The University of Birmingham

The University of Birmingham is one of the top twenty recruiters of international students in the UK (UKCOSA, 2003). In 1958 there were 40 international students at the University. By 1974 this number had increased to 169, 45 of whom were undergraduates. The majority (91) were studying Science and Engineering, although courses in Commerce and Social Science (39) and Education (20) were also popular. The highest number of students coming from a single country was 31, and that country was Turkey. There were also significant numbers coming from Iran (11), Iraq (11), Greece (11) and Malaysia (9). No students came from China.

Statistics produced by the University for the 2001-2002 session indicated that, of the 23,000 students studying at Birmingham, 3,914 were international. These students came from 140 different countries. However, over 1000 were from China. In addition, Business and Economics had become the most popular programmes. One criticism to be levelled at UK universities is that international students have received a lack of support both in terms of language development and social interaction:

> British universities need to manage expectations better. The better universities offer specially tailored induction courses for new Chinese arrivals – ranging from tips on shopping and public transport to thorough training in how to write essays and give presentations. (The Economist, 2003: 3)

The University of Birmingham provides such courses via the English for International Students Unit.

English for International Students Unit

The linguistic and academic demands on a student from abroad studying at a university in Britain are very heavy. The English for International Students Unit (EISU) was the first unit to be set up at a university in the UK, in 1964, with the specific task of providing support for international students (Jordan, 2002). In its infancy the Unit provided:

> A four-day induction course for overseas students;
> A two-week pre-sessional course;
> A diagnostic test to ascertain which grammatical areas students required particular help with;
> An in-sessional academic programme of lectures including covering such topics as grammar, listening for note-taking, vocabulary and writing academic texts;
> A one-to-one tutorial service; and,
> A general advisory service.

The increase in international student numbers has led to an increase in the support provided. Currently, the main objectives of EISU are:

- to provide in-sessional English language and study skills support for international students at the University of Birmingham;
- to help international students develop their English language and study skills prior to their enrolment at the University through 20 (initiated in 2001), 10 and 6 week pre-sessional courses (initiated in 1990);
- to test incoming international students and identify students with potential English language difficulties;

- to offer 20, 15, 10 and 6 week programmes in Business and Management English (initiated in 2001);
- to offer programmes in Executive English (under Birmingham International Business Communications) and training in Communication Skills;
- to offer programmes in General English for other groups of tertiary level international students.

In 1990, 81 students attended the EISU pre-sessional courses. These students came from 32 countries. The countries sending the most students were Indonesia (12), Pakistan (10), Thailand (7), and Turkey (6). No students came from China. In 2002, 473 students attended EISU pre-sessional (235), pre-MBA (149) and General English (89) programmes. 47% of these students were Chinese.

In 2002, an exploratory questionnaire was produced with the purpose of aiming to ascertain what reasons may lie behind these changes in international student numbers and country of origin, and thereby determine the potential impact this may have on student provision. Before the findings of the questionnaire are presented and discussed, brief recourse will be given to the questionnaire design and objectives.

PART TWO: RESEARCH FOCUS AND METHOD

1. Questionnaire Use and Design

Questionnaires are only one of several ways researchers can gather information, test hypotheses, and obtain answers to research questions. A well-formulated planning structure, with clear objectives is key when producing an effective questionnaire:

> The questionnaire may be considered as a formalised and stylised interview, or interview by proxy. The form is the same as it would be in a face-to-face interview, but in order to remove the interviewer the subject is presented with what, essentially, is a structured transcript with the responses missing. (Walker, 1985: 91)

Viewed in this way questionnaires can be designed to gather information and test and suggest new hypotheses. As Munn and Drever (1991: 1) state:

> a questionnaire can provide you with:
> * descriptive information
> * tentative explanations associated with testing of an hypothesis

Subjects responding to the questionnaire must be able to understand the questions posed and their relevance. The designer should also be aware, particularly when dealing with respondents who are working in their second language, that there is a tendency for only those who are competent to reply. Therefore the questionnaire designer should ensure that all questions are easy to understand and answer at various levels of second language proficiency.

Although the sample size is dependent to a large extent on the purpose of the study, a minimum of 30 respondent as a selection base is suggested (Cohen and Manion, 1994). Since validity is related to the size of the sample, researchers suggest that at least 100 respondents is desirable, as Munn and Drever (1991: 15) demonstrate:

Sample size	95% confidence range
100	+/- 10%
250	+/- 6%
1000	+/- 3%

The general rule for questionnaire design is that each item must measure a specific aspect of the objective. The questions can be open or closed, although quantification and analysis can be more easily carried out with closed questions. General questions should be placed first, followed by those that are more specific (Cohen and Manion, 1994).

2. Questionnaire Aim and Objectives

Following the considerations raised above, an exploratory questionnaire (see Appendix 1) was produced in order to reach a better understanding of the needs and expectations of international students in the university community and, as a result, improve the provision made for the international students in terms of English language teaching and support.

The specific objectives of the questionnaire were to:

1. establish the current international student profile at the University of Birmingham;
2. discover the reasons why the students had come to study in the UK and specifically at the University of Birmingham;
3. determine the needs and expectations of the international students with regard to English language teaching and support.

In order to achieve this the questionnaire was divided into three sections:

a) General Information
b) Reasons for Study
c) English Language Teaching and Support

The questionnaire was distributed to incoming international students in September 2002 following the administering of the EISU diagnostic test. From the questionnaires distributed, 177 were returned, of which 81 (46%) were students from the Far East (FE).

PART THREE: QUESTIONNAIRE RESULTS AND DISCUSSION

1. General Information

Wolf (1997: 423) emphasises the 'natural ordering or flow necessary to produce a well-made questionnaire'. With this in mind, and the belief that a logical progression will make a questionnaire easier to complete, the questionnaire began with a section on general information. The data requested covered student age, gender, nationality, subject department and status. Figures 1 and 2 illustrate the age and nationality of the population respectively. There were 177 respondents in the entire population, 86% of which were between 20 and 30 years old. A similar figure was present for FE students, with 84% being between 20 and 30; 12% between 30 and 40; and 4% under 20. FE students provided the highest number (81) from any given area, with Europe following in second place with 63 students. This is representative of the trend in international student numbers both nationally and regionally (UKCOSA, 2003). In terms of gender the total population was evenly split, with 89 being male and 88 female. This proportioning was duplicated in the FE students' data, with 41 being female and 40 male.

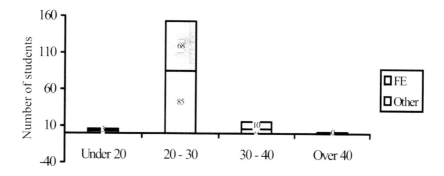

Figure 1. International Student Age Profile

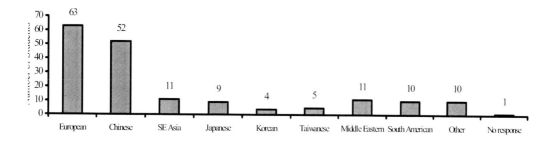

Figure 2. International Student Nationality

The most popular subject of study nationally is Business and Administration. This fact is also reflected in the data obtained from the exploratory questionnaire, as shown in Figure 3.

However, this is largely due to the FE students, 63% of which are taking the aforementioned courses, whereas only 29% of the remaining students are taking business-related programmes. This is again representative of the national (UKCOSA, 2003) and regional trend. In EISU, 87% of students attending summer courses from April to September in 2002 came from the Far East. 90% of students were postgraduate with over 60% of these students studying on pre-MBA programmes (preparation for business-related courses, such as Commerce, and Accounting and Finance). Not surprisingly, therefore, the vast majority of FE students (91%) were postgraduates (Figure 4). The FE undergraduates were studying Economics, Computer Science, Mathematics and Political Science. Some reasons for this are given in the following section.

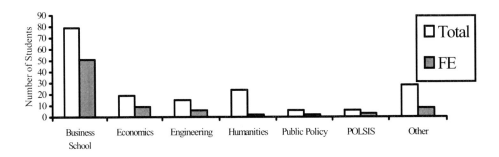

Figure 3. International Student Department

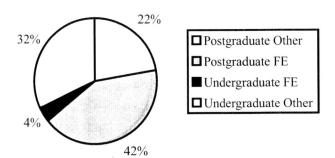

Figure 4. International Student Status

2. Reasons for Study

As mentioned in Part One, historically China's reasons for learning English have been to facilitate technological and scientific advances. Other FE Asian countries have experienced similar developments. The Ministry of Education in Japan, for example, has sought to respond to the changing nature of Japan's relationship with the rest of the world, particularly its business and economic relationship, by placing higher emphasis on the importance of English (Shimahara, 1992).

The reasons international students gave for choosing to pursue courses at the University of Birmingham (Figure 5) centred on a suitable course, English language development (although not for the FE students), and reputation. This may have more to do with question phraseology, where the emphasis may have been placed too greatly on 'Birmingham', and less with deep-seated reasons why students actually left their home countries. More indicative of the business impact is, as previously presented in Figure 3, the propensity for students to take courses in Business Studies, Commerce, Accounting and Finance, and Economics.

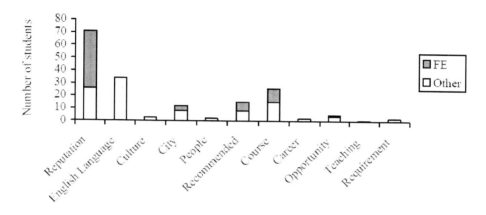

Figure 5. Reasons for Chosing Birmingham

A clearer picture is given in the students' responses to the question, *Why have you chosen your particular course?* Over 30% of FE students stated that interest was an important factor:

I am interested in it. (Student #1 Chinese)
I like it. (S #13 C)
I'm interested in this field. (S #38 C)

Knowledge of English correlates highly with income and social prestige (Lord and Cheng, 1987). This may lead to a strong abstract motivation for study abroad. Over 50% of FE students cited skill-based and career development reasons:

To establish a solid foundation in business and grasp the necessary skills.
(S #35 C)
To get a higher position in my country. (S #41 C)
To have an academic background in order to get a better job in the future.
(S #56 Taiwanese)
I feel I can use the knowledge I get from this course to develop my country in the future.
(S #64 Thai)

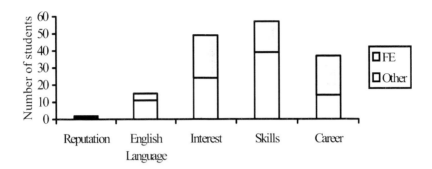

Figure 6. Reasons for chosing course

English language development was also considered to be of some importance, although it was stated more explicitly in the following section.

3. English Language Teaching and Support

Students naturally come to university to study their subject courses, and this was shown to be a priority in their reasons for attending the University of Birmingham. However of vital importance to many international students is the English language support provided. Over 80% of all students, and 85% of FE students, considered it to be of importance, as displayed in Figure 7.

Figure 7. English Language Support Required

The major reason for requiring English language support for the majority of students in the entire population was that their English ability needed to increase in order to fulfil the obligations of their academic study, as illustrated in Figure 8. Another key area, particularly with FE students, was the need for a development in Speaking and Listening. Given the traditional nature of teaching and learning still prevalent in FE countries (Lamie, 2001), this is an understandable response:

Chinese university teaching is different to that in British higher education. Class discussion and questioning the teacher are rare and often discouraged. Exams are important; group-based activities and course-work hardly feature. Memorising and regurgitating texts matter a lot; use of other source material and critical thinking skills, especially at undergraduate level, are minimal. (Economist, 2003: 3)

Historically, in China, the method of English language teaching has seen a focus on reading and translation. As with Japan (Ito, 1978) the emphasis was placed on the rote learning of grammar and vocabulary. This has served to produce students reasonably competent in Reading, and Writing (although not necessarily Academic Writing), but less comfortable with Speaking and Listening. This is in contrast to students coming from Europe, as can be seen in Figures 9 and 10.

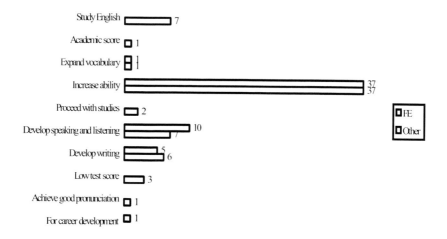

Figure 8. Reasons for needing English Language support

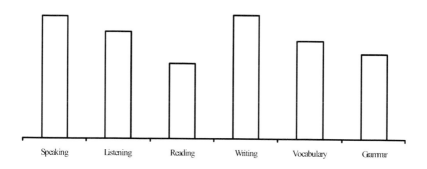

Figure 9. Most important area in terms of English language support: International Students Other

This has serious implications for the content, method and delivery of English language support classes. Up to the present day, although a variety of courses have been delivered at universities, such as Listening for note-taking, and Writing academic texts, as presented in Part One, the focus in the English language has been on the studying of grammar in the academic context.

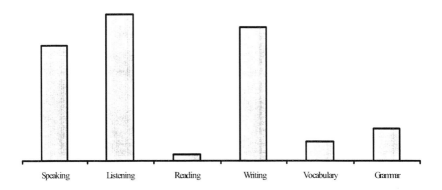

Figure 10. Most important area in terms of English language support: International Students FE

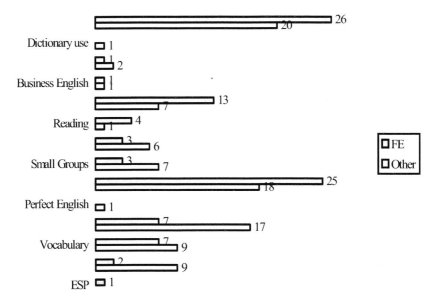

Figure 11. Kind of English support required

This has been largely due to the nationality base of the students, the majority coming from Europe, the Middle East or Africa. The recent trend, presented in this paper and supported by both national and regional data, of increased numbers of students coming from the Far East shows no signs of abating. In addition, there has been a shift in subjects studied, with Science and Engineering, hitherto the most popular, being replaced by business-related courses. With students now coming from different countries, taking different courses, perceiving the need for different requirements, as shown in Figure 11, English language support providers must find ways of catering for divergent needs.

The development of business-related pre-sessional courses (pre-MBA courses) in EISU was a direct response to this change of student profile. Course components include:

- English language improvement
- Writing academic essays and business reports
- Listening to business and management lectures and note-taking
- Presentation skills
- Strategies for reading and summarising business literature
- Reading, analysing and critically evaluating business case studies
- Individual tutorials

The entire range of English language provision at the University of Birmingham is now undergoing review. This is essential if we are to provide effective and efficient support for all of our students, from all countries.

CONCLUSION

There has been a dramatic growth in the numbers of international students studying in the UK in recent years. The reason for this development would appear to the increase in students arriving from the Far East, in particular from China, where numbers have risen by 92%. This national growth has been mirrored at the University of Birmingham. With nearly 4000 international students studying at Birmingham, over 1000 of whom are from China, the University has begun to take this development extremely seriously.

This study has reinforced the indication that a shift has taken place in the international student profile. The majority of students no longer come from Europe, but from the Far East. They are no longer coming primarily to study Science and Engineering, or Education, but are focussing on business-related courses and Economics. This has directly lead to a change in the perceived requirements in terms of English language support. The study concludes that a review of English language provision and international student support needs to take place if the needs and wants of all students are to be fulfilled. A review is underway at the University of Birmingham and changes have already begun to take place, as the introduction and focus of the pre-MBA programme delivered by EISU demonstrates.

There are also other areas of equal importance which must be taken into consideration, as Ballard and Clanchy (1997: viii) state:

Many of the difficulties international students experience in their study derive not from 'poor English' (though lack of language competence is in many cases a real problem), but from a clash of educational cultures.

Therefore any review of support and provision needs to take this into account. This goal would also be assisted by developments in international students' home countries, both in terms of a raising of awareness as well as potential changes in language learning and teaching at school and tertiary levels. If Chinese students are to achieve their personal goals, and if China is to successfully launch itself into the global educational arena then the implications of such a move must be considered and acted upon, and this must happen soon.

REFERENCES

Ballard, B. and Clanchy, J. (1997) *Teaching International Students.* Deakin: IDP Education.

Boyle, J. (2000) A brief history of English language teaching in China. *IATEFL Issues,* 155.

British Council, The (2001) UK's global offer attracts more international students. At *http://www.britishcouncil.org/learning/intstudspr.shtml*

Cohen, L. and Manion, L. (1994) *Research Methods in Education.* London: Routledge.

Cowan, J. Light, R. Matthews, B. and Tucker, G. (1979) English teaching in China: a recent survey. *TESOL Quarterly*, 12, 4: 465-482.

Economist, The (2003) Western promise. March 27th 2003.

Hamp-Lyons,L. and Hyland, K. (2002) EAP: issues and directions. *Journal of English for Academic Purposes,* 1,1: 1-13.

Ito, K. (1978) *Traditional methods and new methods.* In, Koike *et al:* 208.

Jordan, R.R. (2002) The growth of EAP in Britain. *Journal of English for Academic Purposes,* 1,1: 69-80.

Keeves, J.P. (ed) (1997) *Educational Research Methodology and Measurement: An International Handbook.* Oxford: Pergamon.

Koike, I., Matsuyama, M., Igarashi, Y., and Suzuki, K. (eds) (1978) *The Teaching of English in Japan.* Tokyo: Eichosha Publishing.

Lamie, J.M. (2001) *Understanding Change.* Nova Science Publishers: New York.

Leestma, R. and Walberg, H. (eds) (1992) *Japanese Educational Productivity.* University of Michigan: Michigan.

Lord, R. and Cheng, H.N. (1987) *Language Education in Hong Kong.* Hong Kong: Chinese University Press.

Maley, A. (1995) *Landmark review of English in China.* The British Council.

Munn, P. and Drever, E. (1991) *Using Questionnaires in Small Scale Research.* Glasgow: SCRE.

Shimahara, N. (1992) Overview of Japanese education: policy, structure and current issues. In, Leestma R., and Walberg, H. (eds).

Shimahara, N. (1998) *The Politics of Classroom Life.* London: Garland.

UKCOSA (2003) Higher Education Statistics. At, *http://www.ukosa.org.uk.*

Walker, R. (1985) *Doing Research.* London: Routledge.

Wolf, R.M. (1997) *Questionnaires.* In, Keeves, J.P. (ed): 422-427.

APPENDIX 1
International Students Questionnaire 2002

Part A: General Information   (*Please tick the appropriate box)

1. Age*:   under 20 years   20 – 30 ⌐   30 – 40 ⌐   Over 40 ⌐
2. Gender*:   Male   Female
3. Nationality: _____
4. Department: _____
5. Student status*:   Undergraduate   ⌐Postgraduate ⌐   Other _____
                                                                    (please specify)

Part B: Reasons for Study

1. Why have you decided to come and study at the University of Birmingham?

_____

_____

2. Why have you chosen your particular course?

_____

_____

Part C: English Language Teaching and Support

1. Will you need English Language support while you are studying here*? Yes ⌐ No ⌐
Why? _____

2. Which of the following areas do you think you will need MOST help with in terms of English language support (please write **1** for the most important, **2** for the next, and so on, **6** will be for the least important):

Speaking: How to participate in group discussion and debate _____
Listening: How to listen to lectures and take notes   _____
Reading: How to read and summarise texts   _____
Writing: How to write an academic essay   _____
Vocabulary: How to choose appropriate vocabulary   _____
Grammar: How to use the correct grammar   _____

3. What kind of English language support do you want during your time here at Birmingham?

_____

_____

In: China in Focus Economic, Political and Educational Issues
Editor: Ernest P. Nolan, pp. 97-105

ISBN 1-60021-543-8
© 2007 Nova Science Publishers, Inc.

Chapter 7

COMPREHENSIVE SCHOOL IMPROVEMENT IN THE CONTEXT OF SOCIAL TRANSFORMATION IN CHINA: A CASE OF NEW BASIC EDUCATION PROJECT

Ye Lan

East China Normal University, China

SURVEY OF NATIONAL EDUCATION REFORM IN CHINA IN THE PAST TWENTY-FIVE YEARS

During the past twenty-five years, China has experienced and is still experiencing rapid and deep transformative change and, in this process, Chinese school education has also undergone unprecedented development. With the adoption of the policy of economic reform and opening up to the outside world in 1978, basic education in China entered a new era of progress. From that time to the mid-1980s, conscious efforts were made by the government to adjust the educational structure, increase the educational budget and raise the social status of teachers.

From 1985 to the early 1990s, national education reform in China was focused on reform of the educational structure. In 1985, the Central Committee of the Communist Party of China (CPC) issued the *Decision on the Reform of the Educational Structure*, laying down the principle that local governments should be responsible for basic education and local government and schools should have more autonomy in educational decision-making. In 1986, the National People's Congress promulgated the *Compulsory Education Law of the People's Republic of China,* which is the first educational law in the history of the People's Republic of China (PRC), thus placing the implementation of nine-year compulsory education in China on a legal basis. During this period, generally speaking, efforts for educational reform were mainly focused on re-organizing the educational structure and adjusting educational management systems. School level educational change still gained little attention.

In 1993, the CPC Central Committee and the State Council jointly issued the *Guidelines for the Reform and Development of Education in China*, clarifying the directions and basic policies for the development of basic education till the early years of the 21st century. This document also points out that the development of education should not only emphasize quantity, but also quality and efficiency. In early 1999, the State Council ratified the *Action Plan for Educational Vitalization Facing the 21st Century* formulated by the Ministry of Education, putting forward national curriculum reform and teacher in-service training in the following years. In the same year, the CPC Central Committee and the State Council jointly promulgated the *Decision on the Deepening of Educational Reform and the Full Promotion of Quality Education*, mandating change of educational structure, system, aims, curriculum, and methods to suit the needs of social development in the twenty-first century. Since then national educational reform efforts in China have begun to focus on school level change, the beginning of a concern with the question of how to promote comprehensive school improvement.

The simple description above is only an illustration of national educational reform initiated by the CPC Central Committee, the State Council or the Ministry of Education during the past twenty-five years. Besides such top-down educational reform strategies, there are still two kinds of non-governmental school improvement efforts that have an important impact on the development of educational theory and practice in China. One is grass-roots educational changes initiated by schools or teachers, such as 'Happy Education' initiated by the No.1 Attached Primary School of Shanghai Normal School, 'Success Education' originated by the No.8 Middle School of Shanghai Jabei District, and 'Situational Chinese Teaching Method' originated by a Chinese teacher named Li Jilin from the Attached Primary School of Nantong Normal School. These changes usually focus on teaching methods that first show their effectiveness in one school and then gain the attention of the media or the educational authority and are then adopted by other schools.

The other kind of non-governmental school improvement efforts are university-school collaborative educational change projects. With little or no governmental funds, these projects usually conduct long-term collaborative inquiry in one school or several schools or even in several school districts. Comparatively, these projects are concerned more with school level improvement. They always start from one educational theme such as curriculum or classroom instruction, and then extend to strategies fostering comprehensive school improvement. Influential examples of this kind of project are the 'Comprehensive Curriculum Change Project' conducted by a university-school team led by Professor Yun Zhaoshi from the Shanghai Normal University, and the 'Subjective Education Project' conducted by a team led by Professor Pei Dina from the Beijing Normal University. The case we take to illustrate school improvement in China in this chapter, the New Basic Education Project, is one of the collaborative school improvement projects. Different from the two kinds of school-based educational changes described above, the scope of change in the New Basic Education Project is wider and it aims at comprehensive school transformation.

NEW BASIC EDUCATION PROJECT: AN OVERVIEW

Beginning in 1994, the New Basic Education Project may be divided into two phases. The first phase, from 1994 to 1999, we call the 'exploring phase'. This was conducted in five primary and five middle schools in Shanghai by a collaborative research team led by Professor Ye Lan from the East China Normal University. Emphasis was mainly put on the improvement of classroom teaching and class construction during this period.

The second phase, which we call the 'extending phase' began in 1999 and will last till 2005. In this phase, more schools will join this project, and currently there are 57 schools drawn from seven provinces participating in this project. The project also extends its scope of change during this period. Except for changes in classroom teaching and class construction, the project also takes measures to improve school administration and enhance the professional development of teacher and principals, and consciously fosters local (district and school level) change agents.

The aim of the New Basic Education Project is to explore the transformation of schooling in a social transformation era in China, by forming a mutually-transformative and inter-constructive relationship of theory and practice. Schooling transformation means the internal nature and daily practice of schools should change from the pre-modern status to a modern one. The pre-modern schools which 'produce' students according to the models of industrialization and mass production and aim at knowledge transmission will no longer suit the developmental needs of the changed social context in China, and must be transformed.

The New Basic Education Project develops a framework of school transformation. In our view, this school transformation should include:

1) *Value promotion.* The value of modern schools lies not only in transmitting and inheriting knowledge that human beings have already mastered, or reproduction of culture and productivity; modern schools should also serve social renewal development and personal lifelong development.

2) *Re-focusing.* Modern schooling should care for the active development of *all* students rather than paying attention to only a few 'elite' students. Modern schooling should emphasize the communication of subject matter and students' lives and social context, rather than be concerned solely with subject matter, and modern schools should have more autonomy in school administration, school-based curriculum development, teacher professional development, and school-based educational inquiries.

3) *Open structure.* The whole system of education should retain a certain degree of openness and flexibility. At the school level, modern schools should be open to the outside world, including the internet, the media, the society in general, local communities, and other schools, and be open to the possibilities of student development.

4) *Interactive process.* Unlike the typical linear teacher-students relationship in the process of education in pre-modern schools, the process of schooling in modern schools should be active, purposeful and multi-orientated in interaction among multiple factors, multiple levels, and multiple groups. During the process of this

interaction, the creative potential of teachers and students should produce creative practice.

5) *Motivation internalization.* The development motivation of pre-modern schools is always affected by external factors, such as external standards, explicit and measurable outcomes, and recognition of public opinion. Modern schools should develop internal development and motivation.

CONTENT OF NEW BASIC EDUCATION PROJECT

The New Basic Education Project is a collaborative project aiming at integrated and comprehensive school improvement. Apart from theoretical research, the practical changes focus mainly on the following four aspects:

a) Improvement of Curriculum and Instruction

In the area of curriculum and instruction, the core concern of the Now Basic Education Project is to study the richness and explore the vitality of teacher-student activities in classroom teaching. Even in current China, the most commonly shared conception of classroom teaching in the circle of basic education is that the main value of teaching is to transmit knowledge from the textbooks. We try to replace this conception with another one: the main value of classroom teaching is to foster the active and healthy development of students in the current social context. In the New Basic Education Project, we try to reshape the theory and practice of teaching by making classroom teaching an interactive process of the teacher and students according to certain educational aims, by making classroom teaching a dynamic process of teaching and learning during which teaching and learning form a relationship of mutual promotion, mutual creation, and inter-construction. In this project, the students' developmental needs are the starting point for curriculum and instruction improvement. We try to construct a new form of classroom teaching by helping teachers understand the importance of students' development in curriculum and instruction improvement, extend the educational value of certain disciplines, and change their teaching behaviors. We have published a series of papers on the topic of curriculum and instruction improvement[1]. We take many measures to promote curriculum and instruction improvement in the project, including 'teaching content structuring', 'flexible teaching planning', 'dynamic evolving in the teaching process', and 'multiple progressive teaching evaluation'.

b) Improvement of Class Construction

In China, the school class is the basic organization to which a student belongs in his or her school life. From the very beginning, the New Basic Education Project put emphasis on

---

[1] Ye, Lan (200a2) Reconstruct the value of classroom teaching, Educational Research, 23, 5, 3-7; Ye, Lan (2002b) Reconstruct the conceptions of teaching process, Educational Research, 23, 10, 24-30; Ye, Lan and Wu, Yaping (2003) Reform of classroom teaching and reform of classroom teaching evaluation, Educational Research, 24, 8, 42-49. These papers are the theorization of change practice in this project.

the value of class construction in students' personal development. We make great efforts to help teachers in the project both understand these conceptions and try to follow them in practice: students are the authentic masters of the class, the class is every students' class, everybody in the class has the right and responsibility to participate in activities and management of the class; and daily class life is the most important part of class construction. We should try our best to form a kind of harmonious, tolerant, healthy, abundant, and active class culture and environment in which every student will have opportunities to attain certain developments.

In the New Basic Education Project, we employ a dynamic, changing system of class role assigning, which means more students will have the opportunity to take charge of one part of the class management to serve his/her classmates. We also try to make students share more autonomy in their class management, encourage students to be 'One Day Class Masters', to help the teacher in charge of the class manage the class. In periodic class activities (usually monthly or bi-monthly) we encourage teachers, in cooperation with students, to select activity themes which are near to the students' lives and to organize class activity in multiple forms (such as debates, discussions, contests, demonstrations) so as to give students more chances for personal development during such activities.

c) Improvement of School Administration

Partly because of the centralized educational policy, most principals in China lack the idea of comprehensive planning of school educational affairs. This has not changed much even after the 1985 *Decision on the Reform of the Educational Structure* according to which the local educational authorities and schools began to have more autonomy in educational decision-making. We eventually realized during the process of the New Basic Education Project that principals' lack of whole school planning is one of the most important obstacles to school improvement. From the second phase of the project, we have strengthened the research and practice of comprehensive school planning and reform of the school level system. We have helped the principals both to construct visions of school development by situation analysis and to take more responsibilities in the role of curriculum leadership (Glatthorn, 1994), rather than being simple implementers of executive orders from educational authorities. To help the principals have access to educational theories and update their understandings of education, the New Basic Education Project offers an in-service professional development course for principals during its second phase. The project also offers opportunities for the principals to discuss aspects of school improvement with teachers and to form comprehensive and systematic change strategies. Innovations during the change process in schools are then institutionalized to improve daily school practice and democratic school administration.

d) Teacher Development

From the beginning of the New Basic Education Project, we clearly realized that the teacher is the key factor in school improvement. In schools, there will be no students' development without teachers' development, no students' emancipation without teachers' emancipation, no students' creation without teachers' creation, and no school transformation without teachers' transformation. Thus we take teacher development as the most important part of school improvement in this project. In addition to being concerned with the enrichment of teachers' professional knowledge and skills, we also emphasize teachers' recognition of professional values and the awakening of teachers' professional consciousness and enthusiasm. We encourage teachers to deepen and widen educational understandings and accumulate practical wisdom by continuous reflection and practice reconstruction.

MEASURES TO PROMOTE SCHOOL IMPROVEMENT

In the New Basic Education Project, we take a series of measures to promote school improvement. Some of these measures are traditionally used in Chinese schools and are revised in the project according to our needs; some of these measures are created and improved during the process of the project.

1. In order to maintain continuous and long-term effects of school improvement, emphasis should be put on the change of 'persons' rather than merely on the change of 'matters' in schools. This means that first we should change the principals and the teachers, help them gain deeper understandings of themselves, of the students, and of their educational practice. And then, the changed principals and teachers will bring about changes in the students. The New Basic Education Project focuses on 'personal development' and it seeks to achieve comprehensive school improvement by changing persons in the schools.

   During the process of the project, we have realized that the change of teachers' educational conceptions and behaviors will not happen authentically until we have based the process of change firmly on teachers' daily practice, helping teachers to internalize what she/he learns during this process. We employ a kind of practice-inquiry that we have called 'Deliberative Reform Practice' during which teachers are required to change their conceptions of the role as a teacher first, to learn educational theories, to reflect personal theories leading their professional behavior, to change those conceptions and behaviors that are not good for students' development, and to transform desirable ideas into their personal practice.

   The core idea of Deliberative Reform Practice is to make the process of teaching a process of professional learning and practice-based educational research. In a typical Deliberative Reform Practice, teachers are encouraged to expose fully their professional behaviors and educational conceptions through classroom observation, teacher interviews, professional dialogues between partners in the project, and collective discussion in the real context in which teachers work. In a following group activity, possibilities of improvement and specific suggestions for change are discussed and teachers are advised to implement these suggestions in their future practice.

Numerous research studies have found that if the process of change costs too much of teachers' extra time this may become an obstacle to change (Singh and Shifflette, 1996; Day, 1999). We completely agree with this. In the New Basic Education Project, we have tried our best to conduct the Deliberative Reform Practice based on teachers' daily professional activities or activities schools have already employed in the past such as classroom observation, lesson plan presentation, post-teaching discussion, collective lesson planning and collective professional learning. Little extra time is required for teachers to conduct the Deliberative Reform Practice in this project.

2. In order to maintain the effects of school improvement, certain inter- and intra-school communities and cultures should be cultivated. From the second phase of the New Basic Education Project, we began to make use consciously of the interactive influences among schools and the change forces of teacher collective activities inside a school. We have formed a Research Community of the New Basic Education Project as a platform for the 57 member schools to share experience and conduct intra-school collaboration. We have also constructed a website for this project http://www.needu.com.cn where principals and teachers can discuss questions concerning the project, share experience and opinions and present their outcomes. Inside member schools, we encourage principals to construct school level research communities among teachers as the organizational support for Deliberative Reform Practice by re-organizing the structure of school system.

These measures have enhanced the process of school improvement by offering platforms for social interactive learning among schools and teachers, and, what may be more important, have cultivated local district-based or school-based change forces that will become important guarantees of continuous and long-term school improvement.

3. School improvement is a complex process that demands collaboration among different stakeholders. We have made great efforts in the New Basic Education Project to form a kind of constructive partnership and co-learning relationship between researchers from the university and team members from schools. To make the collaboration more effective and productive, we insist that all the schools and teachers take part in the project voluntarily and steps have been taken to guarantee smooth sharing and commitment among partners in the project.

The New Basic Education Project has also striven for support from the local educational authorities and parents. Our experience shows that these forces may become the most supportive forces for school improvement.

CONCLUSION

After nearly ten years' trial and self-renewal, member schools in the New Basic Education Project have improved much in classroom teaching, class construction, school administration and teacher development (Ye, 1999; Wang, 2002). The influence of the project has extended during this period, more schools from different parts of China have joined in, and the achievement this project has made has attracted the attention of educational scholars and schools in Mainland China and overseas regions such as Hong Kong. In the current national educational reform, many of the conceptions and practical strategies developed in the New Basic Education Project during its nearly ten-year-long journey have been widely adopted.

As a project, the New Basic Education Project will end soon. However, the nearly ten years' of research has left for us too many questions to re-consider. During the past two decades, Chinese education circles have been making great efforts to learn from Western countries especially from English-speaking countries. We have introduced numerous educational conceptions and we have employed numerous strategies from these countries. We agree with many Western scholars on the general direction of educational reform or school improvement, such as the idea of 'second order change' (Watzlawick, Weakland and Fisch, 1974; Cuban,1988; Fullan,1991; Marzano and Zaffron, 1995) or the conceptions of school restructuring, reculturing, and retiming developed by Fullan (1995). The New Basic Education Project has many things in common with these ideas, yet the project is conducted in the context of Mainland China and aims to study and practice the process of comprehensive school transformation in an era when the whole Chinese society is experiencing rapid and deep transformation. We work in a unique context that is quite different from that of most English-speaking countries. The problems we face are unique and we cannot find ready-made tools and strategies to resolve them. We have unique responsibilities both in theory and in practice and we must develop our own system of conceptions and developmental strategies. We hope that in the future educationists from the western world and educationists from China will have more opportunities to understand each other deeply and to co-operate authentically with each other to promote school improvement.

REFERENCES

Cuban, L. (1988) A fundamental puzzle of school reform, *Phi Delta Kappan*, 70, 5, 341-344.

Day, C. (1999) *Developing Teachers: The Challenge of Lifelong Learning,* London: Falmer Press.

Fullan, M. G. (1991) *The New Meaning of Educational Change (2nd ed.)*, London: Cassell.

Fullan, M. (1996) Professional culture and educational change, *School Psychology Review*, 25, 4, 496-500.

Glatthorn, A. A.(1994) *Developing a Quality Curriculum,* Alexandria, Virginia: Association for Supervision and Curriculum Development.

Marzano, R. J. and Zaffron, S. (1995) A new paradigm for educational change, *Education*, 116, 2, 162-73.

Singh, K. and Shifflette, L. M. (1996) Teachers' perspectives on professional development, *Journal of Personnel Evaluation in Education*, 10, 2, 145-160.

Wang, Jianjun (2002) Professional development of teachers involved in curriculum change: A case of the New Basic Education Project in Shanghai (in Chinese). Unpublished doctoral thesis submitted to The Chinese University of Hong Kong.

Watzlawick, P., Weakland, J. H. and Fisch, R. (1974) *Change: Principles of Problem Formation and Problem Resolution,* New York: W.W. Norton.

Ye, Lan (1999)(ed.) *Reports on the New Basic Education Project: The Exploring Phase* (in Chinese), Shanghai: Sanlian Publishing House.

Ye, Lan (2002a) Reconstruct the value of classroom teaching (in Chinese), *Educational Research*, 23, 5, 3-7.

Ye, Lan (2002b) Reconstruct the conceptions of teaching process (in Chinese), *Educational Research*, 23, 10, 24-30.

Ye, Lan and Wu, Yaping (2003) Reform of classroom teaching and reform of classroom teaching evaluation (in Chinese), *Educational Research*, 24, 8, 42-49.

In: China in Focus Economic, Political and Educational Issues
Editor: Ernest P. Nolan, pp. 107-118

ISBN 1-60021-543-8
© 2007 Nova Science Publishers, Inc.

Chapter 8

SCHOOL IMPROVEMENT IN TAIWAN: 1987-2003

Jenq-Jye Hwang[1], Chia-Chen Yu[2] and Chia-Yu Chang[3]
[1]National University of Tainan, Taiwan
[2]National Taiwan Ocean University, Taiwan
[3]National Taipei University of Technology, Taiwan

INTRODUCTION

Hargreaves and Fullan asserted, "Beyond the walls of our schools, the world is changing dramatically; and it is pushing and pressing down hard on those who work within" (Hargreaves and Fullan, 1998: v). There is always a close connection between schooling and social changes in a country. Educational authorities and educators should devote themselves to improving their schools and to coping with the change. Taiwan has made these same endeavors.

In order to meet the great challenge of social-political change since martial law was lifted in 1987, Taiwan has been striving to launch many educational reforms to improve her schooling. The 1990s were a critical era for rapid reforms to education in Taiwan. Reacting to the conservative education policy and the chronologically accumulated dissatisfaction with the performance of schools, Taiwan not only has put decentralization of educational policy and deregulation into action, moving away from improper governance and domination of central authority, but also empowered schools and teachers to expand their professional autonomy.

Especially, the Ministry of Education (MOE), the highest authority of education in Taiwan, has launched *The Action Program for Educational Reform*, which was approved by the Executive Yuan on May 14, 1999. A total of NT $ 157 billion was allocated to carry out the following twelve projects:

- consolidation of elementary education;
- making pre-school widely accessible;
- consolidating existing systems for teacher training and continuing education;
- creating dynamic and quality technological and vocational education;

- achieving excellence within higher education;
- encouraging lifelong education and information education;
- promoting family education;
- improving education for disabled students;
- enhancing education for aboriginal students;
- making the paths of education more accessible;
- re-establishing counseling systems; and
- advancing education research and funding (MOE, 1999a, 1999b).

Most of these are focused on elementary and secondary education, especially on school improvement projects.

This chapter is arranged as three parts to elaborate the current measures of Taiwan's improvement in elementary and secondary schools and it examines the practical consequences of implementation as well as the issues surrounding school improvement.

THE DIVERSIFIED SCHOOL SYSTEM AND MULTIPLE SCHEMES FOR ADMISSION

The most significant objectives of current education reform are: to establish a modern school system fitted for Taiwan's environment and special needs, such as the education of outstanding citizens who are democratic and autonomous; to contribute to a humanistic and learning society which keeps a balance between spiritual culture and material civilization; and to create a state that is competent to be a global villager successfully participating in international organizations. Educational reform used to be and will continue to be the key to achieving these objectives, and the establishment of a diversified school system is the fundamental strategy to undertake the promotional reform program.

The Diversified School System

Taiwan's elementary and secondary schools are organized as a '6-3-3 school system', providing 6 years of elementary school education, 3 years of junior-high school education and 3 years of senior-high school education. Traditionally, there were three types of formal senior-high schools: academic, vocational and special, each having its own path to access post-secondary or higher education institutions, and there were no bridges between the three paths. Consequently, the education structure became rigid and could not accomplish its intrinsic functions of exploration, differentiation and integration (Wang, 1999).

In order to fulfil the functions of a modern education structure, the MOE has diversified the secondary school system. There are now five paths: complete high school (combined junior- and senior-high schools), academic senior-high, vocational senior-high, comprehensive senior-high (combined academic and vocational high schools), and special high schools; across these paths there are bridges to connect them (MOE, 2002a). After completing junior-high school education, students are assigned to one path according to their

Test Scores, and a flexible mechanism has been introduced for students to transfer from one path to another when necessary during their learning process.

Furthermore, the Taiwan government is trying to localize senior-high schools in communities, to achieve the following goal: each community should have elementary schools, junior-high schools, and senior-high schools for its students (Hwang, 2000: 71-83; Sue *et al.*, 2000). This reform project, adopting measures of 'admission localization', 'curriculum localization', and 'resources localization', aims to establish adaptive learning communities and build a foundation for extending compulsory education from 9 years to 12 years (MOE, 2001; Young, *et al.*, 2003).

The diversified system of senior-high schools has brought new prospects for Taiwan's secondary education and provided effective access routes for achieving educational equity and equality. However, there are many problems and dilemmas challenging Taiwan's education authorities and educators. They are:

1) the proportion of academic and vocational senior-high school students regulated and controlled by the government does not conform to principles of educational deregulation and the trend of adaptive education that empowers students to choose senior-high schools according to their abilities and potentials and under the guidance of teachers and parents;

2) the curricula designed for complete high schools are not articulated very well, and the elective courses are not rich enough for students to choose according to their interest and needs (Hwang and Lee, 1995);

3) the quality of teachers, curriculum and instruction, and learning outcomes in comprehensive high schools are in doubt and should be evaluated systematically in the near future (National Institute of Educational Resources and Research, 2002: 61);

4) to promote each school to become excellent, not only should the government invest a substantial amount of money and other resources, but also the public should break the mystique surrounding traditional star schools and participate positively in school management (Hwang, 2000: 82-83); and

5) no consensus about extending 9 years of compulsory education to 12 years has been achieved yet among the public and among educators. Besides, the disputes focus on extending compulsory education either upward to senior-high school or downward to kindergarten, and on the priority of whether to improve the quality of current 9 years compulsory education or to plan and implement 12 years compulsory education.

Multiple Schemes for Admission

Enrolment and entrance to secondary schools are two key elements affecting school improvement. The former involves the authority of schools to select students, and the latter refers to the right of students to choose schools. Traditionally, these two used to be substituted by the 'Joint Entrance Examination', which might be fair or impartial for every student, but conduced to misshape teaching and learning. Hence, the MOE abolished the senior-high school joint entrance examination in 2001 and promulgated 'Multiple Schemes for Entering Senior-High School'.

The schemes provide three avenues for entering high schools:

1) 'recommendation and selection entrance scheme" for students recommended by junior-high schools to senior-high schools,
2) 'application entrance scheme' for students to choose and apply to senior-high schools by themselves, and
3) 'assigning entrance scheme' for the majority of students entering senior-high schools by Basic Ability Test Scores.

In line with the implementation of these schemes, the MOE (1999b) has drawn up and launched *Implementation Policies for Recommendation and Selection Scheme for Entering Senior-High Schools*, *Implementation Policies for Application Entrance Scheme for Senior-High Schools*, and *Policies for Students to be Assigned to Senior-High Schools*.

The multiple schemes for entering senior-high schools are not the only goal of education reform. Improving the quality of schooling effectively and efficiently is the other goal. Therefore, the reform policies should ensure the credibility and validity of the Basic Ability Tests, maintain the equality and equity of different schemes, and empower each senior-high school to adopt one or multiple schemes and to assess or evaluate junior-high school graduates by multiple standards (Hwang, 2000: 95-108).

Innovative Instruction and Deregulated Curriculum

The ultimate justification of curriculum and instruction reform is to improve conditions for learning. Continuing social and cultural changes are the significant characteristics of modern societies. In the light of these changes and the need to produce more effective instruction, the content of the curriculum, methods of teaching and the physical environment of learning have to be changed.

Reducing Class Size

A large class size, that used to be over 45 pupils per class, has been seriously criticized as one of the main factors contributing to the low quality of Taiwan's schooling. In the late 1990s, the Taiwan government launched '*The Program on Reducing the Class Size*'. This aims at reducing the number of students in the classrooms of elementary and junior high schools to 35 pupils per class in 2007. It also encourages teachers to make their lessons more lively, individualized, and innovative. It seeks to improve the environment of schools and to enhance their educational quality (MOE, 1998a). There has been considerable progress in this program and the official statistics show that the number of pupils per class in the elementary schools has been reduced to an average of 30 and the number in junior-high school has been reduced to an average of 35 (MOE, 2002a).

In line with reducing class size, the MOE (1998b) implemented *The Small Class Teaching Plan* to improve the quality of teaching and learning. This plan encouraged teachers to introduce teaching strategies and evaluation methods that are more adaptive, individualized, and meaningful to students.

Deregulating Curriculum Governance

The National Curriculum Standard, promulgated by the MOE, regulates what should be taught and the number of hours per week for each course in elementary and secondary schools. Due to the centralization of curriculum policy and practice, the MOE was in charge of all aspects of curriculum decision-making. Then, based on the Curriculum Standard, the related official organization, the National Institute for Compilation and Translation (NICT), engaged in the compilation, publication, and issuing of official textbooks with the titles of 'National Edition' or 'Unified Edition'. Therefore, the government monopolized the schools' curricula, and textbooks were rife with what Apple (1993) called 'official knowledge' and biased ideologies relating to politics, culture, ethnicity, or gender. Besides, those textbooks were criticized severely by the public for being too subject-based and disconnected from the living world to attract the students' interest in learning. Moreover, the teaching materials, teaching methods, and even teaching schedules were so prescriptive that teachers could not exert their professional autonomy to provide their students with adaptive curriculum and instruction (Hwang, 1993; Chen and Yu, 1995; Yu, 2002). Then, the only thing the individual teacher can do is to think how to deliver their lessons to students in accordance with the prescriptive National Curriculum Standard.

All the social and educational changes in Taiwan since the late 1980s have led to a more diverse school curriculum and instruction. In the first place, the central government has introduced a curriculum policy that provides for the sharing of the responsibility for curriculum control with local authorities, schools, and teachers. It also shifts the national edition textbook system to a 'textbook censorship system', allowing private publishing companies to participate in textbook compiling and, at the same time, permitting schools to select textbooks that are suitable for students' needs and local culture and environment. Soon, textbook compilation and publication were open to non-governmental publishers and the right of textbook selection was returned from the hands of the government back to schools and teachers. The concerns of schools and teachers about curriculum and instruction moved to how to design their curriculum and instruction at each school site and, at classroom level, to develop a more appropriate and updated curriculum.

Secondly, the ideologies identified in the textbooks have been eliminated and the increasingly multicultural curricula and instruction in the elementary and secondary schools was implemented over the last decade.

Thirdly, after educational deregulation, the local educational authorities engaged in a number of projects (most importantly, school-based curriculum experiments) under local autonomy. What is more, the latest revised curriculum guideline for elementary and junior-high schools (1998), senior-high schools (1996) and vocational high schools (1998) laid more emphases on flexibility, localization and applications to real life. Especially, *the Nine-year Articulated Curriculum Guideline*, that was enacted in 1998 and has replaced the curriculum standards of elementary schools in 2001 and junior-high schools in 2002, has undergone an essential change in underlining: (a) curriculum integration; (b) the spirit of school-based curriculum and the articulation of elementary and junior high schools curriculum; and (c) the setting up of the key competency for students of elementary and junior-high schools (MOE, 2000).

Among the three, curriculum integration aims to improve the school curriculum and overcome the problems of over-divided subjects and disconnected contents. The advocacy of school-based curriculum policy, together with the urge for schools to invoke more autonomy in reforming and developing programs by themselves, requires individual schools to reflect on their own conditions and to cater for the specific needs of each student. In other words, the curriculum autonomy of schools has now become one priority in Taiwan's school improvement, and the empowered teachers are considered as the pivots of the school improvement plans.

School improvement is not a new topic in Taiwan. The school curriculum was not perceived as providing our children with the kind of education needed for the changing times. Appeals from all circles of society for improving schools have been made time after time. Encouraged by the trend of democratization of schooling and curriculum autonomy since the late 1980s, the local education authorities and schools have been offered an impetus to study their own schools and to adopt their own curriculum improvement plans.

Yet the advance to school-based curriculum development (SBCD), regardless of its advantages, also brings about some misunderstandings and panic among teachers and parents. As the curriculum elasticity is increasing, things like teachers' competencies for designing curriculum, curriculum evaluation, and other supplementary measures must be put in place. What is more, whether curriculum autonomy is implemented with teachers' active involvement is called into question (Chou, 1996; Lin,1997; Pung,1999; Chen, 2000). In fact, some teachers and administrators misinterpret SBCD in this way: SBCD means teachers have to develop their school's courses totally different from another school, and even have to construct all teaching materials by themselves. For the time being, how to fulfil the SBCD, how to promote educational quality, and how to justify educational equity are further issues of curriculum deregulation (Chang, 1999).

Additionally, there are some pending issues in need of exploration. First, because the content of local culture is so multifarious, the already heavy learning load becomes even heavier, making these new courses hard to integrate with other existing courses and bringing doubt to this new policy. Secondly, in an age of globalization, how to make the school curriculum become more responsive to the needs of both localization and globalization is also a big challenge. Thirdly, it is argued that the various editions of textbooks will add to the learning load of pupils, since there are too many editions of textbooks for them to read in order to obtain high scores in the Academic Proficiency Tests at ages 5 and 18. These tests are the basis for entering senior-high school or college and universities. Further, this change in textbook provision forces each family to pay more for buying textbooks. Fourthly, the curriculum deregulation policy requires the establishment of national key competency indicators as the criteria for evaluating pupils' performance, which deviates from the traditionally content-centered curriculum making and instruction in Taiwan and as a consequence frustrates many subject specialists and educators.

School-Based Decision-Making and Management

Encompassed by an authoritarian political atmosphere, before 1987, Taiwan's society had been under strict surveillance and control. This centralized management style permeated each social organization, including schools. Education then was simply considered as an apparatus for implementing political policies. As the authoritative politics faded away, the concepts of school accountability and decentralization of management emerged. School-based decision-making and management (SBDM) has become the new management model replacing the long-lasting centralized school management model of the MOE and local educational authorities (Hwang, Yu and Chang, 1993).

The central premise of SBDM is that a school's flexibility and responsiveness will be enhanced, so as to provide schools with the ability to adapt resources and procedures and to make schools more responsive to their constituencies. Such flexibility is critically important to address a school's specific problems; therefore, SBDM appears to be the most important aspect of several comprehensive attempts to improve schools. The characteristics of SBDM in Taiwan feature the reconstruction of school organization, curriculum deregulation, extensive involvement of stakeholders, new measures of principal selection and teacher employment, and school-based staff development.

Reconstruction of School Organization

In order to embody or achieve the autonomy at the school site and to develop teachers' ownership of the school improvement program, the structure of school organization has been transformed. According to the 'Teachers Law', promulgated in 1995 and revised in 2000 later, *Parents Association, Teachers Association* and *Faculty Evaluation Committee* are newly established in the organizational structure of schools. These are designed both to balance power in each school between principal, teachers, and parents and to create a professional shared decision-making climate beneficial to the deliberation of school improvement.

The *Teachers Association*, the formal and active organization in every elementary or secondary school in Taiwan, takes charge of the following tasks or duties (Teachers Law, 2000):

1) to protect the teacher's dignity and professional autonomy;
2) to negotiate the employment contract with the educational authority;
3) to set up the ethical code of teaching;
4) to undertake educational research or to help solve educational problems encountered by each school, and
5) to participate in the administrative affairs of each school and the meetings called by the *Teacher Evaluation Committee*.

The teachers associations, functioning in the context of each individual school in different ways, have a distinct influence over the progress of school improvement. Some play key roles in becoming the promoting force behind their school improvement programs and achieving remarkable success. However, some play their roles as change resisters and become obstacles on the road to school reform. At worst, power struggles have broken out in a few schools among senior administrators, the teachers association and the parents association, and finally this has transformed the concept 'profession autonomy' into 'profession hegemony'.

As for the *Faculty Evaluation Committee*, it usually consists of five to nineteen members, including the principal and representatives chosen from the parents association and teachers association, and the teacher delegates elected by all teachers. The major tasks of the committee are to review the employment of the school faculty, including appointment, dismissal, or suspension, and to arbitrate in any controversy over the teaching contract and teaching misbehaviors (MOE, 2001). It is the unprecedented right of teachers to share the decision-making of personnel affairs in Taiwan's elementary and secondary schools.

Do the committees operate smoothly and properly? Some committees indeed have done good jobs as they brought their professional judgment into full play, but there were some committees that were lobbied illegally, harming the organizational health of the school and making a mess of school self-governance.

Extensive Involvement of Stakeholders

In the democratization process of schooling, the power of influence on school affairs is redistributed and the key players in the schools - teachers, parents, and community members - have opportunities to make a significant impact on school-level decision-making. This enhances the widespread participation of local stakeholders in the educational activities of a school.

In terms of enhancing the decision-making participation and the sense of ownership of stakeholders as a policy tool for opening up school systems to involve outsiders in school management, it actually offers consumers a greater voice in school activities and enables the stakeholders to exert considerable influence on school policy decisions. The professional development of teachers through their participation in internal and external reviews also makes important contributions to cultivating the skills and knowledge required for the achievement of school development objectives.

Involvement contributes to promoting feelings of shared ownership among group members. But, overall, involvement is actually quite low and that of poor and disadvantaged parents is unusual and virtually non-existent in Taiwan's schools. Besides, there is a downside to stakeholders' involvement in school affairs. Three issues attract special attention: the high costs of participation in terms of time; how to make the involvement appropriate and effective; and the difficulty in reaching a consensus.

With the extensive involvement of stakeholders, time spent in participatory decision-making is very demanding. This social cost can be quite high for both administrators and the stakeholders, including students, parents and community members. One of the most immediate costs of increased teacher involvement in school management is 'time' — especially time away from teaching and other interactions with students. For many teachers, the additional time associated with committee work, and the need to balance priorities among administration, teaching and personal life, contributes to increased tiredness and stress, which in turn affects classroom practice and attendance. One other disturbing effect of limited time is its impact on the decision-making process itself and the quality of the decisions made. When there are time constraints and difficulties associated with co-ordinating a wide range of people and organizing them to meet and achieve some agreement, it is often difficult to evaluate issues critically and to develop appropriate responses. Too often committees go for 'quick and ready' solutions, without really innovating.

Participation can be thought of in terms of a continuum reflecting several levels of actual involvement and the power of influence of organizational members in the decision-making enterprise. While some schools express a desire for greater stakeholder influence, as they think this would increase the support to the school, there are still a few schools that are reluctant to welcome the stakeholders' involvement. For teachers and parents, not everyone will choose to become involved in decision-making and management at the school level. And the participants involved in a school's committee would not always represent the entire community and make decisions based on self-interest as opposed to the needs perceived by significant portions of the community. At worst, they disturb the school improvement plan while they are over-intervening in the school's activities.

Associated with an increased demand for public accountability and the emergence of a new group of interests and agencies, those with their own philosophies and assessments of education have driven the debate on school improvement more openly and vehemently. And this consequently brought about a school improvement plan that is deliberate and elaborate. Thus decentralization and devolution to schools as the units of decision-making have not been unproblematic. How to attune to the different aspirations or educational philosophies of stakeholders and reach a consensus is a prolonged and time-consuming business.

New Measures of Principal Selection and Teachers Employment

There has been a big change since the early 1990s in systems for the appointment of principals and the employment of teachers. The educational authority's monopoly of faculty employment has been replaced by the shared decision-making strategy. According to the revised *Regulations for Educators in Schools and Universities* promulgated in 1997, a selection committee, grouped by members including the representatives of teachers and parents, educationists, and the authorities, takes over part of the employment process. Thus, principals or teachers are no longer assigned to schools directly by the MOE or local educational authorities. Schools themselves employing a new faculty member have the right to select candidates to be interviewed and make suggestions for the final choice in the employment procedure.

Though the new measures make teachers and parents become partners in the process established to select new principals and the teachers who will be hired to lead the school and co-operate in the enterprise of school improvement, it causes some problems that need to be solved. As the new systems were adopted in Taiwan, the mass media and public opinion have alleged that bribery and corruption would ruin the subculture of school organization and stain the professionalism. Particularly, a strange phenomenon of voting is that teachers seem to prefer a candidate for the principal of a school with mediocre talent rather than an aggressive one full of innovative ideas.

School-Based Staff Development

In the late 1980s, it became part of the conventional wisdom that anything 'top-down' was autocratic and ineffective. School-based staff development came with this tide of fashion and in-service teacher training tended to abandon the top-down model of professional development. This used to assemble teachers from different schools or from diverse subject areas at teacher centers and provided a standardized and theoretical training program planned by non-practitioners.

The tendency toward school-based staff development in Taiwan has been emphasized for at least two reasons. One reason is teacher's professional knowledge and techniques would be well developed, and needs and deficiencies revealed at the school site; the other is each school should regard the continued training of its staff as an essential part of school improvement.

Now every Wednesday afternoon is set aside as a school-based staff development day in elementary schools, and one half day a week is set aside for teachers of each subject field to pursue professional development in secondary schools. In other words, each teacher should spend at least 36 hours participating in in-service programs or self-study programs.

Under school-based decision-making and management, intensive and wider participation creates a need to legitimize decisions, enlist enthusiasm or expertise, and delegate responsibilities. School-based staff development is undoubtedly essential to help staff, parents, and administrators understand what school restructuring involves and to learn how to participate effectively in an environment characterized by shared decision-making and collaborative work relationships. Furthermore, they support training for those involved in restructuring to provide them with tools necessary for assuming new roles and responsibilities: for example, assisting teachers to develop decision-making, communication and group-process skills. Yet school-based staff development, without a strong internal support structure and elaborate planning in schools, will largely fail and turn the staff development program into a meretricious one. The staff should ponder deeply over the basic issue, that is, how to prepare and support teachers as curriculum developers and what capacity should the school faculty have for self-management in responding to these recurrent demands for school improvement.

CONCLUSION

The rapidity of social change in Taiwan has caused many social problems that need to be addressed and that surely can be resolved by means of schooling. Rather than closing the classroom door on these external and internal changes and demands, more and more school improvement movements have been initiated by the government and schools. There have been several vital changes in elementary and secondary schools since the late 1980s in Taiwan. The educational authorities and the educators have been searching for new and better ways to adapt the management style, enrich their learning environment, and enhance their professional literacy for better schools and high quality education. The movement toward school improvement in Taiwan is taking shape and has accumulated some outcomes after many endeavors.

However, no reform approach is a panacea for educational disease. Although decentralized management and shared-decision making were seen as the possible antidote to dictatorship in Taiwanese schools, they still carry the risk of causing dysfunction in school organization. Besides, Mau and associates (2000) investigated teachers' and parents' opinions about *The Action Program for Educational Reform* implemented by the MOE and found that over 70% of them approved of the reform program. But Ma's (2002) study came to the conclusions that education reforms in Taiwan were initiated and supported by the national leader; and the rationale of educational policy moved from elitism toward populism, the power of educational change moved from centralization to decentralization; and from educational unity to pluralism.

It seems that none of education reforms could win the approval of all stakeholders, and none of the reforms would have benefited all of the students. School improvement, therefore, is a challenging enterprise and a necessary task to carry out. There is no ending for school improvement. The journey to school improvement in Taiwan is undoubtedly arduous and endless.

REFERENCES

Apple, M. W. (1993) *Official Knowledge*, New York, NY: Routledge.

Chang, C. Y. (1999) *School-based Curriculum Development,* Taipei: Shida Shuyuan.

Chen, B. J. and Yu. C. C. (1995) The Major Problems in the Curriculum and Teaching Material from K to 12. Unpublished Report to the Council on the Educational Reform, Executive Yuan.

Chen, S. Y. (2000) An analysis of teachers' curriculum interpretation and curriculum operation experience in elementary schools. Unpublished Master's thesis, National Cheng Chi University.

Chou, S. C. (1996) The policy trend of curriculum deregulation for compulsory education in Taiwan. Unpublished Doctoral dissertation, National Taiwan Normal University.

Hargreaves, A. and Fullan, M. (1998) *What's Worth Fighting for in Education?* Buckingham: Open University Press.

Hwang, J. J. (1993) The social change, ideology, and the school curriculum. In J. J. Hwang (ed.) *The Transformation of Curriculum and Instruction,* Taipei: Shida Shuyuan.

Hwang, J. J. (1993) *The Transformation of Curriculum and Instruction*, Taipei: Shida Shuyuan.

Hwang, J. J. (2000) *Development and Prospects of Technical and Vocational Education,* Taipei: Shida Shuyuan.

Hwang, J. J. and Lee, L. S. (1995) *An Assessment on Establishment of Complete High School (7-12),* Research project sponsored by MOE, Taipei: Research Center for Educational Research, National Taiwan Normal University.

Hwang, J. J., Yu, C. C. and Chang, C.Y. (1993) *An Analysis of the Issues and Trends of Social Conditions, 2000: Education,* Report to Research, Development and Evaluation Council, Executive Yuan.

Lin, S. C. (1997) A study on teachers' participation in curriculum development of elementary schools. Unpublished Master's thesis, National Taiwan Normal University.

Ma, S. S. (2002) *A Synthetic Review of Educational Research Project Reports*, Taipei: National Science Council.

Mau, L. W., Liu, C. J. and Lin, T. T (2000) l*nvestigation of Teachers' and Parents' Opinions about Educational Reform Action Program*, MOE. Taipei: National Institute for Educational Resources and Research.

Ministry of Education, R.O.C. (1998a) *Program on Reducing the Class Size,* Taipei: Ministry of Education, R.O.C.

Ministry of Education, R.O.C. (1998b) *Small Class Teaching Plan,* Taipei: Ministry of Education, R.O.C.

Ministry of Education, R.O.C. (1999a) *The Idea and Practice of Educational Reform*, Taipei: Ministry of Education, R.O.C. Ministry of Education, R.O.C. (1999b) *1999 Progress Report*, *http://140.111.1.22/english/report/1999Report.htm* (Retrieved September 4, 2003).

Ministry of Education, R.O.C. (1999c) *Implementing Regulations of Teachers Law*, Taipei: Ministry of Education, R.O.C.

Ministry of Education, R.O.C. (2000) *The Nine-year Articulated Curriculum Guideline for Compulsory Education*, Taipei : Ministry of Education, R.O.C.

Ministry of Education, R.O.C. (2001a) *Implementation Program for Localizing Senior- High Schools to Communities*, Taipei: Ministry of Education, R.O.C.

Ministry of Education, R.O.C. (2001b) *Regulation for Establishing Faculty Evaluation Committee in Elementary and Secondary schools*, Taipei: Ministry of Education, R.O.C.

Ministry of Education, R.O.C. (2002a) *2002 Education in the Republic of China*, *http://140.111.1.22/english/index.htm* (Retrieved September 4, 2003).

National Institute of Educational Resources and Research (2002) *Review and Improvement of 2001 Educational Reform,* Taipei: National Institute of Educational Resources and Research.

Pung, Y. Z. (1999) A study on elementary school teachers' professional ability in curriculum design. Unpublished Master's thesis, National Hualian Teachers College.

Sue, C. S. , Kao, C. H., Young, S. W. and Hwang, L. H. (2000) *Program of Implementing Localization of Senior High Schools to Communities*, Research project sponsored by MOE, Taipei: Research Center for Educational Research, National Taiwan Normal University.

Wang, H. S. (1999) A study on the reform of school systems in Taiwan. In Educational Association, R. O. C. (ed.), *Education in a Critical Period*, Taipei: Young Chi.

Young, S. W., Shih, M. F., Hsu, C. Y., Hwang, C. F. and Hwang, W. C. (2003) *A study on Implementation Model of 12 years Compulsory Education.* Research project sponsored by MOE, *http://www.edu.tw/high-school/i1301/k12/k12.htm* (Retrieved August 1, 2003).

Yu, C. C. (2002) *Curriculum Innovation*, Taipei: Shida Shuyuan.

In: China in Focus Economic, Political and Educational Issues
Editor: Ernest P. Nolan, pp. 119-124

ISBN 1-60021-543-8
© 2007 Nova Science Publishers, Inc.

Chapter 9

CHINA'S CURRENCY: A SUMMARY OF THE ECONOMIC ISSUES[*]

Wayne M. Morrison and Marc Labonte

ABSTRACT

In response to international pressure over its policy of pegging its currency (the yuan) to the U.S. dollar, the Chinese government on July 21, 2005, announced it would immediately appreciate the yuan to the dollar by 2.1% and adopt a currency policy based on a basket of currencies (including the dollar). Many Members have long charged that China "manipulates" its currency in order to make its exports cheaper and imports into China more expensive than they would be under free market conditions. They further contend that this policy is responsible for the large and growing U.S. trade deficits with China and the loss of U.S. manufacturing jobs. China's July 2005 reforms have done little to lessen congressional concerns. Several bills addressing China's currency have been introduced in Congress, including S. 295, which would raise U.S. tariffs on Chinese goods by an additional 27.5% unless China appreciated its currency.

Unlike most developed economies, such as the United States, China does not allow its currency to float, i.e., let its exchange rates be determined by market forces. Instead, from 1994 until July 21, 2005, China maintained a policy of pegging its currency (the renminbi or yuan), to the U.S. dollar at an exchange rate of roughly 8.28 yuan to the dollar. The Chinese central bank maintained this peg by buying (or selling) as many dollar-denominated assets in exchange for newly printed yuan as needed to eliminate excess demand (supply) for the yuan. As a result, the exchange rate between the yuan and the dollar basically stayed the same, despite changing economic factors which could have otherwise caused the yuan to either appreciate or depreciate relative to the dollar. Under a floating exchange rate system, the relative demand for the two countries' goods and assets would determine the exchange rate of the yuan to the dollar. Many economists contend that for the first several years of the peg, the

---

[*] From CRS Report # RS21625; March 17, 2006

fixed value was likely close to the market value. But in the past few years, economic conditions have changed such that the yuan would likely have appreciated if it had been floating[1]. Because its currency is not fully convertible in international markets, and because it maintains tight restrictions and controls over capital transactions, China can maintain the exchange rate peg and still use monetary policy to pursue domestic goals (such as full employment[2]).

China Reforms the Peg. The Chinese government modified its currency policy on July 21, 2005. It announced that the yuan's exchange rate would become "adjustable, based on market supply and demand with reference to exchange rate movements of currencies in a basket," (it was later announced that the composition of the basket includes the dollar, the yen, the euro, and a few other currencies), and that the exchange rate of the U.S. dollar against the yuan would be immediately adjusted from 8.28 to 8.11, an appreciation of about 2.1%. Unlike a true floating exchange rate, the yuan would (according to the Chinese government) be allowed to fluctuate by 0.3% on a daily basis against the basket[3]. The Chinese government initially hinted that further reforms would be made over time, but later ruled out making further revaluations in the near future.

U.S. CONCERNS OVER CHINA'S CURRENCY POLICY

Many U.S. policymakers and business and labor representatives have charged that China's currency is significantly undervalued vis-à-vis the U.S. dollar (even after the recent revaluation), making Chinese exports to the United States cheaper, and U.S. exports to China more expensive, than they would be if exchange rates were determined by market forces. They further argue that the undervalued currency has contributed to the burgeoning U.S. trade deficit with China (which has risen from $30 billion in 1994 to $202 billion in 2005) and has hurt U.S. production and employment in several U.S. manufacturing sectors (such as textiles and apparel and furniture) that are forced to compete domestically and internationally against "artificially" low-cost goods from China. Furthermore, some analysts contend that China's currency policy induces other East Asian countries to intervene in currency markets in order to keep their currencies weak against the dollar in order to compete with Chinese goods. Critics contend that, while it may have been appropriate for China during the early stages of its economic development to maintain a pegged currency, it is no longer so today, given the size of the Chinese economy and the impact its policies have on the world economy.

---

[1] Many analysts argue that the sharp increase in China's foreign exchange reserves (which grew from $403 billion at the end of 2003 to $819 at the end of 2005) is a major indicator that the yuan is significantly undervalued.

[2] The currency is convertible on a current account basis (such as for trade transactions), but not on a capital account basis (for various types of financial flows, such as portfolio investment). In addition, holdings of foreign exchange by Chinese firms and individuals are closely regulated by the government.

[3] Theoretically, fixing the yuan to a basket of currencies does not rule out the possibility that the yuan could depreciate or appreciate against the dollar. When the other exchange rates in the basket depreciate against the dollar, so will the yuan, but to a lesser extent. How closely the yuan moves with the dollar against other currencies will depend on how large a weight the dollar has in the basket (which has not been revealed by the Chinese government).

China's Concerns Over Modifying Its Currency Policy

Chinese officials argue that its currency policy is not meant to favor exports over imports, but instead to foster economic stability through currency stability, as many other countries do. They have expressed concern that floating its currency could spark an economic crisis in China and would especially be damaging to its export industries at a time when painful economic reforms (such as closing down inefficient state-owned enterprises) are being implemented. They further contend that the Chinese banking system is too underdeveloped and burdened with heavy debt to be able to deal effectively with possible speculative pressures that could occur with a fully convertible currency. The combination of a convertible currency and poorly regulated financial system is seen to be one of the causes of the 1997-1998 Asian financial crisis. Chinese officials view economic stability as critical to sustaining political stability; they fear an appreciated currency could cause deflation, reduce employment, and lower wages in several sectors, and thus could cause worker unrest.

Implications of China's Currency Policy for its Economy

If the yuan is undervalued vis-a-vis the dollar, then Chinese exports to the United States are likely cheaper than they would be if the currency were freely traded, providing a boost to China's export industries (which employ millions of workers and are a major source of China's productivity gains). Eliminating exchange rate risk through a peg also increases the attractiveness of China as a destination for foreign investment in export-oriented production facilities. However, an undervalued currency makes imports more expensive, hurting Chinese consumers and Chinese firms that import parts, machinery, and raw materials. Such a policy, in effect, benefits Chinese exporting firms (many of which are owned by foreign multinational corporations) at the expense of non-exporting Chinese firms, especially those that rely on imported goods. This may impede the most efficient allocation of resources in the Chinese economy. Another major problem is that the Chinese government must expand the money supply in order to keep purchasing dollars, and hot money has poured into China from investors who are speculating that China will continue to appreciate the yuan. These factors could help fuel inflation.

Implications of China's Currency Policy for the U.S. Economy

Effect on Exporters and Import-Competitors. When exchange rate policy causes the yuan to be less expensive than it would be if it were determined by supply and demand, it causes Chinese exports to be relatively inexpensive and U.S. exports to China to be relatively expensive. As a result, U.S. exports and the production of U.S. goods and services that compete with Chinese imports fall, in the short run. (Many of the affected firms are in the manufacturing sector[4].) This causes the trade deficit to rise and reduces aggregate demand in the short run, all else equal[5].

---

[4] There is a long run trend that is moving U.S. production away from manufacturing and toward the service sector. U.S. employment in manufacturing as a share of total nonagricultural employment has fallen from 31.8% in

Effect on U.S. Consumers and Certain Producers. A society's economic well-being is usually measured not by how much it can produce, but how much it can consume. An undervalued yuan that lowers the price of imports from China allows the United States to increase its consumption through an improvement in the terms-of-trade. Since changes in aggregate spending are only temporary, from a long-term perspective the lasting effect of an undervalued yuan is to increase the purchasing power of U.S. consumers. Imports from China are not limited to consumption goods. U.S. producers also import capital equipment and inputs to final products from China. An undervalued yuan lowers the price of these U.S. products, increasing their output.

Effect on U.S. Borrowers. An undervalued yuan also has an effect on U.S. borrowers. When the U.S. runs a current account deficit with China, an equivalent amount of capital flows from China to the United States, as can be seen in the U.S. balance of payments accounts. This occurs because the Chinese central bank or private Chinese citizens are investing in U.S. assets, which allows more U.S. capital investment in plant and equipment to take place than would otherwise occur. Capital investment increases because the greater demand for U.S. assets puts downward pressure on U.S. interest rates, and firms are now willing to make investments that were previously unprofitable. This increases aggregate spending in the short run, all else equal, and also increases the size of the economy in the long run by increasing the capital stock.

Private firms are not the only beneficiaries of the lower interest rates caused by the capital inflow (trade deficit) from China. Interest-sensitive household spending, on goods such as consumer durables and housing, is also higher than it would be if capital from China did not flow into the United States. In addition, a large proportion of the U.S. assets bought by the Chinese, particularly by the central bank, are U.S. Treasury securities, which fund U.S. federal budget deficits. According to the U.S. Treasury Department, China (as of January 2006) held $263 billion in U.S. Treasury securities, making China the second largest foreign holder of such securities, after Japan. If the U.S. trade deficit with China were eliminated, Chinese capital would no longer flow into this country on net, and the government would have to find other buyers of its U.S. Treasuries. This would likely increase the government's interest payments.

Net Effect on the U.S. Economy. In the medium run, an undervalued yuan neither increases nor decreases aggregate demand in the United States. Rather, it leads to a compositional shift in U.S. production, away from U.S. exporters and import-competing firms toward the firms that benefit from Chinese capital flows. Thus, it is expected to have no medium or long run effect on aggregate U.S. employment or unemployment. As evidence, one can consider that the U.S. had a historically large and growing trade deficit throughout

---

1960 to 22.4% in 1980 to 10.7% in 2005. This trend is much larger than the Chinese currency issue, and is caused by changing technology (which requires fewer workers to produce the same number of goods) and comparative advantage.

[5] Putting exchange rate issues aside, most economists maintain that trade is a win-win situation for the economy as a whole, but produces losers within the economy. This view derives from the principle of comparative advantage, which states that trade shifts production to the goods a country is relatively talented at producing from goods it is relatively untalented at producing. As trade expands, production of goods with a comparative disadvantage will decline in the U.S., to the detriment of workers and investors in those sectors (offset by higher employment and profits in sectors with a comparative advantage). Economists generally argue that free trade should be pursued because the gains from trade are large enough that the losers from trade can be compensated by the winners, and the winners will still be better off. See CRS Report RL32059, Trade, Trade Barriers, and Trade Deficits: Implications for U.S. Economic Welfare.

the 1990s at a time when unemployment reached a three-decade low. However, the gains and losses in employment and production caused by the trade deficit will not be dispersed evenly across regions and sectors of the economy: on balance, some areas will gain while others will lose. And by shifting the composition of

U.S. output to a higher capital base, the size of the economy would be larger in the long run as a result of the capital inflow/trade deficit.

Although the compositional shift in output has no negative effect on aggregate U.S. output and employment in the long run, there may be adverse short-run consequences. If output in the trade sector falls more quickly than the output of U.S. recipients of Chinese capital rises, aggregate spending and employment could temporarily fall. This is more likely to be a concern if the economy is already sluggish than if it is at full employment. Otherwise, it is likely that government macroeconomic policy adjustment and market forces can quickly compensate for any decline of output in the trade sector by expanding other elements of aggregate demand. The deficit with China has not prevented the U.S. economy from registering high rates of growth since 2003.

The U.S.-China Trade Deficit in the Context of the Overall U.S. Trade Deficit. While China is a large trading partner, it accounted for only 14.5% of U.S. imports in 2005 and 24% of the sum of all U.S. bilateral trade deficits. Over a span of several years, a country with a floating exchange rate can consistently run an overall trade deficit for only one reason: a domestic imbalance between saving and investment. This has been the case for the United States over the past two decades, where saving as a share of gross domestic product (GDP) has been in gradual decline. On the one hand, the U.S. has high rates of productivity growth and strong economic fundamentals that are conducive to high rates of capital investment. On the other hand, it has a chronically low household saving rate, and recently a negative government saving rate as a result of the budget deficit. As long as Americans save little, foreigners will use their saving to finance profitable investment opportunities in the U.S.; the trade deficit is the result[6]. The returns to foreign-owned capital will flow to foreigners instead of Americans, but the returns to U.S. labor utilizing foreign-owned capital will flow to U.S. labor.

According to Chinese statistics, more than half of what China exports to the world is produced by foreign-invested firms in China, including U.S. companies, which, in many cases, have shifted production to China in order to gain access to China's low-cost labor.

(The returns to capital of U.S. owned firms in China flow to Americans.) Such firms import raw materials and components (much of which come from East Asia) for assembly in China. As a result, China tends to run trade deficits with East Asian countries and trade surpluses with countries with high consumer demand, such as the United States. Overall, in 2005, China had a $102 billion trade surplus (Chinese data), indicating that China had a $100 billion trade deficit with the world excluding the United States (based on U.S. data on its trade deficit with China of $202 billion). These factors imply that much of the increase in U.S. imports (and hence, the rising U.S. trade deficit with China) is largely the result of China

[6] Nations, such as the United States, that fail to save enough to meet their investment needs must obtain savings from other countries with high savings rates. By obtaining foreign investment (in effect, borrowing), the United States can consume more (including more imports) than it would if investment were funded by domestic savings alone — this results in a trade deficit.

becoming a production platform for many foreign companies, rather than unfair Chinese trade policies[7].

Action in 109th Congress

Multiple bills have been introduced in Congress to address concerns over China's currency policy[8]. On April 6, 2005, the Senate failed (by a vote of 33 to 67) to table an amendment, S.Amdt. 309 (Schumer) to S. 600, which would impose a 27.5% tariff on Chinese goods if China failed to appreciate its currency to market levels. In response, the Senate leadership moved to allow a vote on S. 295 (which has same language as S.Amdt. 309) no later than July 27, 2005. However, on June 30th, Senator Schumer and other sponsors of S. 295 agreed to delay consideration of the bill after they were told by Administration officials that China would soon make significant reforms to its currency policy regime. On November 17, 2005, the Senate agreed to take up the bill no later than March 31, 2006. On July 27, 2005, the House passed H.R. 3283 (English), which would, among other things, apply U.S. countervailing laws to non-market economies (such as China); and require the Treasury Department to define "currency manipulation," describe actions that would be considered to constitute manipulation, and report on China's new currency regime.

China's July 21, 2005 reforms have been hailed by many U.S. policymakers as a good first step, but they have indicated that they expect China to make further reforms to permanently defuse the currency issue. In addition, many have expressed disappointment that China's announcement that the currency would be allowed to float within a daily band of 0.3% has not resulted in any significant appreciation of the yuan, indicating that the Chinese government continues to intervene heavily in exchange rate markets[9]. In its November 28, 2005 report to Congress on exchange rate policies, the Treasury Department did not cite China as a country that manipulates its currency, but concluded that China had failed to fully implement its commitment to make its new exchange rate mechanism more flexible and to increase the role of market forces. Instead, the report stated that China's new currency appeared to strongly resemble the previous mechanism of pegging the yuan to the dollar.

---

[7] Of concern to many economists is not the high U.S. trade deficit with China or the amount of capital coming from China, but rather the low U.S. savings rate that makes the United States so reliant on foreigners to finance its investment opportunities. If the U.S. did not borrow from China, it would still have to borrow from other countries.

[8] For a listing of these bills, see CRS Issue Brief IB91121, China-U.S. Trade Issues.

[9] According to the Bank of China, by the end of December 2005, the yuan had appreciated against the dollar by only 0.49% since the currency reform was implemented.

In: China in Focus Economic, Political and Educational Issues ISBN 1-60021-543-8
Editor: Ernest P. Nolan, pp. 125-137
© 2007 Nova Science Publishers, Inc.

Chapter 10

CHINA'S ECONOMIC CONDITIONS[*]

Wayne M. Morrison

ABSTRACT

Since the initiation of economic reforms in 1979, China has become one of the
world's fastest-growing economies. From 1979 to 2005 China's real GDP grew at an
average annual rate of 9.7%; it grew by 9.9% in 2005. Many economists speculate that
China could become the world's largest exporter within the next few years and the largest
economy within a few decades, provided that the government is able to continue and
deepen economic reforms, particularly in regard to its inefficient state-owned enterprises
(SOEs) and the state banking system. In addition, China faces several other difficult
challenges, such as pollution and growing income inequality, that threaten social stability.

Trade continues to play a major role in China's booming economy. In 2005, exports
rose by 28.4% to $762 billion, while imports grew by 17.6% to $660 billion, producing a
$102 billion trade surplus. China is now the world's third-largest trading economy after
the United States and Germany. China's trade boom is largely the result of large inflows
of foreign direct investment (FDI) into China, which totaled $60 billion in 2005. Over
half of China's trade is accounted for by foreign-invested firms in China.

China's economy continues to be a concern to U.S. policymakers. On the one hand,
China's economic growth presents huge opportunities for U.S. exporters. On the other
hand, the surge in Chinese exports to the United States has put competitive pressures on
various U.S. industries. Many U.S. policy-makers have argued that greater efforts should
be made to pressure China to fully implement its WTO commitments (especially in terms
of protecting U.S. intellectual property rights) and change various economic policies
deemed harmful to U.S. economic interests, such as its currency policy and its use of
subsidies to support its state-owned firms. In addition, recent bids by Chinese state-
owned firms to purchase various U.S. firms have raised concerns among Members over
the impact such acquisitions could have on U.S. national and economic security.

---

[*] From CRS Report # IB98014; March 17, 2006

MOST RECENT DEVELOPMENTS

On February 28, 2006, the Chinese government reported that GDP had grown by 9.9%.

On January 9, 2005, the Chinese National Bureau of Statistics made major revisions to its estimates of China's GDP from 1993-2004. The new revisions indicate that China's economy grew significantly faster than previously recorded.

On November 21, 2005, the International Monetary Fund urged China to adopt greater flexibility in its currency policy in order to obtain balanced growth and development and to help reduce global trade imbalances.

On July 21, 2005, the Chinese government announced major reforms to its currency policy. It stated that China's currency (the renminbi or yuan) would no longer be pegged to the dollar but instead would be a managed float regime with reference to a basket of currencies (including the dollar), and that the exchange rate of the U.S. dollar against the yuan would be adjusted from 8.28 to 8.11 yuan per U.S. dollar, an appreciation of 2.1%.

On June 22, 2005, CNOOC, a Chinese company, made a $18.5 billion bid to purchase Unocal, a U.S. energy company. News of the bid raised concern among several Members, many of who contended that the deal threatened U.S. national security. On August 2, 2005, CNOOC withdrew its bid, citing strong political opposition in the United States. On January 10, 2006, CNOOC announced it had reached $2.3 billion deal to purchase a 45% stake in a block of offshore Nigerian oil fields.

BACKGROUND AND ANALYSIS

An Overview of China's Economic Development

China's Economy Prior to Reforms

Prior to 1979, China maintained a centrally planned, or command, economy. A large share of the country's economic output was directed and controlled by the state, which set production goals, controlled prices, and allocated resources throughout most of the economy. During the 1950s, all of China's individual household farms were collectivized into large communes. To support rapid industrialization, the central government undertook large-scale investments in physical and human capital during the 1960s and 1970s. As a result, by 1978 nearly three-fourths of industrial production was produced by centrally controlled state-owned enterprises according to centrally planned output targets. Private enterprises and foreign-invested firms were nearly nonexistent. A central goal of the Chinese government was to make China's economy relatively self-sufficient. Foreign trade was generally limited to obtaining only those goods that could not be made or obtained in China.

Government policies kept the Chinese economy relatively stagnant and inefficient, mainly because there were few profit incentives for firms and farmers; competition was virtually nonexistent, and price and production controls caused widespread distortions in the economy. Chinese living standards were substantially lower than those of many other developing countries. The Chinese government hoped that gradual reform would significantly increase economic growth and raise living standards.

The Introduction of Economic Reforms

Beginning in 1979, China launched several economic reforms. The central government initiated price and ownership incentives for farmers, which enabled them to sell a portion of their crops on the free market. In addition, the government established four special economic zones along the coast for the purpose of attracting foreign investment, boosting exports, and importing high technology products into China. Additional reforms, which followed in stages, sought to decentralize economic policymaking in several sectors, especially trade. Economic control of various enterprises was given to provincial and local governments, which were generally allowed to operate and compete on free market principles, rather than under the direction and guidance of state planning. Additional coastal regions and cities were designated as open cities and development zones, which allowed them to experiment with free market reforms and to offer tax and trade incentives to attract foreign investment. In addition, state price controls on a wide range of products were gradually eliminated.

China's Economic Growth Since Reforms: 1979-2005

Since the introduction of economic reforms, China's economy has grown substantially faster than during the pre-reform period (see **Table 1**). In January 2006, China made major revisions to its GDP data for 1993-2004. The revisions indicated that, based on new estimates of growth in the service sector, the size of China's economy and its GDP growth were significantly higher than previously estimated. For example, real GDP growth in 2004 had been originally measured at 9.5%, but the revised figure puts this rate at 10.1%. Overall, the size of the economy in 2004 was estimated to be nearly 17% higher than previously thought. Based on these revisions, China's average annual real GDP grew by 9.7% between 1979 and 2005; it grew by 9.9% in 2005.

Table 1. China's Average Annual Real GDP Growth Rates, 1960-2005

Time period	Average annual % growth
1960-1978 (pre-reform)	5.3
1979-2005 (post-reform)	9.7
1990	3.8
1991	9.3
1992	14.2
1993	14.0
1994	13.1
1995	10.9
1996	10.0
1997	9.3
1998	7.8
1999	7.6
2000	8.4
2001	8.3
2002	9.1
2003	10.0
2004	10.1
2005	9.9

Source: Official Chinese government data.

Causes of China's Economic Growth

Economists generally attribute much of China's rapid economic growth to two main factors: large-scale capital investment (financed by large domestic savings and foreign investment) and rapid productivity growth. These two factors appear to have gone together hand in hand. Economic reforms led to higher efficiency in the economy, which boosted output and increased resources for additional investment in the economy.

China has historically maintained a high rate of savings. When reforms were initiated in 1979, domestic savings as a percentage of GDP stood at 32%. However, most Chinese savings during this period were generated by the profits of state-owned enterprises (SOEs), which were used by the central government for domestic investment. Economic reforms, which included the decentralization of economic production, led to substantial growth in Chinese household savings (these now account for half of Chinese domestic savings). As a result, savings as a percentage of GDP has steadily risen; it reached nearly 50% in 2005, among the highest savings rates in the world[1].

Several economists have concluded that productivity gains (i.e., increases in efficiency in which inputs are used) were another major factor in China's rapid economic growth. The improvements to productivity were caused largely by a reallocation of resources to more productive uses, especially in sectors that were formerly heavily controlled by the central government, such as agriculture, trade, and services. For example, agricultural reforms boosted production, freeing workers to pursue employment in the more productive manufacturing sector. China's decentralization of the economy led to the rise of nonstate enterprises, which tended to pursue more productive activities than the centrally controlled SOEs. Additionally, a greater share of the economy (mainly the export sector) was exposed to competitive forces. Local and provincial governments were allowed to establish and operate various enterprises on market principles, without interference from the central government. In addition, foreign direct investment (FDI) in China brought with it new technology and processes that boosted efficiency.

Measuring the Size of China's Economy

The actual size of the China's economy has been a subject of extensive debate among economists. Measured in U.S. dollars using nominal exchange rates, China's GDP in 2005 is estimated at about $2.3 trillion; its per capita GDP (a commonly used living-standards measurement) was $1,700. Such data would indicate that China's economy and living standards are significantly lower than those of the United States and Japan, respectively considered to be the number-one and number-two largest economies (see **Table 2**).

Many economists, however, contend that using nominal exchange rates to convert Chinese data into U.S. dollars substantially underestimates the size of China's economy. This is because prices in China for many goods and services are significantly lower than those in the United States and other developed countries. Economists have attempted to factor in these price differentials by using a purchasing power parity (PPP) measurement, which attempts to convert foreign currencies into U.S. dollars on the basis of the actual purchasing power of

---

[1] In comparison, the U.S. savings rate was about 10% in 2005. Savings defined as aggregate national savings by the public and private sector as a percentage of nominal GDP. (*Economist Intelligence Unit* database.)

such currency (based on surveys of the prices of various goods and services) in each respective country. This PPP exchange rate is then used to convert foreign economic data in national currencies into U.S. dollars.

Because prices for many goods and services are significantly lower in China than in the United States and other developed countries (while prices in Japan are higher), the PPP exchange rate raises the estimated size of Chinese economy from $2.3 trillion (nominal dollars) to $8.4 trillion (PPP dollars), significantly larger than Japan's GDP in PPPs ($3.9 trillion), and about 67% the size of the U.S. economy. PPP data also raise China's per capita GDP to $6,386. The PPP figures indicate that, while the size of China's economy is substantial, its living standards fall far below those of the U.S. and Japan. China's per capita GDP on a PPP basis is only 15.2% of U.S. levels. Thus, even if China's GDP were to overtake that of the United States in the next few decades, its living standards would remain substantially below those of the United States for many years to come.

Table 2. Comparisons of United States, Japanese, and Chinese GDP and Per Capita GDP in Nominal U.S. Dollars and PPP, 2005

Country	Nominal GDP ($ billions)	GDP in PPP ($ billions)	Nominal Per Capita GDP	Per Capita GDP in PPP
United States	12,458	12,458	42,130	42,130
Japan	4,571	3,914	35,880	30,720
China	2,262	8,359	1,700	6,386

Source: Economist Intelligence Unit Data Services and Global Insight.

Note: PPP data for China should be interpreted with caution. China is not a fully developed market economy; the prices of many goods and services are distorted due to price controls and government subsidies.

Foreign Direct Investment in China

China's trade and investment reforms and incentives led to a surge in foreign direct investment (FDI), which has been a major source of China's capital growth. Annual utilized FDI in China grew from $636 million in 1983 to $60 billion in 2005 The cumulative level of FDI in China stood at about $621 billion at the end of 2005. Analysts predict that FDI will continue to pour into China as investment barriers are reduced under China's WTO commitments and Chinese demand for imports continues to increase.

Based on cumulative FDI for 1979-2005 about 42% of FDI in China has come from Hong Kong. In 2005, Japan replaced the United States as second largest overall investor in China. The United States ranked third accounting for 8.2% ($51.1 billion) of total FDI. Other major investors include the British Virgin Islands, Taiwan, and South Korea (see **Table 3**)[2]. U.S. FDI in China for 2005 was $3.1 billion (compared to $3.9 billion in 2004), accounting for

---

[2] According to the Chinese Ministry of Commerce, major U.S. investors in China (based on 2003 sales volumes) include Motorola ($5.8 billion in sales volume), General Motors ($2.2 billion), Dell Computer ($2.1 billion), Hewlett Packard ($1.3 billion), and Kodak ($0.6 billion).

5.1% of FDI for that year, and ranked 5th after Hong Kong, the British Virgin Islands, Japan, and South Korea.[3]

Table 3. Major Foreign Investors in China: 1979-2004
($ billions and % of total)

Country	Cumulative Utilized FDI: 1979-2005		Utilized FDI in 2005	
	Amount ($ billions)	% of Total	Amount ($ billions)	% of Total
Total	620.7	100.0	60.3	100.0
Hong Kong	259.5	41.8	17.9	29.7
Japan	53.3	8.6	6.5	10.8
United States	51.1	8.2	3.1	5.1
British Virgin Islands	45.9	7.4	9.0	14.9
Taiwan	41.8	6.7	2.2	3.3
South Korea	31.1	5.0	5.2	8.6

Source: Chinese government statistics. Top six investors according to cumulative FDI from 1979 to 2005.

China's Trade Patterns

Economic reforms have transferred China into a major trading power. Chinese exports rose from $14 billion in 1979 to $762 billion in 2005, while imports over this period grew from $16 billion to $660 billion (see **Table 4**). In 2004, China surpassed Japan as the world's third-largest trading economy (after the United States and Germany). China's trade continues to grow dramatically: From 2002 to 2005, the size of China's exports and imports more than doubled. In 2005, exports and imports rose by 28.4% and 17.6%, respectively. China's trade surplus, which totaled $32 billion in 2004, tripled to $102 billion.

---

[3] The British Virgin Islands is a large source of FDI because of its status as a tax haven. Much of the FDI originating from Hong Kong comes from non-Hong Kong investors, such as Taiwanese.

Table 4. China's Merchandise World Trade, 1979-2005
($ billions)

Year	Exports	Imports	Trade balance
1979	13.7	15.7	-2.0
1980	18.1	19.5	-1.4
1981	21.5	21.6	-0.1
1982	21.9	18.9	2.9
1983	22.1	21.3	0.8
1984	24.8	26.0	-1.1
1985	27.3	42.5	-15.3
1986	31.4	43.2	-11.9
1987	39.4	43.2	-3.8
1988	47.6	55.3	-7.7
1989	52.9	59.1	-6.2
1990	62.9	53.9	9.0
1991	71.9	63.9	8.1
1992	85.5	81.8	3.6
1993	91.6	103.6	-11.9
1994	120.8	115.6	5.2
1995	148.8	132.1	16.7
1996	151.1	138.8	12.3
1997	182.7	142.2	40.5
1998	183.8	140.2	43.6
1999	194.9	165.8	29.1
2000	249.2	225.1	24.1
2001	266.2	243.6	22.6
2002	325.6	295.2	30.4
2003	438.4	412.8	25.6
2004	593.4	561.4	32.0
2005	762.0	660.1	101.9

Source: International Monetary Fund, Direction of Trade Statistics, and official Chinese statistics.

Merchandise trade surpluses, large-scale foreign investment, and its peg to the U.S. dollar have enabled China to accumulate the world's second largest foreign exchange (after Japan). As seen in **Figure 1**, China's accumulation of foreign exchange reserves has been particularly acute over the past few years. China's total reserves reached $819 billion at the end of 2005, up by $210 billion, or 34%, over the same period in 2004.

($ in billions)

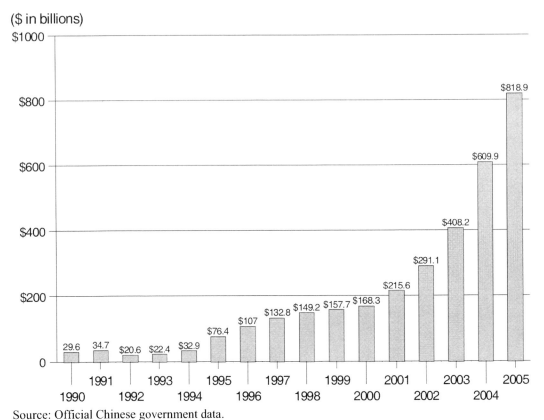

Source: Official Chinese government data.

Figure 1. China's Foreign Exchange Reserves, 1990-2005

China's Major Trading Partners

China's trade data often differ significantly from those of its major trading partners. This is due to the fact that a large share of China's trade (both exports and imports) passes through Hong Kong (which reverted back to Chinese rule in July 1997 but is treated as a separate customs area by most countries, including China and the United States). China treats a large share of its exports through Hong Kong as Chinese exports to Hong Kong for statistical purposes, while many countries that import Chinese products through Hong Kong generally attribute their origin to China for statistical purposes. According to Chinese trade data, its top five trading partners in 2004 were the European Union (EU), the United States, Japan, Hong Kong, and the 10 nations that constitute the Association of Southeast Asian Nations (ASEAN) (see **Table 5**). China's largest export markets were the United States, Hong Kong, and the EU, while its top sources for imports were Japan, the EU, and Taiwan (the United States ranked sixth).

Table 5. China's Top Five Trading Partners: 2005 ($ billions)

Country	Total trade	Chinese exports	Chinese imports	China's trade balance	Trade Balance as Reported by Partner
Hong Kong	246.8	124.5	122.3	2.2	-4.7
European Union	219.3	143.7	75.6	68.1	-132
United States	211.6	162.9	48.7	114.2	-201.6
Japan	184.5	84.0	100.5	-16.5	-28.5
ASEAN*	130.4	55.4	75.0	-19.6	N/A

Sources: Official Chinese trade data and Global Trade Atlas.

Note: Chinese data on its bilateral trade often differ substantially from the official trade data of other countries on their trade with China.

* Association of Southeast Asian Nations (ASEAN) member countries are Indonesia, Malaysia, the Philippines, Singapore, Thailand, Brunei, Cambodia, Laos, Myanmar, and Vietnam.

U.S. trade data indicate that the importance of the U.S. market to China's export sector is likely much higher than is reflected in Chinese trade data. Based on U.S. data on Chinese exports to the United States (which, as noted, do not agree with Chinese data), and Chinese data on total Chinese exports, it is estimated that Chinese exports to the United States as a share of total Chinese exports grew from 15.3% in 1986 to 32.0% in 2005.

A growing level of Chinese exports is from foreign-funded enterprises (FFEs) in China. According to Chinese data, FFEs were responsible for 58% of Chinese exports in 2005, compared with 41% in 1996. A large share of these FFEs are owned by Hong Kong and Taiwan investors, many of whom have shifted their labor-intensive, export-oriented, firms to China to take advantage of low-cost labor. A significant share of the products made by such firms is likely exported to the United States.

Major Chinese Trade Commodities

China's abundance of cheap labor has made it internationally competitive in many low-cost, labor-intensive manufactures. As a result, manufactured products constitute an increasingly larger share of China's trade. A large share of China's imports, such as raw materials, components and parts, and production machinery is used to manufacture products for export. For example, China imports cotton and textile-production machinery (and cotton) to produce textile and apparel items. A substantial amount of China's imports is comprised of parts and components that are assembled in Chinese factories (major products include consumer electronic products and computers), then exported. China's top five exports in 2005 were (1) automatic data processing machines and units, (2) garments and clothing accessories, (3) textile products, (4) parts of data processing machines, and (5) radio telephone handsets (**see Table 6**). China's top imports were (1) electronic integrated circuits and micro-assemblies, (2) crude oil, (3) liquid crystal display panels, (4) steel products, and (5) plastics (see **Table 7**)[4].

---

[4] Rankings differ according to which trade classification is used and at what digit level.

Table 6. Major Chinese Exports, 2005
($billions and % change over previous year)

	Amount	Percent Increase over 2004
Automatic data processing machines and units	74.5	28.6
Garments and clothing accessories	73.4	20.0
Textile products	40.9	23.9
Parts of data processing machines	27.7	20.4
Radio telephone handsets	19.7	44.8

Source: China's Customs Statistics. Estimated, based on January-November 2005 data.

Table 7. Major Chinese Imports, 2005
($ billions and % change over previous year)

	Amount	Percent Change over 2004
Electronic integrated circuits and micro-assemblies	79.3	32.0
Crude oil	47.2	43.5
Liquid crystal display panels	26.8	27.5
Steel products	25.0	20.7
Plastics	24.1	18.6

Source: China's Customs Statistics. Estimated, based on January-November 2005 data.

Major Long-Term Challenges Facing the Chinese Economy

China's economy has shown remarkable economic growth over the past several years, and many economists project that it will enjoy fairly healthy growth in the near future. However, economists caution that these projections are likely to occur only if China continues to make major reforms to its economy. Failure to implement such reforms could endanger future growth.

- **State-owned enterprises (SOEs)**, which account for about one-third of Chinese industrial production, put a heavy strain on China's economy. Over half are believed to lose money and must be supported by subsidies, mainly through state banks. Government support of unprofitable SOEs diverts resources away from potentially more efficient and profitable enterprises. In addition, the poor financial condition of many SOEs makes it difficult for the government to reduce trade barriers out of fear that doing so would lead to widespread bankruptcies among many SOEs.

- **The banking system** faces several major difficulties due to its financial support of SOEs and its failure to operate solely on market-based principles. China's banking system is regulated and controlled by the central government, which sets interest rates and attempts to allocate credit to certain Chinese firms. The central government has used the banking system to keep afloat money-losing SOEs by pressuring state banks to provide low-interest loans, without which a large number of the SOEs would likely go bankrupt. Currently, over 50% of state-owned bank loans now go to the SOEs, even though a large share of loans are not likely to be repaid. Ernst & Young estimates that the level of nonperforming loans by Chinese banks in 2002 was

$480 billion (equal to about 43% of China's GDP).[5] The high volume of bad loans now held by Chinese banks poses a serious threat to China's banking system. Three out of the four state commercial banks are believed to be insolvent. The precarious financial state of the Chinese banking system has made Chinese reformers reluctant to open the banking sector to foreign competition. Corruption poses another problem for China's banking system because loans are often made on the basis of political connections. This system promotes widespread inefficiency in the economy because savings are generally not allocated on the basis of obtaining the highest possible returns.

- **Public unrest over pollution, government corruption, and growing income inequality poses threats to social stability.** The Chinese government reported that there were over 74,000 protests (many of which became violent) involving 3.8 million people in 2004 (up from 53,000 protests in 2003) over such issues as pollution, government corruption, and land seizures. Pollution in China continues to worsen, posing series health risks to the population. The Chinese government often disregards its own environmental laws in order to promote rapid economic growth. According to the World Bank, 16 out of 20 of the world's most polluted cities are in China, and the direct costs to the economy (such as health problems, crop failures and water shortages) is estimated to be hundreds of billions of dollars yearly. The Chinese government estimates that there are over 300 million people living in rural areas that drink unsafe water (caused by chemicals and other contaminants). Toxic spills in China in recent months have threatened the water supply of millions of people. Rising income inequality, particularly between people living in the urban coastal and those living in the inner rural regions of China, has become another source of tension. A number of protests in China have stemmed in part from frustrations among many Chinese (especially peasants) that they are not benefitting from China's economic reforms and rapid growth, and perceptions that those who are getting rich are doing so because they have connections with government officials. Protests have broken out over government land seizures and plant shutdowns in large part due to perceptions that these actions benefitted a select group with connections. A 2005 United Nations report stated that the income gap between the urban and rural areas was among the highest in the world and warned that this gap threatens social stability. The report urged China to take greater steps to improve conditions for the rural poor, and bolster education, health care, and the social security system.

- **The lack of the rule of law** in China has led to widespread government corruption, financial speculation, and misallocation of investment funds. In many cases, government "connections," not market forces, are the main determinant of successful firms in China. Many U.S. firms find it difficult to do business in China because rules and regulations are generally not consistent or transparent, contracts are not easily enforced, and intellectual property rights are not protected (due to the lack of an independent judicial system). The lack of the rule of law in China limits competition and undermines the efficient allocation of goods and services in the economy.

---

[5] Ernst & Young Asia Pacific Financial Solutions, Nonperforming Loan Report, Asia, 2002.

Outlook for China's Economy and Implications for the United States

The short-term outlook for the Chinese economy appears to be positive, but it will likely be strongly influenced by the government's ability to reform the SOEs and banking system to make them more responsive to market forces, to fully implement its WTO commitments, and to assist workers who lose their jobs due to economic reforms (in order to maintain social stability). Global Insight, an economic forecasting firm, projects that China's real GDP will average 8.0% over the next five years, indicating that China could double the size of its economy in less than 10 years.[6] The Economist Intelligence Unit projects that China will become the world's largest exporter by 2010 and the world's largest economy by 2020.

China's rise as an economic superpower is likely to pose both opportunities and challenges for the United States and the world trading system. China's rapid economic growth has boosted incomes and is making China a huge market for a variety of goods and services. In addition, China's abundant low-cost labor has led multinational corporations to shift their export-oriented, labor-intensive manufacturing facilities to China. This process has lowered prices for consumers, boosting their purchasing power. It has also lowered costs for firms that import and use Chinese-made components and parts to produce manufactured goods, boosting their competitiveness. Conversely, China's role as a major international manufacturer has raised a number of concerns. Many developing countries worry that growing FDI in China is coming at the expense of FDI in their country. Policymakers in both developing and developed countries have expressed concern over the loss of domestic manufacturing jobs that have shifted to China (as well as the downward pressures on domestic wages and prices that may occur from competing against low-cost Chinese-made goods).

Many analysts contend that China's currency policy, despite reforms undertaken in July 2005, is having a negative impact on the economies of many of its trading partners by artificially making its exports cheaper, and imports more expensive, than they would be under a floating system. They have urged China to move toward a floating exchange rate regime as soon as possible, contending that such a move would benefit China's economy and those of its trading partners.[7] Chinese officials have expressed concern that further currency reforms, if implemented too quickly, could prove disruptive to the economy. A number of bills have been introduced in Congress to address Chinese currency policy, including some that would impose a 27.5% tariff on Chinese goods unless China appreciated its currency to market levels.[8] Failure by China to implement further reforms to its currency regime could prompt Congress to take up currency-related legislation. On the other hand, some analysts have raised concerns that China's move toward a managed float tied to a basket of currencies may diminish China's purchase of U.S. Treasury securities, which could affect U.S. interest rates.

China is attempting to establish and promote companies that can compete globally, especially in advanced technologies. In some cases, China has attempted to purchase large foreign companies. For example, in December 2004, Lenovo Group Limited, a computer company primarily owned by the Chinese government, purchased IBM's personal computer division. In June 2005, the China National Offshore Oil Corporation (CNOOC) made a bid to buy a U.S. energy company, UNOCAL, for $18.5 billion, although strong opposition in

---

[6] Global Insight, China: Interim Forecast Analysis: Economic Growth, December 15, 2005.
[7] For a discussion of this issue, see CRS Report RS21625: *China's Currency Peg: A Summary of the Economic Issues*, by Wayne Morrison and Marc Labonte.
[8] For a listing of these bills, See CRS Issue Brief IB91121, *China-U.S. Trade Issues*, by Wayne M. Morrison.

Congress forced CNOOC to withdraw its bid. China's possession of large currency reserves and desire to become a world leader in the production of a variety of goods and strategic commodities will likely lead the Chinese government to expand efforts to take over major international corporations. Many Members charge that China's use of extensive subsidies to support state-owned firms, especially to fund takeover bids, threatens U.S. economic interests and may violate its WTO commitments.

China's rapid economic growth and continued expansion of its manufacturing base are fueling a sharp demand for energy and raw materials, which is becoming an increasingly important factor in determining world prices for such commodities. China is now the world's second largest consumer of oil products (after the United States) at 6.7 million barrels per day, and that level is projected to double to 13.4 million barrels per day by 2025.[9] According to the U.S. Energy Information Administration, around 40% of world oil demand growth over the past four years came from China and this demand is "a very significant factor in world oil markets."[10] China has also reportedly become the largest consumer of steel, cement, and copper.

Some U.S. policymakers have expressed concern over China's rising ownership of U.S. government debt, due to fears that China might attempt to use its holdings as leverage in its dealings with the United States on economic and/or political matters. China is the second largest foreign holder of Treasury securities (after Japan), and both the level of those holdings and China's share of total foreign holdings have increased sharply over the past few years. These went from $51.8 billion in 1999 to $257 billion at end of 2005. China's U.S. Treasury securities holdings as a share of total foreign holdings over this period have grown from 4.1% to 11.8%. Some have raised concerns that threats by China to halt future purchases, or to sell existing holdings, could cause the value of the dollar to depreciate in world markets (raising import prices), increase U.S. interest rates, lead to a decline in U.S. stock and bond markets, and possibly cause the U.S. economy to slow. However, any such disruption to the U.S. economy would also hurt China's economy since about a third of China's exports go to the United States.

---

[9] Global Insight, Global Petroleum Outlook Forecast Tables (Long-Term), January 2005.
[10] Global Insight, China: Interim Forecast Analysis: Economic Growth, December 1

In: China in Focus Economic, Political and Educational Issues
Editor: Ernest P. Nolan, pp. 139-177
ISBN 1-60021-543-8
© 2007 Nova Science Publishers, Inc.

Chapter 11

CHINA, THE UNITED STATES AND THE IMF: NEGOTIATING EXCHANGE RATE ADJUSTMENT[*]

Jonathan E. Sanford

ABSTRACT

In recent years, the United States and other countries have expressed considerable concern that China's national currency (the yuan or renminbi) is seriously undervalued. Some analysts say the yuan needs to rise by as much as 40% in order to reflect its equilibrium value. Critics say that China's undervalued currency provides it with an unfair trade advantage that has seriously injured the manufacturing sector in the United States. Chinese officials counter that they have not pegged the yuan to the dollar in order to gain trade advantages. Rather, they say the fixed rate promotes economic stability that is vital for the functioning of its domestic economy.

On July 21, 2005, China announced a new foreign exchange system which is intended to allow more flexibility and to permit the international value of the yuan to be established by market forces. The yuan was increased in value by 2% and a "managed float" was introduced. However, the value of the yuan has changed little since then. Despite the publication of many studies, scholars do not agree whether or by what percent the yuan is undervalued. The wide range of estimates suggests that there is no reason to believe that any particular figure is correct. It is not clear that the U.S. trade deficit would be lower or U.S. manufacturers would benefit if China raised the value of the yuan. In the short run, U.S. producers might be able to sell higher-priced products to U.S. consumers if the inflow of Chinese goods were reduced. In the long run, though, as long as the United States is a net importer of capital, it will have a trade deficit and other countries will ultimately replace China as suppliers of low-cost goods to the U.S. market.

The Treasury Department has strongly urged China in recent years to adopt procedures that would allow the yuan to rise in value. Congress is considering legislation that would penalize China if its currency is not revalued. The United States has pursued the yuan-dollar exchange rate issue as a bilateral U.S.-China issue. Other countries are also affected by the presumably undervalued yuan — some more than the U.S. — but they have allowed the United States to take the lead.

---

[*] Order Code RL33322 March 13, 2006

There are at least five ways the United States could deal with the yuan exchange rate issue. Some of these would involve other countries more explicitly in the process. First, the United States could continue pressing China publicly to raise the value of the yuan on the assumption that change will not occur without foreign pressure. Second, it could stop pressing China publicly, on the expectation that China might move more rapidly towards reform if it is not pressured. Third, the United States could restrict imports from China pending action to revalue the yuan. Fourth, the U.S. could ask the IMF to declare that China is manipulating its currency in violation of IMF rules. Fifth, the United States could refer the issue to the World Trade Organization (WTO), asserting that the United States has been injured by unfair trade practices linked to the undervaluation of China's currency. The WTO, in turn, could authorize trade remedies (tariffs on Chinese goods, for example) aimed at correcting this abuse.

SCOPE AND CONTENT

Overview

In recent years, there has been growing concern in the United States and elsewhere that China may be manipulating the value of its currency to gain unfair trade advantages. Many believe that China's national currency, the yuan or renminbi (RMB), may be seriously undervalued compared to the dollar and other major currencies.[1] The United States and other countries have urged China to raise the value of its currency. Chinese officials say they want to make their exchange rate system more flexible, but theysayChina also needs long-term stability in its currency value in order to avoid internal dislocations. Discussion of this question has taken place at the International Monetary Fund (IMF) and at other multilateral fora such as the periodic meetings of the G-8 (the seven largest industrial countries plus Russia.) The United States and other countries have also spoken directly to China on a bilateral basis about this issue.

The key issue is what — if the yuan is undervalued — China and the world should do about it. China is currently undergoing a major shift from a state-dominated to a market-based economy. It has pursued a policy of export-led growth in order to generate the employment and income necessary to facilitate change in the overall structure of its economy. It has priced its currency in order to facilitate that policy.

In July 2005, China adopted reforms aimed at giving market forces a possible role in the valuation of the yuan. Most observers say the initial changes (a 2% rise in value) were too small and they note that little change has occurred since. Chinese officials retain firm control over the mechanisms which produce the yuan-dollar exchange rate and the criteria they use in this process remain opaque. International discussions have sought to persuade China to accelerate the process but — while the concerns of other countries may bear weight in the thinking of Chinese officials — there are no effective "teeth" in the International Monetary

---

[1] For a comprehensive discussion of the China exchange rate issue, see CRS Report RS21625, China's Currency Peg: A Summary of the Economic Issues and CRS Report RL32165, China's Exchange Rate Peg: Economic Issues and Options for U.S. Trade Policy. See also CRS Issue Briefs IB91121, U.S.-China Trade Issues and CRS Report RS22338, China's Currency: A Brief overview of U.S. Options. The term "renminbi" means "people's currency" while "yuan" is the unit of account (one yuan, two yuan, etc.) In this report, for simplicity, China's currency will be called the "yuan" except in instances where the term "renminbi" is used in a quotation or official statement.

Fund that could compel China to change its policies and procedures more rapidly than it wishes to do so.

Many in the United States believe that the large volume of Chinese exports to the United States is damaging the U.S. manufacturing sector and feeding the U.S. trade deficit. They believe that the undervalued yuan is an important reason why China is able to price its goods so competitively and why production in many areas is shifting to China. Other analysts believe that — by virtue of its undervalued currency — China is damaging the world trading system and denying export opportunities to other countries whose currencies are more fairly priced. Congress is considering legislation which would place countervailing duties or special tariffs on Chinese goods entering the U.S. in order to offset the trade benefits China presumably gains from its present exchange rate policies.

This Report in Four Parts

Events and Issues. This report has four parts. The first part discusses the issues and events surrounding the yuan-dollar controversy. It describes the actions which Chinese authorities have taken to revalue the yuan and, arguably, to lay the groundwork for a larger future role for market forces in its valuation. It also describes the methods the Chinese authorities have used and still use to hold the value of the yuan at the level they prefer. This section discusses the efforts the International Monetary Fund, the U.S. Government and other governments have made to encourage or press China to revalue its currency. It also reviews the U.S. Treasury Department's discussion of China in its semi-annual report on currency manipulation and legislation currently pending in Congress which would levy special duties on Chinese goods if the yuan is not increased considerably in value.

Five Questions which Frame the Controversy. The second part of this report looks at five central questions.

First, is the yuan undervalued and, if so, by how much? This question may be harder to answer than many people assume. Most economists agree the yuan is undervalued, but the 17 studies reviewed in this report show widely different conclusions. Some say the yuan is slightly *overvalued*, others say it is 15% or 25% or perhaps 49% *undervalued*, while several say it is impossible to make an accurate computation. The data are poor, China is changing rapidly, and scholars use different assumptions in their studies. Moreover, new economic data published in December 2005 seem to render all previous studies obsolete, as they give a very different picture of the Chinese economy than was available before. In recent studies, IMF experts say the yuan is undervalued but they also say it is impossible to know how large the distortion might be. The IMF also says that it is impossible to separate the trade effects of that distortion from the other factors (labor costs, productivity, etc.) which also affect the price of Chinese goods.

Without some objective way of determining what the "real" value of the yuan might be, it may be difficult for China and other countries to agree what size increase is "enough." Likewise, without knowing the proper rate, it might be difficult to design special U.S. tariffs which the world would consider fair and compensatory rather than arbitrary or punitive. It might be helpful if China, the United States and other countries could agree on criteria by which to decide how an appropriate exchange rate for the dollar and yuan might be determined.

Second, does China manipulate the value of the yuan? The IMF rules state that countries may not manipulate the value of their currency in order to gain unfair trade advantage. The second section of this report examines China's behavior in light of the five standards the IMF uses to judge whether manipulation is taking place. For whatever reason, the IMF has not publicly declared that China is manipulating its currency. However, China's actions seem to meet three of the IMF's criteria in this regard. The IMF has no "teeth," however, nor any means other than persuasion to make countries comply with its rules. In this context, it is not clear that an IMF announcement that China was violating its rules would help or hinder the current discussions aimed at persuading China to raise the value of the yuan.

Third, how fast could China revalue the yuan if it wanted to? Theoretically, the People's Bank of China could raise the exchange value of the yuan to any specified level overnight. However, Chinese officials are concerned about the growth and employment effects any change in the value of the yuan may have on their economy. A too-rapid increase might have serious negative effects on employment, output and growth. Some also worry that "hot money" could complicate the process of revaluation and may require China to delay any changes until the perceived speculative pressure abates. Many experts believe that a gradual and measured approach to currency revaluation is appropriate for China. The IMF says, for example, that emerging market countries generally do not handle rapid and large exchange rate movements well and that serious dislocations can occur. Others believe, however, that basic fairness to other countries requires China to raise the value of its currency. Some analysts believe China could suffer serious damage to its economy if it does not change is economic strategy. Its heavy reliance on export-led growth makes it vulnerable, for example, to a slowdown in world demand. Higher currency values would stimulate growth of its domestic economy.

Fourth, has China "cooked the books" in terms of its trade surplus? Some analysts believe that China's actual net income from trade is many times larger than that which China's publishes in its official trade statistics. Indeed, data published by the IMF show that, while China reports that it had a net trade surplus of $41 billion in 2004, its trading partners report that they had a combined trade deficit of $267 billion with China. Some people say that a trade surplus this large is proof that China's currency is substantially undervalued.

Others would ask, however, where — if China is accruing an extra $200 billion annually in trade income beyond the amounts accounted for in its balance of payments figures — that money might be. It might be hard, for example, for China to hide all this additional income year after year in secret undeclared foreign exchange reserves without somebody discovering that it exists.

Trade date for other countries also show (though on a smaller scale) this same mismatch between the amount reported by exporter countries and the amounts reported by those who import their products. Bad data collection by individual countries and methodological problems in the reporting system seem to be better explanations for these discrepancies than is the uniform prospect that exporters fudge their data while importers report their incoming trade data correctly.

Fifth, would the U.S. economy benefit if China revalued the yuan? Correcting the international value of the yuan may improve the efficiency of international trade. But will it reduce the U.S. trade deficit and strengthen the U.S. manufacturing sector? Most economists believe not. The U.S. and Chinese economies have become increasingly interdependent in recent years. China is pursuing a policy of export-led growth and the United States provides a ready market for its goods. Meanwhile, the United States imports large quantities of capital from abroad (by borrowing or by opening its economy to foreign investment) and — in order (more money chasing the same quantity of goods) to avoid turning that imported money into inflation — it must also import goods and services for the imported money to buy. If China raised the value of the yuan, its exports to the United States will likely shrink and the amount of money it could place in the U.S. economy would decline.

Temporarily, the decline in these imports might allow U.S. producers to take some of the market (albeit at higher prices) previously supplied by China. From a longer perspective, though, it is likely that production will shift to other low-cost countries and these will ramp up their exports in order to supply the U.S. market previously supplied by Chinese goods. On the other hand, the inflow of foreign goods will decline and U.S. manufactured goods might be more competitive in U.S. and foreign markets if the U.S. savings rate increased, the United States borrowed less and received fewer investments from abroad, and the international value of the dollar declined.[2]

Three Dilemmas for China. The third section of this report looks at some of the monetary and financial dilemmas which affect China's views about exchange rate policy. **First, what should China do about its foreign exchange (forex) reserves?** China has $819 billion in foreign exchange reserves (rough 70% in dollars). These are an important source of income, influence, and future spending power. However, they are also a problem. For one thing, the growth in China's forex reserves fuels domestic inflation. For every dollar the People's Bank of China buys (to hold down the value of the yuan and to increase its reserves), it injects 8 yuan into China's economy. China's reserves grew by $100 billion in 2005, so this is a lot of new "printing press" money. The central bank has tried with limited success to bottle up the inflationary effect of this money with public debt transactions and tight monetary policy. If China raised the value of the yuan, the growth in its foreign exchange reserves would slow or stop and — if it relaxed its monetary policy — the growth and reform prospects of its internal economy might be enhanced.

On the other hand, revaluation would cost China a great deal of money. If the yuan increased in value by 20%, the purchasing power of China's foreign reserves would go down corresponding. It would lose, from China's perspective, about 1.3 trillion yuan (about $200 billion) in purchasing power. If China began withdrawing assets from the U.S. market and converting them to other currencies, in order to reduce its exposure, it would lose money because its actions would push down the value of the securities and the dollars it sold. When it purchased other currencies and foreign assets to replace its former U.S. holdings, it would lose money again because its actions would also push up their prices. Chinese officials may want to reduce the inflationary pressure which comes from growth in their foreign exchange reserves but they may not be happy about the prospect of major financial losses if they revalue or if they move their current assets elsewhere.

Second, where is the money coming from that fuels those growing reserves? Many people believe that exports and incoming foreign investment account for most of the increase

---

[2] For a further discussion of the effects of the undervalued yuan on the U.S. economy, see CRS Report RS21625, *China's Currency Peg* , pp. 4-6 and CRS Report RL32165, *China's Exchange Rate Peg*, pp. 19-2, note 1.

in China's foreign exchange reserves. Some suggest, however, that "hot money" — speculative inflows of foreign funds seeking to profit from revaluation of the yuan — may account for most of the growth in China's reserves.

Depending on the source of the money, the policy implications for China are very different. If trade and investment are the main source of the funds, then — if Chinese officials want to slow the growth in reserves — they should raise the value of the yuan. However, if speculative inflows are the primary source, then China's policy choices are more difficult. A large quick revaluation would stop the speculative pressure but it might also damage China's economy. Gradual increases would allow the Chinese economy to adjust but it might also encourage speculators to bring more money into China in hopes of profiting as the currency goes up in value. A refusal to consider any change in the value might discourage the speculators over a long period of time But if the status quo prevailed during that period, this would also make China's trading partners angry and give them reasons to doubt whether Chinese officials are sincere when they say they want to revalue the yuan.

Third, would revaluation strengthen or weaken China's banking system? China's banks are riddled with bad debt and their competitiveness weakened by years of state control. If the yuan were increased in value, would the shock cause Chinese banks to strengthen their procedures or would it put the system at risk? A change in exchange rates which weakened the export sector without simultaneously stimulating domestic commerce could hold bad news for China's banks.

Some experts point out that Chinese banks hold only a small portion of their assets in foreign currencies and the government has recently established asset management companies (similar to the mechanisms the U.S. Government used in the 1980s to resolve the U.S. savings and loan crisis) to take bad debt off the books of the banks. However, export-related activities account for a major share of the customers in China's banking system. Nevertheless, most experts agree that bad debts (non-performing assets) account for perhaps 30% of the assets of Chinese banks and they say the government will need to spend hundreds of billions of dollars in yuan to recapitalize and restructure the major banks. The IMF says that the strength of China's banking system should not be an impediment to a gradual increase in the value of the yuan. However, Chinese officials have expressed reservations and may not be willing to revalue the yuan very quickly until their concerns about the impact on their national banking system have been alleviated. External pressure to revalue rapidly might be seen as an effort by foreigners to create more opportunities for their firms to buy ailing Chinese banks.

Policy Options for the United States. The fourth part of this report identifies five major options which U.S. policy-makers might consider if they want to encourage China to revalue the yuan. They are not mutually exclusive, though it might be difficult for some of them to be pursued simultaneously.

First, the United States could continue pressing China publicly for further changes in its foreign exchange system, in order that the yuan's value would better reflect market conditions and economic realities. If Chinese reformers need outside pressure to help them persuade other officials to consider reform, this strategy might help. Second, as a reciprocal of the first option, U.S. policy-makers might refrain from pressing China to move more quickly with its reforms. This might be an effective strategy if the Chinese proponents of change find that outside pressure strengthens the hand of those resisting reform.

Third, the United States could levy special tariffs on Chinese imports in an effort to encourage China to be more accommodating in their discussions with the United States about the yuan. However, such duties may violate WTO rules. Also, Chinese exporters may be able to absorb some of the cost of the new duties. Further, if the yuan were revalued, the price of Chinese exports would need not increase by the same rate as did the yuan. Chinese exports include a high proportion of inputs imported from other countries. The price of those inputs would not change if the yuan went up in value. To break even, producers in China would only need to increase the price of their exports by an amount which reflects the higher dollar-equivalent cost of Chinese-produced inputs and labor paid in yuan.

Fourth and fifth, the United States might refer the dollar-yuan controversy to the IMF or the World Trade Organization. As noted above, this issue has been discussed at the IMF for some time. Proposed changes in the power of the IMF might give it more authority over country exchange rate policies, including authority to address problems of manipulation. Whether China would be the main country affected, whether the United States and other countries would allow the IMF to determine their exchange rates, and what impact these rule changes might have on the policies of the countries with the world's largest economies are matters for speculation.

An appeal to the WTO might be based on the grounds that China's undervalued currency allegedly constitutes a subsidy to its export sector. The WTO can evaluate trade disputes and it can authorize countries to levy trade penalties in order to enforce its decisions. However, it has no authority to judge exchange rate issues. The WTO and IMF have an agreement, though, specifying that any exchange rate issues which arise in WTO deliberations shall be referred to the IMF and the IMF's decision shall be final. In effect, the WTO would be the enforcer if the IMF decided that a country was manipulating its currency to gain unfair trade advantage.

ISSUES AND EVENTS

Yuan-Dollar Exchange Rate Issue

The Controversy. In 1994, the People's Bank of China (PBC) lowered the value of its currency from 5.8 to about 8.3 yuan to the dollar. During the next decade, despite the rapid growth and modernization of the Chinese economy and the enormous expansion of its exports, the pegged value of the yuan remained essentially unchanged. The PBC bought dollars in the market in order to keep the value of the yuan virtually unchanged. Many argue that this constitutes manipulation.

Arguments Pro and Con. Many argue that China is manipulating the value of its currency in order to gain unfair trade advantage.[3] They believe this has seriously injured the manufacturing sector in the United States and contributed significantly to the U.S. trade deficit.

---

[3] See, for example, a report and data published by the China Currency Coalition. *Chinese Currency Manipulation Fact Sheet, April 2005.* The Coalition is a group of U.S. industrial, service, agricultural, and labor organizations seeking change in the yuan exchange rate. In addition to labor unions, most of its members appear to represent import-sensitive products. Available at [http://www/chinacurrencycoalition.com/factsheet.html].

The act of currency manipulation is often hard to see. However, the effects of manipulation on currency prices is more apparent. Critics of China's exchange rate policies argue that China's currency is perhaps 25% to 50% undervalued compared to the U.S. dollar. They cite various studies which support their view. They say the undervalued yuan adds to the U.S. trade deficit and hurts U.S. output and employment. Many have urged the Administration to put pressure on China in order to make it stop manipulating the yuan. They say China should either raise the value of the yuan by official action ("revalue") or let it trade freely in foreign exchange markets ("float") so that the free market can determine its real international value.

The issue of manipulation is controversial. The IMF says, in its Articles of Agreement (Article IV), that countries shall "Avoid manipulating exchange rates or the international monetary system in order to prevent effective balance of payments adjustment or to gain an unfair competitive advantage over other members."[4] Member countries are supposed to comply with this requirement. In addition, the

U.S. Omnibus Trade and Competitiveness of 1988 requires that the Secretary of the Treasury determine whether other countries "manipulate the rate of exchange between their currency and the United States dollar for the purpose of preventing effective balance of payments adjustments or gaining unfair competitive advantage in international trade."[5]

Chinese officials argue that the fixed exchange rate between the yuan and the U.S. dollar is not intended to promote exports but rather to promote economic stability. They worry that, if the value of the yuan increased sharply against the dollar or if its value fluctuated widely in world currency markets, China could suffer a major economic crisis that would seriously injure its prospects for growth, employment, and economic reform. Chinese officials have not entered into the debate concerning the "real" value of China's currency, though some say there is no convincing evidence that the yuan is undervalued. They could cite econometric studies (see below) which support the view that China's currency is slightly overvalued or perhaps only a little undervalued compared to the dollar.

Many economists doubt that China's actions have had any appreciable impact on the long-term value of the dollar. The dollar plays a broad role in international finance and the amount of dollars in circulation globally is very large. A recent survey by the world's leading central banks indicated that the daily trading of foreign currencies totals more than $1.9 trillion, 90% of which is in dollars.[6]

China Announces a Change. On July 21, 2005, China's central bank announced a new exchange rate system for China's currency. First, it increased the value of the yuan, which rose from 8.28 to 8.11 to the dollar.[7] Second, the yuan would be referenced, not just to the dollar but to a basket of currencies, and it would be allowed to vary by 0.3% each day above or below a central parity. Third, the central bank said that "the closing price of...the US dollar

---

[4] Articles of Agreement of the International Monetary Fund. 60 Stat. 1401, TAIS 1501.

[5] The Omnibus Trade and Competitiveness Act of 1988, P.L. 100-418, sec. 3004.

[6] Triennial Central Bank Survey: Foreign Exchange and Derivatives Market Activity in 2004. Bank for International Settlements, March 2005, pp. 1-2. A copy of this report is available at [http://www.bis.org/publ/rpfx05t.pdf]. The 2001 survey is : Central Bank Survey of Foreign Exchange and Derivatives Market Activity in April 2001: Preliminary Global Data. Bank for International Settlements, October 2001.

[7] A currency is said to "rise" in value compared to the U.S. dollar when one dollar buys a smaller amount of that currency than before. By convention, it is said that the yuan or renminbi rose in value by a little over 2% (even though the number gets smaller) when it went from Rmb 8.28 to Rmb 8.11 to the dollar on July 21, 2005.

traded against the RMB [yuan]...after the closing...of the market each working day" would become "the central parity for the...following working day."[8] This seemed to be an exchange system which economists call a "crawling peg."

If the new procedure had been allowed to function as announced, the yuan could have increased in value by 30% in five months. On July 27, 2005, however, the central bank announced that no further changes in the value of the yuan should be expected. Rather, it said, China's new system would be a "managed float." The central bank would compare the value of the yuan to a "basket" of currencies issued by its major trading partners. However, the Chinese authorities made it clear that they would decide what the value of the yuan would be and they would determine when and how liberalization might occur. The yuan might fluctuate compared to other currencies, but they said its dollar value would be fixed.

Too Small? To many observers, the 2% increase in the value of the yuan announced in July 2005 was too small and the process for possible future increases was too obscure and uncertain. Some might argue that the changes in the new system reflect the current debate about economic policy within the Chinese leadership. Some Chinese officials may believe that reform, including liberalization of the yuan, is in China's best interest. Others may believe that China must continue the policy of export-led growth and the advantages of the old system should not be disposed of lightly.

From this perspective, some might say the new system was adopted in order to buy time, to delay reform, and to forestall outside pressure. China was scheduled to discuss its exchange rate policies with the IMF executive board in August 2005 and the advent of a new system gave the Chinese something new to present. The IMF board was critical of China's exchange rate policies in 2004 and IMF staff had strongly urged China in mid-2005 to introduce market forces into China's exchange rate regime. The change was also announced just before Congress was scheduled to consider several bills which sought to put pressure on China if it did not revalue its currency. Arguably, a series of ambiguous steps which seemed to herald change might buy China time to consider its options and lay its plans. It might give the IMF board a reason not to press for faster action and it might persuade Congress to postpone action on the pending bills.[9]

Alternatively, instead of seeing the new system as the product of internal debate, one might say that it is obscure because it seeks to confuse and frustrate speculators. The inflow of "hot money," is serious. An official with China's State Administration of Foreign Exchange reportedly observed that "Whether we [can] effectively refrain speculation on yuan is the key to the success or failure of the reform."[10] If China wants to avoid instability and sharp changes in currency prices, its actions must not invite speculators to bring in more foreign currency and buy more yuan. In effect, China must do what the speculators expect — increase the value of the yuan — without encouraging them to capitalize on their expectations.

---

[8] The new procedure was widely discussed in the press. See, for example, "2% Solution: China lets Yuan Rise vs. Dollar, Easing Trade Tensions Slightly." *Wall Street Journal*, July 22, 2005, p. 1; Richard McGregor *et al.* "China revalues the renminbi." *Financial Times*, July 22, 2005, p. 1; and Peter Goodman. "China Ends Fixed-Rate Currency." *Washington Post*, July 22, 2005, p. 1.

[9] See, for example: "Richard McGregor. "Aim is to allow greater flexibility while still keeping firm control." and "Making sense of China's choice." *Financial Times*, July 22, 2005, pp. 2 and 4.

[10] "Chinese bank reaffirms revaluation policy." *BBC Monitoring Asia Pacific.* September 21, 2005.

The old system offered speculators a one-way no-risk bet, since there was little chance the yuan would fall in value whereas there seemed a real possibility that the value would eventually rise, perhaps substantially. This offered potentially large rewards to those who owned yuan or yuan-denominated assets.[11] The inflow of speculative money puts pressure on China to revalue the yuan to reduce the flow.[12] However, if the increase were not sudden and massive, speculators might be encouraged to buy more yuan in hopes of profiting as it goes up in value. As long as there is a general expectation that the yuan is underpriced and as long as these speculative flows continue, Chinese officials are reluctant to allow the market to determine the yuan's value. They worry that it might increase too much in value ("overshoot") if it were opened suddenly to market forces and this could also have negative consequences for the Chinese and world economies.

New Initiatives Since July 2005. More recently, the Chinese authorities have taken other steps that could allow market forces to eventually play a role in the valuation of the yuan. In mid- 2005, they created a system of non-deliverable forward contracts which let individuals take positions and make predictions as to the future value of the yuan.[13]

In January 2006, China's State Administration of Foreign Exchange (SAFE) authorized 13 local and foreign banks[14] to buy and sell yuan for dollars in the yuan spot market. An experiment allowing some banks to trade yuan for euros and Hong Kong dollars had begun in 2005. The new arrangement is supposed to improve liquidity and allow market forces a role in the valuation of the yuan. Under the new rule, the opening price for the yuan would be determined by the average closing price of the 13 banks (with the two most extreme eliminated.) In principle, this would allow yuan to move up or down in value in response to market forces. However, observers note that the central bank remains the biggest trader in the yuan-dollar market and any bank which quotes too high a rate will be vulnerable if it floods the market with yuan in order to keep the rate at its preferred price.

In December 2005, the Chinese authorities took two additional steps that would either reduce the demand for yuan or increase the demand in China for dollars. The central bank announced that it was raising the interest rate for deposits held in U.S. or Hong Kong dollars, widening the gap between those rates and those paid for accounts denominated in yuan.[15] This was aimed at discouraging speculators from buying yuan in hopes they can turn a profit by converting them back into dollars if, in the near future, the yuan should increase substantially in value.

---

[11] See, for example: Morris Goldstein and Nicholas Lardy. "China's revaluation shows size really matters." *Financial Times,* July 22, 2005, p. 13.

[12] This argument is the author's synthesis of conversations he and other members of his group had with Chinese and U.S. officials and other persons in early January 2006 during a congressional staff visit to China and Hong Kong.

[13] Patrick Higgins and Owen F. Humpage. "Nondeliverable forwards: can we tell where the renminbi is headed?" *Economic Commentary.* September 1, 2005. Federal Reserve Bank of Cleveland. Settlement on these contracts is in dollars, not in yuan. Keith Bradsher. "China Loosens Limits on Trading Against Other Currencies but Keeps Rein on Dollar." *New York Times*, September 24, 2005, p. C6.

[14] These included five foreign banks (ABN Amro Holding NV, Bank of Montreal, Standard Chartered PLC, Citigroup Inc. and HSBC Holdings PLC) and eight Chinese banks (Bank of China, China Construction Bank, Industrial & Commercial Bank of China, Agricultural Bank of China, Bank of Communications Co., China Merchant's Bank Co., Citic Bank Co. and Industrial Bank Co.) Jane Lanhee Lee. "International Investor: China approves banks as renminbi market makers; Move is set to bring more-active trading of domestic currency." *The Wall Street Journal Asia* (Hong Kong), January 3, 2006, p. 32.

[15] Prashant Rao. "Rates ease pressure on yuan to strengthen." *International Herald Tribune* (Paris), December 29, 29005, p. 17.

The central bank also announced that it would soon scrap the existing limits on the amounts that Chinese firms could take out of the country.[16] This could marginally push down the value of the yuan when Chinese firms sold their national currency in order to purchase the dollars needed to expand their overseas operations.

Market Expectations. The dollar exchange rate for the yuan has changed by only a little more than one-half of 1% since the new system was introduced, going from Rmb 8.11 to the dollar on July 21, 2005 to Rmb 8.0424 to the dollar on February 26, 2006. The People's Bank of China retains firm control of the exchange rate through its transactions in foreign exchange markets. In January 2006, futures contracts suggested that traders believed the value of the yuan would rise 2.1% (to Rmb 7.86 to the dollar) in six months and 4.3% by the end of 2006. A global markets analyst for Goldman Sachs predicted, by contrast, that the value of the yuan would increase by 9% (to Rmb 7.34) by the end of the year.[17] The Economist Intelligence Unit said the yuan would rise 4.4% in 2006 (to Rmb 7.9) and 3.7% in 2006 (to Rmb 7.6.)[18]

These predictions assume that the People's Bank of China will bring these results about through its exchange market transactions or (to say the same thing) that it will not act to prevent market forces from generating these rates of exchange.

International Views

Efforts by the IMF. The IMF staff proposed, in its June 2005 report on its recent Article IV consultations, that China should revise its foreign exchange policies and allow the market to play a larger role in the valuation of the yuan.[19] The IMF executive board had the report prior to its formal review of China's policies, though the actual document was not published until September.

The IMF executive board discussed China's new exchange rate policies during its August 2005 annual Article IV consultation review. Many people believe that China announced its new policies two weeks before that meeting in order to show they were addressing the issue. The previous year, during its August 2004 review of China's policies, the board had said that greater exchange rate flexibility was in China's best interests.[20] It also welcomed China's statement that it would "introduce, in a phased manner, greater exchange rate flexibility." Some observers suggest that it might have been awkward for China to go to the 2005 meeting and report that it had done nothing.

In its August 2005 review, the IMF executive board "welcomed the change in the exchange rate regime — an important move toward greater exchange rate flexibility — and encouraged the authorities to utilize the flexibility afforded by the new arrangement." It reiterated its earlier point that greater exchange rate flexibility was both necessary and in

---

[16] Shai Oster. "Beijing hints at a shift in its foreign holdings; Desire to diversify may hurt the dollar; Controls to be eased." *The Wall Street Journal Asia* (Hong Kong), January 6, 2006, p. 1.

[17] Both cited in Steve Johnson, "Traders price in surging renminbi." *Financial Times* (London), January 6, 2006, p. 38.

[18] *EIU ViewsWire*. New York, December 8, 2005.

[19] Article IV of the IMF Articles of Agreement require it to meet annually with member countries to discuss their economic and foreign exchange policies.

[20] International Monetary Fund. *IMF Concludes 2004 Article IV Consultation with the People's Republic of China*, August 25, 2004. Public Information Notice 04/99. It appears from context that "greater flexibility" meant an upward valuation of the yuan. The statement by China is taken from the IMF's summary the board discussion.

China's best interests.[21] It also said that "a more flexible exchange rate, not simply a revaluation, is the key to providing scope for monetary policy independence and enhancing the economy's resilience to external shocks." According to the summary of the board discussion, most directors supported a gradual and cautious approach but many others recommended that China move quickly to a foreign exchange level which reflects underlying market forces.

Other Countries' Views. No other country has taken as strong a public position on the Chinese exchange rate issue as has the United States, even though the low cost of Chinese exports has been a source of concern to interests in their countries as well. Nevertheless, some other countries reportedly have been vigorous in their private discussions with Chinese officials, urging them to give market forces a larger role in determining the value of the yuan. Their public statements have tended to show patience with China's concerns. Some observers suggested that they preferred to let the United States do the "heavy lifting."

Some countries have spoken out. In early June 2005, for example, David Dodge, Governor of the Bank of Canada, called on China to free its currency from the fixed rate against the U.S. dollar or to risk sparking U.S. and European trade protectionism.[22] At the same time, Japan's finance minister urged China to reform its tight currency peg on grounds that the current yuan-dollar exchange rate was hurting the Chinese economy and causing it to overheat.[23]

European ministers reportedly have been more accommodating in their remarks. For example, Chinese Premier Wen Jiabao told an Asia-Europe ministerial meeting in June 2005 that China would adopt a more flexible currency policy only when it believed itself ready. European ministers replied, in their public statements, that they hoped it would not take too long[24] but they agreed that China should not be pressured and it had the right to determine when and how it would reform its currency.[25]

Since July 2005, observers have been waiting for an announcement by China that it would further liberalize its exchange rate policy. The IMF executive board urged this at its discussion of China's policies in August 2005. The governing boards of the IMF and World Bank urged it at their joint annual meetings in late September 2005. Treasury Secretary Snow

---

[21] International Monetary Fund. *IMF Concludes 2005 Article IV Consultation with the People's Republic of China.* September 12, 2005. Public Information Notice 05/122. Available from the China page of the IMF website as well as in an annex (pp. 69-72) to the 2005 Article IV staff report. See IMF. *People's Republic of China: Staff Report for the 2005 Article IV Consultation.* July 8, 2005, p. 14. Available from the China page on the IMF website.

[22] Paul Brent. "Dodge's call to free the Chinese yuan has strong backing." *National Post* (Don Mills, Ontario), June 6, 2005, p. FP2.

[23] "Tanigaki says quick action on yuan needed." Economic Times of India., The Electronic Times Online, July 9, 2005. See the Economic Times of India's website at [http://economictimes.indiatimes.com /articleshow/1165902.cms]. By contrast, Japan previously had called for China to take immediate action. The Japanese Finance Minister told the G7 finance ministers in February 2003 meeting, that change was urgently needed and "Too much importation of China's cheap goods" was "the root-cause of the global economic depression." Yang Jian and Melinda Moore. "Renminbi" Eurobiz Magazine, July 2003, found at [http://www.sinomedia.net/eurobiz/v200307/rmb.html].

[24] Kervin Yao and Yoko Nishikawa. "Yuan Dominates Asia-Europe meeting." *Reuters*, June 26, 2005, reported at [*http://news.yahoo.com/s/nm/economy_china_dc&printer*].

[25] Cindi Sui. "Europe backs off on yuan value." *The Australian*, June 27, 2005, at [*http://theaustralian. news.com.au/common/story_page/0,5744,15741709%255E31037,00 .htm*]. Cary Huang. "World clamours for Beijing to revalue yuan; But there is agreement that China should dictate timing of any currency reforms." *South China Post* (Hong Kong), June 27, 2005, p. 5.

urged it during his October 2005 trip to China. President Bush reiterated the point during a state visit to China in November 2005.

In September 2005, the finance ministers of the G-7 countries said, in the communique following a meeting in Washington, D.C., that "we welcome the recent decision by the Chinese authorities to pursue greater flexibility in their exchange rate regime."[26] This was the first time a G-7 communique had called on China by name to take action. "We expect the development of this more market-oriented system to improve the functioning and stability of the global economy and the international monetary system," they added. China's President told the G-8 leaders that China wanted to base the yuan's value on market forces but it would do this on its own time and not as a result of foreign pressure.[27]

The G-7 finance ministers were even more specific in their communique following their meeting in London on December 3, 2005. They said that "further implementation of China's currency system would improve the functioning and stability of the global economy and the international monetary system." They said, in language not directly mentioning China, that such disparities, along with high oil prices, were a threat to a "solid" world economy.[28] They also said that "exchange rates should reflect economic fundamentals" and that they would monitor exchange markets closely. This was much stronger language than the "welcome" the ministers had expressed three months earlier.

Individual leaders were even more specific in their remarks. European Central Bank president Jean-Claude Trichet said at the time that the G-7's public comments were "in continuity with the message that we have been giving." He also said, referring to Asia, that "this part of the world has to contribute to the solution of global imbalances."[29] Japan's finance minister, Sadakazu Tanigaki, said, at the same time, that "we believe China needs some time to get accustomed to their new currency regime, but a considerable time has already passed. I expect China to make its currency a bit more flexible."[30] Treasury Secretary Snow said, on this occasion, that "this rigidity constrains exchange rate flexibility in the region and thus poses risks to China's economy and the global economy." Jin Renqing, China's finance minister, did not comment directly but did say that China would over time allow market forces to play a greater role in determining the value of the renminbi.

U.S. Views. In the United States, both the Administration and Congress have spoken to the issue of China's currency.

Action by the Executive Branch. In January 2004, President George W. Bush told a crowd in Toledo, Ohio that "we expect countries like China to understand that trade imbalances mean that trade is not balanced and fair. They have got to deal with their currency."[31] On July 21, 2005, responding to China's announcement that it was adopting a

---

[26] "G-7 Ministers Urge China to Make More Progress on Exchange Rate." *Bloomberg News*, September 26, 2005, available from Bloomberg News at [*http://www.bloomberg.com/apps/news?pid=10000080&sid=a86iuRuMx. 4g&refer=asia*]. "G7 demands more flexible yuan regime." *The Daily Yomiuri*, Sept. 25, 2005, p. 1.

[27] Scott Hills. "China's Hu sidesteps yuan debate in G8 address." Reuters, July 1, 2005, at [http://today.reuters/PrinterFriendlyPopup.aspx?type=live8News&StoryiD-uri:2005-o.html].

[28] Simon Kennedy and Gonzalo Vina. "G-7 prods China to let yuan rise; Beijing is accused of "rigidity" as currency appreciates little." *International Herald Tribune* (Paris), December 6, 2005, p. 20.

[29] Jane Wardell. "Economic officials chide China." (Associated Press) *Deseret News*, December 4, 2005, p. A12; "G-7 prods..." *ibid.*

[30] Gonzolo Vena and Simon Kennedy. "G7 pushes China on the yuan; Rates 'should reflect' fundamentals, it says." *International Herald Tribune*, December 5, 2005, p. 15.

[31] White House. "President Discusses Job Training and the Economy in Ohio." January 21, 2004. See [*http://www.whitehouse.gov/news/releases/2004/01/200401221-2.html*].

new exchange rate system, Treasury Secretary John Snow said that he welcomed the announcement but "we will monitor China's managed float as their exchange rate moves to alignment with underlying market conditions."[32] He agreed that the initial 2% change was small, but he said the important thing was China's willingness to change. "This is the start of a process," he said, "and the Chinese have indicated they want to get their currency based on markets rather than a peg."[33]

The United States has urged the IMF to press China to introduce market forces in its foreign exchange process more quickly. (This is discussed further in Part IV below.) In January 2006, at the World Economic Forum in Davos, Switzerland, Under Secretary Tim Adams told Bloomberg Television that China was not doing enough. "China needs to undertake serious reforms. They're on the road to reform but they need to move faster."[34] He also told a panel at the Forum that the United States had never asked China to float its currency as it does not think the Chinese financial system could withstand it. Rather, he said, the United States had urged China to allow more flexibility in their exchange rate. "All we've asked them to do is what they've agreed to do and what they know is in their best interest to do," he said.[35]

The Omnibus Trade and Competitiveness Act of 1988 (sec. 3004) requires the Secretary of the Treasury to determine, in consultation with the International Monetary Fund, whether countries are manipulating their currency in order to gain unfair trade advantage. In May 2005, Treasury reported that China was not manipulating its currency.[36] Some observers said the Treasury Department was more critical of China in this report than earlier in part due to congressional pressure. "If current trends continue without substantial alteration [i.e., revaluation]," the report said, "China's policies will likely meet the statute's technical requirements" for designating China as a country which unfairly manipulates its currency value. Nevertheless, the report said that Chinese authorities had assured Treasury Secretary Snow that they were laying the groundwork for a future revaluation of the yuan. It was on this basis that the Department found that China was not manipulating its currency. Snow reportedly gave China six months to rectify the situation and he called for an immediate 10% revaluation.[37] No such change occurred.

In November 2005, Treasury reported that China's actions "are not sufficient and do not represent fulfillment of the Chinese authorities' [earlier] commitment."[38] It said, though, that

---

[32] Snow Welcomes China's Currency Reforms, at [*http://www.treas.gov/news/index1*.html].

[33] Susie Gharib. "Secretary of State John Snow Sounds-off On China's Money Move." *Nightly Business Review*, July 21, 2005. Interview, available at [*http://www.nightltybusiness.org/transcript.html*].

[34] Bloomberg News. "Dickering at Davos: Which way yuan; Pace of China yuan reform takes center stage at World Economic Forum." January 25, 2006: 2:17 PM EST. Available at [*http://207.25.71.61/2006/01/25/news/ international/bc.davos.china.reut/index.htm*].

[35] World Economic Forum Annual Meeting 2006, *Fixing Up Fixed Exchange Rates*, summary of discussion, January 1, 2006. Available by searching Google by title or at [*http://www.weforum.org/site/ knowledgenavigator.nsf/Content/_S15322?open&event_id=*].

[36] [U.S. Department of the Treasury.] *Report to Congress on International Economic and Exchange Rate Policies, May 2005*. Obtained from [*http://www.treas/gov*], the Treasury Department website. See especially pp. 11-14.

[37] See, for example Andrew Balls, "US sets out revaluation deadline for China," *Financial Times*, USA edition, May 18, 2005, p. 1. See also Edmund L. Andrews, "Bush's Choice: Anger China or Congress over Currency," *The New York Times*, May 17, 2005, p. 1, and Andrew Balls, "FT.com site: China told to revalue by 10% by US," *Financial Times*, May 24, 2005, p. 1.

[38] [U.S. Department of the Treasury.] *Report to Congress on International Economic and Exchange Rate Policies, November 2005*. Available from [*http://www.treas/gov*], the Treasury Department website. See especially pp. 17-21.

Chinese authorities had pledged in October 2005 "that they would enhance the flexibility and strengthen the role of market forces in their managed floating exchange rate regime." It also said that "President Hu told President Bush that China would unswervingly press ahead with reform in its exchange rate mechanism." Therefore, by implication, they were not manipulating the yuan. The Chinese authorities should act, the report concluded, "by the time this report is next issued" (i.e., in six months.)

The Treasury Department's report did not discuss what impact China's new multi-currency exchange rate system might have on U.S. credit markets. Under the new system, China will not need to hold or acquire as many dollars as before in order to stabilize the price of its currency. To stabilize the value of the yuan compared to the currency basket, it may need to buy euros or yen or some other currency instead. If China is accumulating fewer dollars than before, it will have less need to purchase dollar-denominated assets. Many analysts believe that if China's future purchases of U.S. securities go down, the sellers of dollar-denominated notes and bonds may find that they need to offer higher interest rates than before in order to attract new buyers for the securities previously bought by China. This might lead to an increase in market interest rates in the United States.

Action by Congress. In late 2005, Congress passed legislation which urged the President to create a comprehensive plan to address diplomatic, military and economic issues relating to China.[39] In particular, it said the Administration should encourage China to revalue its currency further against the U.S. dollar by allowing the yuan to float against a trade-weighted basket of currencies. Congress is currently considering several bills which would require the United States to limit trade with China if it does not revalue the yuan or direct the President to take the yuan-dollar exchange rate issue to the IMF or WTO for action.

Three bills are prominent among this legislation. In July 2005, the House of Representatives passed legislation (H.R. 3283) introduced by Representative Phil English which would make imports from non-market economies (such as China) subject to U.S. countervailing duty.[40] Exports from China which were found to be subsidized on account of exchange rate manipulation might be subject to these trade rules and monetary penalties could be assessed which would raise the price of those goods in U.S. markets. The bill also required the Treasury Department to define the term "currency manipulation" for the purpose of U.S. law and to report periodically on China's implementation of its new exchange rate regime.[41]

The House is also considering another bill (H.R. 1498), introduced by Representatives Tim Ryan and Duncan Hunter, that would make it clear under U.S. law that exchange rate manipulation by China would make goods imported from that country actionable to U.S. countervailing duties.[42] No action has been taken on the bill, though it currently has 158 co-sponsors.

The Senate is also considering legislation that would limit China's access to the

U.S. market if it does not stop manipulating the value of its currency. Senators Charles Schumer and Lindsey Graham proposed on April 6, 2005, for example, that Congress enact a

---

[39] The fiscal 2006 defense appropriations act, H.R. 1815, approved by Congress in December 2005 and signed into law (Public Law 109-163) on January 6, 2006. The relevant language is found in Section 1234 of that act.

[40] H.R. 3283, passed by the House (255 to 168) on July 27, 2005. Senator Susan Collins introduced a similar bill (S. 1421) in the Senate in July 2005 but no action has been taken.

[41] For more on the issue of countervailing duties and nonmarket economies, see CRS Issue Brief IB10148, *Trade Remedy Legislation: Applying Countervailing Action to Nonmarket Economy Countries.*

[42] H.R. 1498, the Chinese Currency Act of 2005, introduced April 9, 2005.

27.5% tariff on all Chinese products entering the United States if China does not raise the value of its currency.[43] This is deemed to be the average degree of undervaluation identified by several studies. The Senate voted 67-33 for this proposal, as a rider on another bill, but it was later introduced as a separate bill

(S. 295). Originally scheduled for consideration in mid-2005, action was postponed. The bill is expected to come up again for consideration by the Senate in sometime in 2006.

FIVE KEY QUESTIONS

Is the Yuan Undervalued? By How Much?

The IMF said in its 2004 evaluation of the Chinese economy that it was "difficult to find persuasive evidence that the renminbi [yuan] is substantially undervalued."[44] Since then, many economic studies have been published seeking to determine the yuan's "equilibrium" exchange rate. (This is the exchange rate that would prevail if the value of the yuan was not controlled and if the U.S. and Chinese economies were both at macroeconomic equilibrium.) The results of these studies differ widely. Consequently, there is sufficient research available to support any position about the value of the yuan that one might wish to take.

The IMF's China experts found in their 2005 evaluation that the yuan is undervalued and the rate of undervaluation is increasing. More flexibility is needed, they said, to avoid disruption of the domestic economy.[45] The difficulty, however, one expert told the author, is the lack of any reliable way of knowing how large the distortion may be or how its effects can be separated from the other factors (such as labor costs and productivity) which affect the international price of Chinese goods.

In a market economy, the exchange rate of a currency (vis-a-vis another currency) can be affected by many things. These including interest rates, trade relationships, institutional arrangements the international flow of money between currency markets, and interventions (purchases or sales of currency) by the central bank. Market forces will balance these factors and establish an exchange rate which is supposed to reflect the actual value of goods and services in one country compared to those in another country but sometimes — depending on other considerations affecting the economy of either country — it does not.

The task of assessing exchange rates is more difficult when market forces are constrained and currency values are set by official action. A simple method would have one look at the price of a single product in world markets, on the theory that properly functioning currency markets should adjust to equalize product costs. One example is the *Economist*'s well known "Big Mac Index," a light-hearted procedure which compares the cost of McDonald's hamburgers around the world.[46] By its calculation, based on the price of hamburgers sold in both markets, the yuan is 59% undervalued compared to the U.S. dollar. Most economists

---

[43] Greg Hitt. "Senate Slams China's Currency Policy." *Wall Street Journal.* April 7, 2005, p. 1.

[44] International Monetary Fund. *People's Republic of China: Staff Report for the 2004 Article IV Consultation.* July 6, 2004, p. 12. This report is available from the China page in the country section of the IMF website at [*http://www.imf.org*].

[45] IMF, 2005 Article IV Staff Report, note 21.

[46] See [http://www.economist.com/markets/bigmac/displayStory.cfm?story_id=5389856]. See also [*http://www. stanford.edu/class/msande247s/bigmac02.htm*] for a reference to the "light hearted" nature of the measure.

agree that this index provides only a general suggestion of the relative valuation of currencies.[47] The disparity in hamburger prices around the world can also be read as a comment on the valuation of the U.S. dollar. The *Economist* says that the index shows that the U.S. dollar is more overvalued now, compared to most other currencies, than at any time since measure was introduced 16 years ago.

A more substantive effort to calculate the equilibrium value requires construction of an econometric model for the countries whose currencies are being compared. Much statistical information is required as well as a clear concept of the way the institutions and sectors relate to each other. Often, information is not available and analysts have to substitute data based on their understanding as to how each economy works and what the correct number would be if it were available. [48]

In 2005, the Chinese Currency Coalition published a report citing eight reports or statements (in addition to the Big Mac Index) which said that, to varying degrees, the yuan was substantially undervalued.[49] Two of the sources dated from 1998 or 2000. The others dated from 2002 or 2003. These included (in addition to the hamburger index) a reference saying that the World Bank thought the yuan was 75% undervalued and other studies, statements or testimony to Congress saying the yuan was priced 10% to 40% below its "real" value.50

The IMF published a paper in late 2005 which compared eight major studies released in 2004 and 2005 that sought to calculate China's "real" exchange rate on the basis of macroeconomic and econometric analysis.[51] One scholar found, in two studies using 2003 data, that the yuan was either slightly undervalued or slightly overvalued that year. He found in a later study (using the next year's data) that the yuan was 5% overvalued in 2004. Another analyst found, using the same data, that the yuan was only slightly undervalued in 2004. By contrast, others scholars have found, using essentially the same statistics, that the yuan has been substantially undervalued in recent years. One team concluded, for example, that the yuan was pegged (in a study using 2002 data) at a rate that 18-to-49% and (in another study using 2003 data) 23% below its "real" value. Another researcher found, in a study using 2000 data, that the yuan was undervalued by 35% that year. Yet another scholar concluded, on the basis of 2004 data, that the official rate that year was 15to-30% below its "real" market equilibrium value.

[47] For one thing, consumption patterns for this product varies from country to country. Also, while the hamburgers are the same worldwide, most of their inputs are supplied locally. Few hamburgers are exported from China to the United States. Labor, rent and paper products are cheaper in China, for instance, than in the United States. Other factors besides currency valuation can influence the cost of these local components.

[48] For a simple guide to the process of calculating equilibrium exchange rates, see Sergio Da Silva. *Classroom Guide to the Equilibrium Exchange Rate Model*. It is available at [*http://ideas.repec.org/p/wpa/wuwpif/0405019. html*].

[49] See Chinese Currency Manipulation Fact Sheet, cited in note 3.

[50] The full names and citations to sources were not provided. Many economists would argue that the World Bank data were misconstrued, as the Bank's figures are not measures of the extent to which currencies are over- or undervalued compared to the dollar but rather two ways that per capita income levels in poor countries may be compared internationally. The question whether the World Bank's purchasing power parity index can be used to measure deviations in exchange rates is also discussed in CRS Report RL32165, *China's Exchange Rate Peg*, pp. 12-13, note 1.

[51] Steven Dunaway and Xiangming Li. *Estimating China's "Equilibrium" Real Exchange Rate*. IMF Working Paper WP/05/202, October 2005. Available from the China page in the country section of the IMF website: [*http://www.imf.org*]. The eight studies referenced in the IMF report were by Virginie Coudert and Cécile Couharde (2 studies), Tao Wang (3), Morris Goldstein, Jeffrey Frankel, and J. Lee. Full citations may be found in the report.

Meanwhile, Funke and Rahn, two scholars from Hamburg University in Germany, found "compelling evidence that the renminbi is not substantially undervalued."[52] They seem to have employed the same econometric equilibrium modeling techniques used by scholars cited in the recent IMF paper. The claims by some that China's currency is grossly undervalued are incorrect, they argue. Rather, they say, it seems in some circles to be "politically expedient to scapegoat the Chinese currency for economic difficulties elsewhere." Higgins and Humpage, two economists with the Federal Reserve Bank of Cleveland, report that it "is next to impossible"to determine the equilibrium exchange rate for developing countries through econometric modeling.[53] China is particularly difficult, they say, because institutions and patterns of economic activity are changing very rapidly.

Data on the Chinese economy are incomplete, uncertain or unreliable. In late December 2005, China announced that — when services previously omitted from official statistics were taken into account — its gross domestic product (GDP) was 17% larger than expected. This was like discovering a province the size of Turkey or Indonesia that was previously not counted in national statistics. The new data make the Chinese economy the sixth largest in the world in dollar terms. If it grows by 10% in 2006 and its currency appreciates by a like amount, China could surpass Germany, Britain and France to become the world's third largest economy.[54] All the previous macroeconomic ratios — investment to GDP, exports as a share of GDP, rate of growth, etc. — changed with the advent of the new data. None of the studies cited above used the new data. Thus, even if they are correct in their use of the old data, their calculations do not reflect this more recent data on the Chinese economy.

The variations in the conclusions of the 17 studies mentioned above may be due in large part to the way scholars define the relationships among the different segments of the Chinese economy and the different assumptions they use to fill in gaps when they lack adequate information. Without careful analysis of the methodology and assumptions used in each study, there is no way of knowing whether the results of any of these studies are more accurate than others.[55]

It appears that few of the participants in the debate about the value of China's currency have studied the methodologies or the assumptions of the various studies. Rather, it seems that advocates select the studies they quote more because they like their conclusions than because they believe they are the best research available. Few of the participants in the debate cite findings which support conclusions other than those they support or provide reasons why their preferred studies are superior on substantive grounds to others which disagree.

---

[52] Michael Funke and Jörg Rahn. "Just How Undervalued is the Chinese Renminbi?" *The World Economy* 28:4 (April 2005), pp. 465-489.

[53] Patrick Higgins and Owen Humpage. "The Chinese Renminbi: What's Real, What's Not." August 1, 2005, at [*http://www.clevelandfed.org/Research/Com2005/0815.pdf*].

[54] See, for example: Clifford Coonan. "Services sector plays major role in surging Chinese economy." *Irish Times* (Dublin), December 27, 2005, p. 16. The calculation that China could move from sixth to third place was made by the Congressional Research Service using data in this and other newspaper reports.

[55] Some prominent studies which argue that the yuan is substantially undervalued seem to have been based on back-of-the-envelope calculations rather than on systematic econometric analysis. Others use questionable assumptions or weak economic logic. For a discussion, see CRS Report RL32165, *China's Exchange Rate Peg*, pp. 8-13, note 1.

Is China Manipulating Its Currency?

The IMF and Exchange Rate Policy. In the past thirty years, the role of the IMF in the international financial system has changed. Until the early 1970s, the IMF had a central role in determining world exchange rates. All currencies had a fixed value ("par value") compared to the U.S. dollar and the U.S. dollar was worth a specified amount of gold. If countries wanted to change their par value compared to the U.S. dollar, the IMF had to first approve. Since 1976, however, with passage of the Second Amendment to the IMF Articles of Agreement, each country is free to determine the exchange rate system it will use. Some countries have floated the value of their currency in world money markets, others have fixed the value of their currency to that of another major country, and others have pursued a mixed strategy.

IMF Surveillance. The IMF is no longer the arbiter of world exchange rates. Rather, in the modern world, it exercises surveillance over exchange rates in order to encourage and to help countries comply with the basic rules. Article IV of the IMF charter prohibits countries from manipulating their exchange rates in order to gain unfair trade advantage. It also says that "the Fund shall exercise firm surveillance over the exchange rate policies of members, and shall adopt specific principles for the guidance of all members with respect to those policies." Its current principles for surveillance were adopted by the IMF executive board in 1979 and have been revised periodically since.[56] The principles say that countries may peg the value of their currency to another currency but they cannot do this in ways which violate the requirements of Article IV. Basically, the pegged rate needs to reflect a country's underlying economic realities. These include, for example, changes in the volume and composition of its domestic output, in the size, composition and direction of its foreign trade, in its domestic rates of growth and national income, in the size of its reserves and in shifts in its domestic fiscal and monetary policies, relative rates of productivity and of change and technological advance.

Countries are allowed, under the guidelines, to use their exchange rates to promote growth and development. The IMF rules for surveillance say the Fund's appraisal of country policies "shall take into account the extent to which the policies of a member, including its exchange rate policies, serve the objectives of the continuing development of orderly underlying conditions that are necessary for financial stability, the promotion of sustainable economic growth, and reasonable levels of employment." However, countries are also required to "take into account in their intervention policies the interests of other members, including those of the countries in whose currencies they intervene." In other words, countries can use exchange rate policy to help sustain growth and employment in their domestic economy but they cannot use an unrealistic exchange rate to prevent balance of payments (BOP) adjustment or to gain unfair trade advantages. Adjustment includes such things as increased imports, capital inflows to fund BOP deficits or outflows to offset BOP surpluses, increased domestic interest rates or price levels, and the accumulation of excess reserves. If

---

[56] These are published in the IMF's *Selected Decisions and Selected Documents of the International Monetary Fund*, 24th issue. Washington, D.C. June 30, 1999, pp.10-29. Reference here is to the General Principles, Principles for the Guidance of Members' Exchange Rate Policies, and Principles of Fund Surveillance over Exchange Rate Policies specified in the IMF board decision *Surveillance over Exchange Rate Policies: Review*, Decision No. 6026-(9/13), January 22, 1979, as amended, pp. 10-16.

one country does not adjust its BOP imbalance, the burden of adjustment will be thrown upon its trading partners through monetary contraction, unemployment and the like.

China and Manipulation. The IMF has six criteria which might be used to identify situations where countries are manipulating their currencies in order to gain unfair trade advantage. Any one of the criteria would be sufficient to note the likely presence of manipulation. It appears that China's foreign exchange practices are congruent with at least four of the IMF criteria.[57]

Persistent Intervention. The IMF says (its criterion number 1) that "protracted large-scale intervention in one direction in the exchange market" is one indication that a country may be manipulating the value of its currency. Countries may intervene in foreign exchange markets to counter short-term disorderly conditions that cause disruptive short-term movements in the exchange value of their currencies. However, the IMF guidelines say that persistent one-way intervention"might indicate the need for discussion with a member."[58]

If China's currency were properly priced and the goal were exchange rate stability, the central bank would intervene in the market in both directions, buying and selling yuan in order to dampen the effect of temporary shocks and to spread the effects of change over a longer period of time. Instead, China routinely sells yuan in order to keep the market price from rising. It rarely buys yuan to keep the market price from sinking too low. This would seem to be the kind of "protracted large-scale intervention in one direction" which the IMF specified in its first operational definition of manipulation.

An Unchanging Peg. The IMF's second criterion which indicates that a country might be manipulating its currency is "behavior of the exchange rate that appears to be unrelated to underlying economic and financial conditions including factors affecting competitiveness and long-term capital movements." Countries may peg the value of their currency to another currency but the pegged rate needs to reflect the country's economic realities. These include, for example, changes in the volume and composition of its domestic output, in the size, composition and direction of its foreign trade, in its domestic rates of growth and national income, in the size of its reserves and in shifts in its domestic fiscal and monetary policies, relative rates of productivity and of change and technological advance.

The yuan-dollar exchange rate was largelyunchanged from1994 to 2005. Since reforms were announced in mid-2005 it has changed very little. Some might argue that the fact that China held its exchange rate constant during this period is evidence that China was not manipulating the yuan through fine-tuning of its valuation. However, manipulation can be as much a *lack* of change as an *act* of change.[59]

Whether an unchanging exchange rated is a violation of Article IV depends on the way the country holds the rate constant. China did not have to micro-manage the daily rate for its currency in order to maximize its export opportunities. They merely sold yuan whenever the yuan-dollar exchange rate increased beyond the level the central bank desired. Chinese

---

[57] In addition to the four cited here, the other IMF criteria include numbers three (a prolonged reductions or incentives for BOP purposes affecting current transactions or the inflow or outflow of capital) and six (unsustainable flows of private capital.)

[58] IMF. *Selected Decisions*, note 55. See "Principles of Fund Surveillance over Exchange Rate Policies," pp. 12-15, section 2(i), (iv) and (v).

[59] See, for example, Morris Goldstein's argument to that effect. "China and the Renminbi Exchange Rate" in C. Fred Bergsten and John Williamson, eds. *Dollar Adjustment: How Far" Against Whom?* Washington, D.C.: Institute for International Economics, November 2004. Special Report 17.

authorities used domestic monetary policy and other domestic economic practices to offset the effects of the fixed yuan-dollar rate.

Economic conditions have changed markedly in China since 1994. Production and consumption patterns changed. Import and export patterns changed. The relative value of goods and services and the relative value of labor, capital and other factors of production changed. The international value of China's currency should have changed as well to reflect these changes. Among other things, this would have produced price signals that could have changed consumption and production patterns, promoted efficient and effective utilization of resources, and improved the Chinese people's standard of living and level of real income. The behavior of the yuan-dollar exchange rate after 1994 "appears to be unrelated to underlying economic and financial conditions" and is therefore consistent with the IMF's second criterion for identifying currency manipulation.

Prolonged Foreign Lending. The IMF's fourth criterion says that "excessive and prolonged short-term official or quasi-official lending for balance of payments purposes" can be evidence that currency manipulation is taking place. Prolonged borrowing for the same purpose is also evidence of manipulation.

Since 1994, China's foreign exchange reserves have grown sixteen-fold, from $53 billion to $819 billion. Some of the funds in China's foreign exchange reserves are equity investments. Most, however, are loans to foreign governments or private borrowers. For example, China's investment in U.S. Government debt has more than tripled in the past five years, from $71 billion in 2000 to $242 billion in 2005. By definition, these are loans to the U.S. Government and they are short-term, in the sense that they can be liquidated at any time through sales in security markets. They help the United States cover its balance of payments (current account) deficit and they help China adjust its balance of payments in a way which does not require it to spend its international income on purchases of goods and services from abroad. At least on the part of China, this appears to be the kind of behavior "to prevent effective balance of payments adjustment" (in the words of Article IV) that meets the IMF's fourth test for currency manipulation.

Influence on Capital Movements. The IMF's fifth criterion says that a conversation with a country might be in order if it evidences "the pursuit, for balance of payments purposes, of monetary and other domestic policies that provide abnormal encouragement or discouragement to capital flows." Many observers say that the growing size of China's reserves shows that its government is promoting an abnormal outflow of capital for BOP purposes.

The Chinese government purchases large amounts of foreign exchange in order to maintain the price of its currency. Thus, foreign money is less available to Chinese citizens and firms than it might be otherwise. Consequently, instead of being cleared on the current account through imports and other current activity, China's balance of payments is cleared through the capital account by large additions to China's foreign exchange reserves.

Many analysts agree that China's reserves are larger than its normal trade or financial needs would require. They are larger, for example, than any need China is likely to face if its international income suddenly declined — as a result, for instance, of an economic shock originating elsewhere in the world economy — and it needed money for a while to pay for imports or to service debt. In this light, many would argue with reference to the IMF criterion noted above, that continued expansion of China's foreign exchange reserves is not just an encouragement for the outward flow of capital but an encouragement for "abnormal" flows as well.

Some would argue in addition that the continued growth of China's reserves is inconsistent with provisions of the IMF charter. Article IV also stipulates that all members shall seek to promote stability by fostering orderly underlying economic and financial conditions and a monetary system that does not tend to produce erratic disruptions." Every dollar that China adds to its reserves is a dollar that some other country adds to its foreign debt. Arguably, the accumulation of large reserves and large debts does not enhance the stability of the world financial and trading system.

Countries with large foreign exchange reserves do not import as much as they could and debtor countries have difficulty retiring their foreign obligations by trade. In that sense, high reserves are not a formal trade barrier but they have the same effect. They hamper "the expansion and balanced growth of international trade" (one of the purposes, stated in its Articles of Agreement, for which the IMF was created.) China is not the only country accumulating large reserves but many would argue that its practices are a source of concern.

China's View. Chinese officials say they are not seeking unfair trade advantage. They only want exchange rate stability to protect their economy from destabilizing change. The result, however, is the same. Chinese officials say that, whatever the technicalities might be, the economic benefits of stability are important and are shared by many countries. Moreover, they could argue, their efforts to influence exchange rates through intervention in currency markets differ little in their effect from similar action which countries with floating exchange rates take to influence their currencies' exchange rates — changes in interest rates and other policies, for example. Furthermore, they might say, Japan and other Asian countries also buy dollars in order to keep down the value of their currencies and to stimulate their exports. Arguably, they would argue, it is unfair to single out China in this regard when others do the same thing and their trade impact on the U.S. economy is at least as great as that of China.[60]

How Fast Should China Revalue?

If China can continue to contain the inflationary pressures caused by rapid growth in its economy and its foreign exchange reserves, it can probably delay for some time any need for a major change in the dollar value of its currency. Unlike countries with overvalued currencies, it will not run out of foreign exchange if it postpones the decision. Rather, its foreign exchange reserves will grow.

China could increase the value of the yuan overnight to a much higher level if it wished to do so. However, Chinese officials are concerned that too-fast and too-steep an increase could hurt the growth rate, employment rate, and reform prospects of the Chinese economy. Chinese officials say they want to shift away from export led growth towards an economic program focused more on growth in the internal economy. However, they do not want to slow down the export sector until their internal economy is able to provide the growth they need to

---

[60] For discussion of Japan's efforts at currency manipulation, see CRS Report RL33178, *Japan's Currency Intervention: Current Issues,* updated January 12, 2006. See also J.T. Young. "Japan's subtle subsidy." *The Washington Times,* December 5, 2005, p. A19. Japan's foreign exchange reserves are larger than those of China and its exports have had a greater impact arguably on the U.S. manufacturing sector than have those of China.

continue the transformation process now underway. These considerations seem to suggest that revaluation should take place gradually. However, if speculative capital flows are a problem, as discussed below, they may want to delay the process considerably.

Most experts agree that China's current situation is not sustainable and they cannot postpone revaluation of the yuan indefinitely. If nothing is done to slow the growth of China's foreign exchange reserves, for instance, inflation may eventually push up domestic prices in China and raise its export prices. Experts differ, though, as to how quickly China should move towards a market-based exchange system. The IMF says a gradual approach is needed. In July 2005, the IMF staff proposed that China adopt a phased approach in moving towards full exchange rate flexibility.[61] More recently, the director of the IMF's research department urged a deliberate pace.[62] Experience has shown, he said, that emerging markets do not handle large, rapid exchange rate movements well. In China, he suggested, rapid change might disrupt or bankrupt major segments of the economy — particularly the banking system — and make reform a long, drawn-out and painful process.

Other experts believe that policy reform must occur more quickly. Some say that China's undervalued currency is hurting other countries and fairness requires rapid action to remedy the situation. Some suggest that China risks a financial crisis if it does not revalue soon.[63] One says that rapid revaluation is needed because China's emphasis on export-led growth makes it vulnerable to any slowdown in global demand.[64] Otherwise, they say, China risks being another "Asian miracle" country, like those that went bust during the Asian financial crisis in the 1990s.

Many also believe quick action is needed because the current economic relationship between the United States and China is unstable and harbors serious risk. Roubini and Setser argue, for instance, that change is inevitable and the only question is how it will take place.[65] A smooth landing is possible, they say, if Chinese officials lessen China's emphasis on exports and the accumulation of reserves and U.S. policy makers reduce their country's dependence on foreign loans and capital. Otherwise, they believe, some unforseen event may trigger a crisis which could have serious negative consequences for both countries.

Is China Hiding its Real Trade Surplus?

Some people argue that China's trade surplus is many times larger than the amount which China publishes in its official statistics. The China CurrencyCoalition says, for instance, that China's trade balance was nearly six times larger in 2003 than its official statistics suggest.[66] IMF data show that in 2004 the 156 countries it categorized as "world" had a combined trade

[61] Ibid., p. 14.

[62] Raghuram Rajan. *Remarks on Global Current Account Imbalances and Financial Sector— Reform with Examples from China.* Address to the Cato Institute, November 3, 2005. Available from the China page on the IMF website.

[63] See, for example, the argument to this effect in *Chinese Currency Manipulation*, note 3.

[64] Brad Setser. The Chinese Conundrum: External financial strength, Domestic financial weakness. October 31, 2005. Available (with registration) from the RGEmonitor website at [http://www.rgemonitor.com/redir.php?sid=1&tgid=10000&cid=108028].

[65] Nouriel Roubini and Brad Setser. *The sustainability of US external deficits and Chinese external surpluses.* November 22, 2005. PowerPoint Slides. Available from the RGEMonitor website at [*http://www.rgemonitor.com/redir.php?sid=1&tgid=10000 &cid=108683*].

[66] See the Chinese Currency Coalition factsheet cited in note 3.

deficit with China of $267 billion, roughly six and one-half times more than trade surplus of $41 billion that China reported that year.[67] If China's trade income were the larger of these figures, this would be strong evidence the yuan is undervalued.

In theory, the net trade figures reported by exporter and importer countries should match. In practice, the data are often inconsistent. There is strong reason to believe that methodological reasons account for much of the discrepancy in data. Perhaps countries keep better count of their imports than their exports. Perhaps the figures are confused and intermingled when products are imported and re-exported or when inputs from several sources are channeled through a final exporter countries.

The IMF's *Direction of Trade Statistics* (DOTS) shows, in any case, that — when the exports of all countries to every country are subtracted from the imports every country receives from all countries, the world had a $269 billion trade deficit with itself in 2004.[68] Other countries show similar disparities between the trade balances they report and those reported by their trade partners.[69] In 2005, the IMF executive board noted weaknesses in China's BOP statistics in its annual Article IV review in 2005 and it urged the Chinese authorities to take advantage of Fund's technical assistance to help improve them.[70]

The China Currency Coalition says, however, that China is "hiding the ball" by deliberately reporting incorrect trade statistics. It believes the figure reported by importer countries more accurately reflects China's net income from trade. This is further evidence, the Coalition says, that the yuan is seriously overvalued.

If this is correct, China must be receiving over $200 billion more each year from trade income than it reports. In that case, the money must be somewhere. China could not have spent this money on imports, as it would have then shown up in the trade statistics of the exporter countries. It seems unlikely that Chinese exporters would have brought this additional foreign currency back into China. If they had, the People's Bank of China would have had to spend three times more yuan than the amount officially announced to keep the yuan at the pegged rate. The inflationary impact of these additional yuan would be substantial and would have manifested itself through rapidly increasing domestic price levels.

Alternatively, the presumed $200 billion in extra annual revenue might have been held abroad. This would require the cooperation of Chinese officials, since it would mean that roughly 80% of China's trade income each year does not come back to China. It seems unlikely that China has been giving the money away, since this would make it the world's largest foreign aid donor (ten times the size of the United States) and international effects of its generosity would be evident. Possibly, if the money exists and is not the product of a

---

[67] For a discussion of China trade data, see CRS Report RL31403, *China's Trade with the United States and the World.* Updated January 23, 2006. IMF figure cited on p. 9.

[68] IMF. *Direction of Trade Statistics,* 2005 yearbook, p. 2. The DOTS data are computed on a somewhat different basis than are those for individual countries. On this table, industrial countries are net exporters and developing countries are net importers. For purposes of this table, China has a net trade deficit of over $300 billion.

[69] China reported net exports of $80.29 billion to the United States for 2004 while the United States reported net imports of $176.8 billion from China. India reported a net trade surplus of $6.86 billion with the United States while the United States reported a net deficit of $10.56 billion with India. France reported a surplus of $6.28 billion while the U.S. figures show a $11.06 billion deficit. Malaysia reported a surplus of $8.49 billion while the United States reported a $18.15 billion deficit with Malaysia. . Senegal reported a deficit of $89 million while the United States reported a surplus of $86 million. *Direction of Trade, 2005,* pp. 133, 203, 252, 322, and 431.

[70] See IMF Article IV 2005 staff report, p. 73. See note 21 above.

methodological flaw, the government of China might have accumulated it annually into secret foreign exchange reserves. This would mean, again if the money exists, that China has perhaps $1 trillion in clandestine funds invested in other countries (over and above its announced official reserves.) Even if China were only using this money to acquire revenue, not influence, it would be difficult to hide. If the assets were registered as Chinese at the time of purchase, for instance, they would likely show up in host country statistics.

As another possibility, if the government of China does not control the money, then it might be held by Chinese citizens and companies. In any other country, the fact that people prefer to hold foreign currencies rather than their own currency might be taken as evidence of capital flight. It might suggest that people "in the know" believe the yuan is overpriced and likely to crash. Keeping their assets in foreign currencies would be a way of protecting themselves against that eventuality. For China, however, the general view is one suggesting that the yuan will be going *up* in value and foreign currencies will go *down* in value compared to it. It seems unlikely that Chinese insiders would see the situation so differently from the common view or that they would have been able to hold a secret this big for so long.

The above scenarios are not be impossible, but they seem unlikely. It seems more likely that the $200 billion difference in the trade data reported by China and its trade partners is not real money. Rather, it is probably the result of methodological and procedural error. China's real export figures may be higher or its trading partners' import figures may be lower than the reported amounts. We do not know. Caution in the use of published data would seem appropriate. It is probably not a good idea, though, to ignore or discard the existing body of world trade and finance statistics just because some of the data do not match. The IMF and its member countries might scrutinize their procedures to see whether errors and inaccuracies of this sort can be reduced or eliminated over time.

Would Revaluation Help the U.S. Economy?

A Symbiotic Relationship. The dollar-yuan exchange rate is not determined in a vacuum. Rather, the relationship between the two currencies reflects the broader relationship between the countries which issue them. Even if they are chosen by official action, exchange rates are the consequence of each country's economic priorities and the way those priorities interact. The United States needs to import capital from abroad to finance its present level of economic activity without incurring higher interest rates. Consequently, the international value of the dollar must be relatively high in order to encourage the inflow of capital. China needs to encourage exports in order to stimulate economic growth and facilitate economic reform. Therefore, the value of the yuan must be low enough to encourage export growth. So long as these are the main issues on each country's economic agenda, major changes in yuan-dollar exchange rate or the U.S. trade deficit are unlikely.

The U.S. Imports Capital. The United States does not save enough domestically to finance simultaneously its preferred levels of consumption and investment and to cover the Federal budget deficit. By contrast, other countries (including several in Asia) save more than their economies can effectively absorb. The United States needs more capital than it can generate on its own to sustain the

U.S. economy and foreigners need safe and profitable ways to invest their surplus funds. This generates a continual inflow of foreign funds into the United States. The inflow of funds, in turn, helps generate more demand for imported goods. The U.S. current account deficit equals about 6% of GDP and requires the United States to import more than $2 billion daily from abroad.[71]

This capital inflow pushes up the exchange value of the dollar, which lowers the relative price of imports and generates a corresponding inflow of foreign goods. It is a basic principle of economics that countries which are net borrowers of money from the world must be net importers of goods and services as well.[72] If the value of the yuan increased, the volume of Chinese exports and Chinese capital flows to the United States would likely decrease.[73] In the short run, U.S. producers would probably take over a share of the market previously supplied by Chinese goods, though consumers would likely have to pay more for those goods than they did for Chinese imports. Profits and employments in those firms would likely increase. If China's trade balance declined, under this scenario, its rate of investment in the United States would also likely decline. In that case, many economists believe, U.S. interest rates would probably increase. This would likely have a negative impact, they expect, on the housing market and (with interest taking a larger share of household income) on consumer purchases.

Over the longer run, foreign production is likely to shift from China to other low-cost countries. As their exports to the United States increase, producers in these other countries would likely recover much of the market previously supplied by the Chinese. On the other hand, higher interest rates in the United States might stimulate an inflow of capital from other foreign sources. One can only speculate whether interest rates would eventually decline to their former level and what the impact these changes would have on the U.S. economy.

China Wants Growth. China, for its part, also has priorities other than an accurate valuation of the yuan. Chinese officials believe they need to pursue a policy of export-led growth. They believe their domestic economy is otherwise too inefficient to generate the levels of employment and resources needed for economic reform and conversion of the economy to a market-based system rather than one based on state-ownership and control. They worry that the domestic economy cannot otherwise absorb the unemployment being generated by reform in the rural sector and state-owned enterprises. They also worry that their banking system would be unable to allocate capital effectively or to cope with the speculative pressure that might follow the introduction of a more flexible exchange rate system and more open capital markets.

China's economy has been growing at a rate of about 9% annually for the past decade. Most experts believe this rate cannot be sustained indefinitely, given both the present levels of productivity and the strain and inflationary pressure such growth places on the economy. China needs to slow down its growth rate in order to consolidate recent gains and to correct

---

[71] See, for example: Geoff Dyer and Andrew Balls. "Questions grow over China's forex strategy." *FT.com.* (London) January 6, 2006, p. 1.

[72] For a further discussion of the causes of the U.S. trade deficit, see CRS Report RL31032, *The U.S. Trade Deficit: Causes, Consequences, and Cures,* updated September 15, 2005.

[73] Not all would agree with this view. One manufacturer notes, for example, that labor and other Chinese content account for no more than 30% of total operating costs for Chinese exporters and — with most materials costs denominated in dollars — content priced in yuan accounts for only about 20% of total costs. If China's currency were to increase in value, the cost of the imported components would be unchanged and the price of China's exports would need to be increased only marginally to recover the higher local costs. See, for example, Kathrin Hille, "China's currency shift frays nerves." *Financial Times* August 7, 2005, p. 1, available from its website at [*http://www.FT.com*].

imbalances. They say that raising the value of the yuan would help. It would slow the growth in reserves, lower inflationary pressures, reduce the cost of imports, raise per capita income, reduce distortions and encourage the flow of resources from the export sectors to the domestic economy. However, Chinese officials are reluctant to shift from a policy of export-led growth to one based more on internal growth until they believe their domestic economy is more efficient and productive and economic reform has further progressed.

According to the IMF, most Chinese officials believe they eventually need to liberalize the yuan and shift more to a policy of domestic led growth.[74] Senior Chinese officials told the press in December 2005 that the value of the yuan would be increasingly influenced by the market and the trend is for China's currency to appreciate over time.[75] Yu Yongding, a member of the central bank's policy committee, said at the time that there is a risk that inflation could be ignited if the exchange rate is not allowed to appreciate. He also said that China's foreign exchange reserves had been growing too fast.

Many in the Chinese leadership believe their country is not yet ready for substantial changes in the value of the yuan. In any case, they say, efforts to resolve the imbalances in the world economy will require concerted action by many nations and China should not be expected to solve them alone.[76]

THREE DILEMMAS FOR CHINA

Intervention and Reserves

The People's Bank of China intervenes in the market to buy foreign exchange and sell yuan in order to hold the value of its currency at a relatively constant level. As a result, China has accumulated foreign exchange reserves which now total more than $819 billion. At the present rate of growth, its reserves will surpass those of Japan and total $1 trillion by the end of 2006.[77] If the bank did not sell yuan, the value of China's currency would rise and its volume of exports would fall. Many of China's export industries reportedly operate on very slim profit margins and many might go bankrupt if the yuan rose substantially in price.[78]

Much attention has been paid to the size of China foreign exchange reserves. Many see them as a potential financial threat to other countries. Many believe the growth in China's reserves proves that its currency is undervalued and manipulated.

However, the growth in China's reserves causes problems as well. For one thing, it puts great pressure on China's monetary system. China cannot have an independent monetary policy, since its domestic money supply grows at the size of its foreign reserves expands. For every dollar bought by the central bank to maintain the peg, the People's Bank of China creates new 8 yuan which it gives to the seller. The PBC has reportedly intervened in the currency market at a rate equal to about 12% of China's GDP.[79] The IMF says that only about

[74] Cited in the IMF's staff report on the 2005 Article IV consultation, note 21 above.
[75] "Beijing officials signal support for higher yuan." *The Wall Street Journal Asia* (Hong Kong), December 13, 2005, p. 9.
[76] Ibid., pp. 14-16.
[77] "China's currency reserves hit $819bn." *The Times* (London), January 16, 2006, p. 39.
[78] "Revised growth figures send mixed signals." *South China Morning Post* (Hong Kong),December 27, 2005, p. 1.
[79] Brad Setser. *The Chinese Conundrum,* note 64

half the liquidity caused by the increase in reserves has been sterilized (that is, removed from circulation through sales of government bonds.)[80] Thus, the central bank has had to hold down the growth of credit and lending by state banks in order to keep this excess liquidity from causing inflation. The June 2005 IMF Article IV staff report urged China to wring more excess liquidity from the system and to tighten monetary policy still further.

The growth in China's reserves also creates another problem. Roughly 70% of its reserves are held in dollars or dollar-denominated securities. If the yuan should go up in value compared to the dollar, the value of China's reserves will go down and China would lose a great deal of money.[81] The State Agency for Foreign Exchange announced in mid-January 2006 that it would be "actively exploring more efficient use of our FX [foreign exchange] reserve assets" and "widening the foreign exchange reserves scope." It said it wanted to "optimize the currency and asset structure" of China's reserves and to "actively boost investment returns."[82] Some market analysts thought this meant that China intended to sell some of its dollar-denominated assets.[83] Their alarm abated, however, when it became clear that China simply planned to invest a smaller portion of its new reserves in dollars and more in the currencies of other trading partners.

Where's the Money Coming From?

Hot Money or Trade? China's foreign exchange reserves are growing because the country's central bank is buying dollars and other foreign currencies in order to stabilize the market price of the yuan. The question is where the foreign currency is coming from. Many argue that the growth in China's reserves is the result of its trade policies as well as the inflow of foreign investment. Recent research suggests, however, that speculative inflows ("hot money") may be responsible for over three-quarters of the net increase in China's foreign exchange reserves since 1998.

Accounting the BOP. Table 1 shows (based on IMF data) the size and amount of change which took place in China's foreign exchange reserves and balance of payments (BOP) during the period 1998 to 2004. Foreign exchange reserves and alternative BOP figures have been discussed above. The balance of payments is a comprehensive picture of a country's international financial and commercial transactions. It has three parts: the current account balance, the capital account balance and the total for errors and omissions. The current account balance is the net sum of a country's exports and imports of goods and services plus its net income from foreign investment. The capital account balance is the net sum of all the

---

[80] IMF. Staff Report for the 2004 Article IV Consultation, note 44, p. 9.

[81] China keeps its books in yuan. The dollar value of the Chinese assets would not change but their value from the Chinese perspective would decline. Likewise the international value of assets denominated in yuan would increase.

[82] The Associated Press. "China might diversify investments: U.S. mortgage industry worried; Drop in Treasury purchases could hurt home buyers." *Columbian* (Vancouver, Washington), January 11, 2006. "Forex reserves could be used to set up national investment trust firms." *South China Post* (Hong Kong), January 16, 2006, p. 5.

[83] To dampen concern, the governor of the People's Bank of China personally met with press to affirm that China had no plans to reduce its dollar holdings or to use them to buy other assets, such as oil. See "Forex reserves could be used...." (note 82.) Many analyst predict that, if China reduces its rate of investment in the United States, U.S. interest rates will increase. A large sale of China's dollar assets could also drive down U.S. security prices.

monetary flows to or from a country — net foreign investments, loans made or received, transfers by individuals (remittances from migrant workers, for example) and other transactions needed to finance activity in the current account.

Conceptually, the current account and capital account balances should cancel each other out, one being positive and the other negative. Imports which are not paid for with current revenue, for example, would have to be financed directly or indirectly by capital from abroad. In fact, however, some financial and commercial transactions are not recorded and the current account or capital account is often larger than the other. To make the two parts of the BOP match, economists add a third figure, called "errors and omissions" (E&O), which acknowledges that for unexplained reasons more money is in one account or the other. This may reflect income from illegal trade, mis-measurement, or undisclosed movement of money by individuals ("capital flight") seeking to protect their assets from an expected change in the exchange rates or by speculators hoping to profit from that change.

Table 1. Composition of China's Buildup in Foreign Exchange Reserves (billions of U.S. dollars)

	(1) Average 1998-2000	(2) Average 2001-2004	(3) Amount of Change
Foreign reserve increase a	8.5	122.8	114.3
Current Account balance	23.7	42.2	18.5
Capital Account Balance	0.3	69.3	69.0
Of which FDI b net	*38.5*	*46.6*	*8.1*
Of which other	*-38.2*	*22.7*	*60.9*
Errors and Omissions	-15.4	11.4	26.8
Non-FDI* capital account balance c	*-53.6*	*34.1*	*87.7*

Source: Prasad and Wei.

a. Foreign reserve increase is the sum of the current account and capital account balances plus errors and omissions.
b. FDI is Foreign Direct Investment.
c. Includes errors and omissions.

Analyzing China's BOP

Table 1 breaks China's balance of payments figures into these three components. It also provides separate figures, in the capital account, for foreign direct investment. Prasad and Wei, the authors of the table, identified the annual changes in China's foreign exchange reserves and the amounts recorded for each element of China's balance of payments and they present the average annual amounts for each item for the first three and the last four years of the 1998 to 2004 period.[84] From that data, they derive the amount of change which occurred in each instance between the first and the last halves of that seven-year period.

On first inspection, looking only at the middle column, it seems that most of the growth in China's reserves was due to trade and investment. Between 2001 and 2004, Prasad and Wei note, China's net annual current account balance was $42.2 billion while the net inflow from FDI was $46.6 billion.[85] It appears, therefore, that the $88.8 billion from these two sources accounted for most of the $128 billion average annual increase in China's foreign exchange reserves during that period.

Prasad and Wei find, however, that other factors — particularly the inflow of "hot money" were more important. As **Table 1** also shows, comparing the first and second columns, that the average annual level of China's foreign exchange reserves grew by $8.5 billion from 1998 to 2000 and by $122.8 billion from 2001 to 2004. In column 3, Prasad and Wei found that the annual change in China's trade receipts ($18.5 billion) and FDI ($8.1 billion), shown in column three, were not sufficient to account for the average $114.3 billion in China's reserves. On the other hand, the swing in flows from non-FDI investment and E&O were substantial.

Between 1998 and 2000, they observe, capital flowed out of China openly (non-FDI) or covertly (E&O.) They speculate that initially Chinese firms and families moved money abroad to take advantage of favorable investment and exchange rate opportunities. After 2001, however, they suggest, Chinese firms and families and foreign speculators began moving money back into China in hopes of profiting from the expected increase in the value of the yuan. They observe that, as **Table 1** indicates, the net flow of funds from non-FDI investment and E&O between the two periods amounted to an average $87.7 billion a year, nearly 77% of total change in China's foreign exchange reserves during the 1998-2004 period.

Policy Implications. The policy prescriptions are different, depending on the source, if one wants to reduce the inflow of foreign currencies and to lessen the central bank's incentive to sell yuan in foreign exchange markets. If trade-related factors are the major reason why foreign exchange is flowing to China, then changes in the country's trade policies and exchange rate would help diminish the flow. China's government would need to take steps, in this scenario, to shift resources and employment from the export sector to the domestic economy.

On the other hand, if "hot money" is responsible for the buildup in reserves, then a gradual appreciation in the value of the yuan might encourage further inflows of speculative funds. In that case, the central bank might cool the inflow of "hot money" by holding the value of the yuan constant for a sustained period of time.

The *Economist* reported in late January 2006 that the delay and uncertainty of the new Chinese exchange rate system may have had this effect.[86] The flow of portfolio capital investment, one form of "hot money," declined to about $1 billion a month in late 2005, it

---

[84] Eswar Prasad and Shang-Jin Wei. *The Chinese Approach to Capital Inflows: Patterns and Possible Explanations.* National Bureau of Economic Research. NBER Working Paper Series, Working Paper 11306, April 2005.

[85] The sources of FDI coming to China have changed over the years. In 2004, the major sources were Hong Kong (32%), Virgin Islands (12%), Korea (11%), Japan (9%), European Union (7%), United States (7%), Taiwan (5%), Western Samoa (2%) and Singapore (2%). The sources for the Virgin Islands and Western Samoa money are unknown. The five Asian countries accounted for 60% of the total. See Prasad and Wei, p.79.

[86] "Portfolio Investment in China: Cooling Down." *The Economist*, January 28, 2006, p. 73.

reported, from the average level of $8 billion a month seen from late 2003 through mid-2005. It appears, the *Economist* suggests, that "the speculators who have been furiously pumping money into China for the past three years have at last given up and gone home." The magazine predicts that China's trade surplus may also start to fall and import growth may revive.

If the data for the last part of 2005 are correct and if the *Economist*'s predictions are right — and it is much too soon to know whether these are so — then the People's Bank of China may have an easier time managing monetary policy in the future. There would be less need, for example, for it to print yuan in order to keep down the value of the yuan by buying up the inflow of dollars. This would make it easier, if the PBC wishes to do so, for the central bank to relax its control and to allow market forces more influence on the yuan-dollar exchange rate.

Would Revaluation Hurt China's Banks?

Many believe China needs to reform its financial system before the yuan can rise appreciably in value. If revaluation occurs first, they say, the banking system may not be able to cope and this might have negative effects on economic growth. Others believe, however, that — while more reform is needed — China's banking system should be able to accommodate more flexibility in the value of the yuan. Nevertheless, there is serious worry on the part of many that a floating exchange rate system could lead to destabilizing capital outflows.[87]

The IMF says that major steps have been taken to restructure the banking system (even though further action is required) and the condition of the banking system is no longer an obstacle to exchange rate reform. As a result of recapitalization, sales of nonperforming loans, and other reform efforts, the IMF staff reported, the capital strength, asset quality and operating results for China's banks have significantly improved. In the old days, state banks made loans to state industry with little expectation those loans would be repaid. Thus the savings of Chinese individuals were sunk into subsidizing these money-losing firms.

Most of these "legacy" loans have been transferred to four government-owned asset management corporations (AMCs), so the government budget rather than the banking system will bear the cost of those bad loans. Consequently, the IMF reports, bad loan ratios for the major commercial banks (the four largest state banks and 14 joint stock commercial banks) have fallen from about 24% of loans in 2002 to about 13% in September 2005.[88] These institutions account for about three-quarters of total bank assets. They say that efforts to tighten the banks' balance sheets and to strengthen their internal controls and risk management procedures are still needed.

The IMF does not report figures for the ratio of bad loans (non-performing loans) in the banking system as a whole because the procedures for reporting bad loans by small banks are different from those for large banks. Two IMF economists, Prasad and Wei, reported in their 2005 article that non-performing loans in the banking system amounted to 30% of GDP in

---

[87] As noted earlier, though (text and note 16 above), China has announced that it will soon relax its controls over capital outflows It is unclear if this is a precursor for greater future exchange flexibility or merely a means to limit growth in China's forex reserves.

[88] Author's interview with IMF staff, December 2005.

2003.[89] IMF staff indicates that this larger figure calculates the bad loan ratio for smaller banks in the same way that bad loans are calculated for the larger banks. Prasad and Wei suggest that a major share of China's foreign exchange reserves may need to clear up the accumulated bad debt.

Setser asserts that conditions in the Chinese banking system are grim and the costs of reform will be great.[90] He says the banking system is not ready yet for a more flexible currency. Bad debt in the banking system is equivalent to 20% or 30% of GDP, he says. Officials estimates reported that 40% of all loans in 2002 were non-performing, he indicates, and "legacy" bad loans (debt owed by state firms) totaled $400 billion. Other estimates put the figure at $650 billion, he says, or about 50% of China's 2002 GDP. The recent boom in bank lending may have reduced the level to 25% or so, he says. However, he suggests, the total volume of bad debt may be higher once the bad loans made since 2002 are included in the total.

Setser says that many analysts believe that the government will need to buy out the bad "legacy"debt if it wants to improve the soundness of the banking system. The IMF's statement (see above) that some bad loans were transferred out of the banking system seems to confirm this view. Setser says the government will also need to provide large amounts of money to stabilize its undercapitalized state banks. Some estimates report, he says, that the cost of cleaning up the financial system could equal 20% of national GDP (about $340 billion of China's 2004 GDP) and nearly all of it will be borne by the national government. This could push the national debt-to-GDP ratio, he says, from 33% in 2004 to perhaps 50% overall.

IMF experts say that China does not need to resolve the problem of bad debt in its banking system before its currency can be liberalized. They argue that — so long as capital controls continue — the yuan-dollar exchange rate could be more flexible without harming the Chinese banks. The Chinese banks know how to trade currencies and manage their foreign exchange exposure, the IMF staff reports. They already do this in their worldwide operations. Some economists believe that China cannot have a flexible currency until it ends capital controls.[91] IMF experts argue, however, that China's banks cannot handle full liberalization of the capital account at this juncture. If capital controls were removed, they assert, a substantial outflow of capital from the banks would likely occur and this would be very destabilizing.[92]

OPTIONS FOR THE UNITED STATES

There are several ways the United States might encourage China to move more quickly towards increasing the value of the yuan. These options or policy tools are not mutually

---

[89] Prasad and Wei, note 84, p. 13.

[90] See note 64.

[91] See, for example, comments by Gail Foster, chief economist for the Conference Board, in Peter Bartram, "Insight — Yuan weak link." *Financial Director.* September 30, 2005, p. 14.

[92] See, for example: Edward Prasad, Thomas Rumbaugh, and Qing Wang. *Putting the Cart Before the Horse? Capital Account Liberalization and Exchange Rate Flexibility in China.* IMF Policy Discussion Paper PDP/05/01, January 2005. Available from the IMF website.

exclusive, but it might be difficult or awkward for the United States to pursue some of them simultaneously. [93]

First, the U.S. Government might continue pressing China publicly for additional changes in its foreign exchange system in order to make the international value of the yuan better reflect market conditions and economic realities. This assumes either that China is reluctant to change or that reformers in China will be helped by external stimulus. Second, the U.S. Government might stop pressing China publicly for change. This option is predicated on the expectation that reformers will be able to move China more rapidly towards currency liberalization if China is not pressured from abroad.

Third. the United States could enact legislation restricting Chinese exports to the United States if the value of the yuan is not increased. This assumes that China will change its exchange rate policies only if forced to do so. Fourth, the U.S. Government might refer the question to the IMF, asking the international agency to determine whether China has been manipulating its currency in violation of IMF rules. This assumes that technical findings and persuasion by the IMF and its major member countries may have effect. Fifth, the U.S. Government might refer the issue to the World Trade Organization (WTO), alleging that the United States has been injured by unfair trade practices linked to the undervaluation of China's currency. If the WTO found that the U.S. petition had merit, it could authorize trade remedies to correct the allege abuse. This assumes that exchange rate issues and questions of general system-wide subsidy will fall within the purview of the WTO rules.

Continue Public Pressure

Continued public pressure is one method the United States might use to encourage China to adopt further reforms in its foreign exchange procedures. This might include official findings by the Treasury Department that China is a manipulator or strong exhortations by high-level U.S. officials. Among other things, U.S. officials might press Chinese officials to provide them more information as to the ways they intend to link reform of their domestic economy to reform in their exchange rate regime and the criteria they might use for discerning progress.

In evaluating this option, it would be helpful to know whether Chinese officials really intend to move towards a market-based valuation of the yuan or whether they intend to drag the process out as long as possible. If China adopted the reforms announced to date mainly in response to foreign pressure, then it is possible that further pressure might persuade them to go faster. However, if Chinese officials adopted these reforms because they believe that market-based reform is in China's best interests, foreign pressure may complicate this process. China has a long tradition of not giving in to foreign pressure. Foreign pressure might strengthen the hand of the reformers, but it might also stiffen resistence by the opponents of reform and make it harder for the reformers to achieve their ends.

It also might be helpful if U.S. officials and legislators had more information about China's internal decision making process. How strong are the reformers? What key choices do Chinese officials believe they face as regards the economy and value of the yuan? How do

---

[93] Some of these options are also discussed, with similar conclusions, in CRS Report RL32165, *China's Exchange Rate Peg*, pp. 28-30, note 1.

they think China and other countries can best determine what the true international value of the yuan might be? What criteria do they believe are relevant for determining currency value and their timetable for change?

Given their most recent statements, other G-7 countries will likely support the United States if it continues to press China for more rapid action. However, they may also back away and leave the United States on its own if they believe U.S. efforts are potentially counterproductive.

Pursue a Policy of Restraint

Instead of pressing China publicly for reform, the United States might decide on a policy of restraint. This is not an option in favor of the status quo. Rather, it accepts the premise that Chinese officials want to proceed with their reform program as rapidly as economic conditions and the policy consensus in China permits. This option assumes that overt foreign pressure may be counterproductive if it slows the process and strengthens the hand of those in China who oppose reform. Arguably, the Treasury Department has shown restraint of this sort when it said, in its recent reports, that China was not manipulating the value of its currency.

Some might argued that the United States should view the trade and currency dispute within the context of its overall relationship with China. While economic issues are important, this view would suggest, it is also important not to raise tensions to the point where China becomes reluctant to cooperate with the United States on other issues, such as North Korea's policies on nuclear weapons. Pressing the yuan-dollar exchange rate issue to the exclusion of other important U.S. interests might be seen, from this perspective, as counterproductive. Others might respond, however, that China will cooperate with the United States in other areas when it believes that this serves its interests.

China may have strong reasons for wanting change in its foreign exchange system. As noted before, China faces the prospect of serious inflation if it does not slow or stop the growth in its foreign exchange reserves. An increase in the value of its currency would be a key way of accomplishing that goal.

Ironically, some kind of external encouragement may still be needed to help China accomplish its plans. Even if Chinese authorities want to move forward with their reform program, they may need some external pressure — if only in the form of agreed deadlines and benchmarks — to help them overcome inertia when they encounter difficult choices as they put their currency reform policies into effect.

Restrict Exports to the United States

Instead of exerting public and mostly verbal pressure, the United States could adopt legislation restricting China's access to the U.S. market until it raises the value of its currency. There are several ways this could be done. The English bill (H.R. 3282), Ryan-Hunter bill (H.R. 1498) and Schumer/Graham bill (S. 295), all both mentioned above, would have this effect. By raising the U.S. price of Chinese imports, they would presumably reduce the flow of Chinese exports to the United States, raise the prices paid by U.S. consumers (perhaps helping some U.S. producers) and stimulate the growth of export industries in other countries that would take China's place.

Similar effects would likely occur if the U.S. Government invoked the provisions of Section 301, authorizing the U.S. Trade Representative to respond to unreasonable or discriminatory practices that burden or restrict U.S. commerce. [94] Likewise, if the Treasury Department found in its semi-annual report that China was manipulating the value of its currency to the detriment of the United States, consultations with China and trade actions would also be required. Under the Section 301 mechanism, the United States could impose trade sanctions against Chinese goods if China does not change its trade or foreign exchange policies. The United States could also use other U.S. trade laws to impose special "safeguard" restrictions on Chinese goods if the growth in Chinese imports is found to have caused (or threatens to cause) market disruption to U.S. domestic produce.[95] Measures of this sort are allowable under WTO rules on a temporary or limited basis but it is less clear that they may be used across the board or for longer periods.

It is not clear how much the price of Chinese goods would need to increase, or the volume of Chinese exports to the United States would decrease, though, if the value of the yuan increased. Components purchased from other countries account for a major share of the value of exports bearing the label "Made in China." The cost of Malaysian or Thai inputs would not change for the producer in China if the value of the yuan increased. The price of the final product would only need to increase by an amount sufficient to recover the higher cost of the producer's that were denominated in yuan. Depending on the products and methods of production, it is possible that the overall increase in product costs would be modest and the volume of Chinese exports to the United States would be large even after the value of the yuan increased.

It is uncertain what the Chinese authorities and Chinese firms would do if faced with restrictive import legislation of this sort. They might cut prices and trim profits in order to keep unchanged their share of U.S. markets. They might retaliate against

U.S. exports, setting off a trade war between the United States and China. They might also ask the WTO for authority to levy trade sanctions, on grounds that the United States was not complying with the WTO rules on international trade. Alternatively, they might raise the value of the yuan in hopes that this will eliminate the new U.S. tariffs on their goods.

The WTO trade rules allow countries to levy countervailing duties to offset any subsidies foreign exporters might receive from their home governments. WTO rules do not allow countries to impose tariffs or restrictions merely for the purpose of excluding foreign goods. If the United States hopes to persuade other countries that its special levies on Chinese imports are fair and compensatory, it will likely need to show that the size of the levies match the degree of subsidy which Chinese producers receive through the undervalued yuan. It might be helpful in this regard if there were more agreement among scholars and the affected countries as to whether and by how much China's currency is undervalued.

---

[94] Section 301 to 309 of the Trade Act of 1974, as amended. See also CRS Report 98-454, *Section 301 of the Trade Act of 1974, as Amended: Its Operations and Issues Involving its Use by the United States.* See, for example, China Currency Coalition factsheet, note 3.

[95] See CRS Report RS20570, Trade Remedies and the U.S.-China Bilateral WTO Accession Agreement, updated August 4, 2003.

If the United States put special levies on Chinese goods, China might ask the WTO to rule that the United States acted in a manner inconsistent with its obligations.[96] The countervailing duties and anti-dumping penalties allowed under WTO rules are usually applied to specific goods rather than to all exports coming from a particular country. Exchange rate manipulation might be seen as a type of general across-the-board subsidy for a country's exports. Nevertheless, there is little precedent (but see below) at the WTO for considering exchange rates from this perspective. The WTO may be concerned that the rules governing world trade would be harder to enforce if countries were free to impose countervailing duties whenever they decided unilaterally that the currencies of other countries were undervalued.

If the WTO agreed with China's petition, it could authorize China to retaliate by withdrawing tariff concessions on U.S. goods. The WTO dispute settlement process is adjudicated with reference to the WTO rules and there seems little room for political pressure by the United States and other countries. Other countries could, however, submit briefs in support of the U.S. or the Chinese position. Countries likely will give some thought to the potential impact that a trade dispute between the United States and China might have more broadly on world trade negotiations.

If the volume of Chinese exports to the United States declines because of new trade legislation, the profits of foreign firms located in China which produce those goods will likely go down as well. Exporters could shift their production facilities further to the west in China, where labor costs are lower than on the coast. This might reduce costs enough for Chinese exporters to pay the new tariff and leave their prices unchanged. Alternatively, Chinese companies and international firms might shift production to other countries where the costs of production have become lower than those in China because of yuan revaluation. In that case, these countries might replace China as major suppliers of manufactured products to the United States.

If the United States wants to keep out foreign products (not just Chinese products) which undersell U.S. manufactures, then new legislation would be needed to penalize other countries as they ramp up to take China's place. This would violate WTO rules and the terms of international trade agreements to which the United States is a party. Because the U.S. economy needs to import foreign goods of similar value to the foreign capital it imports each year, it may be hard for the U.S. government to stop countries from expanding their exports to the United States. role. If the volume of imports declines, however, prices for manufactured products in the United States may increase, giving U.S. producers some relief. U.S. consumers would likely need to spend a larger portion of their income in this case to purchase the goods which were previously produced abroad.

Take It to the IMF

The United States could also pursue the issue of China's exchange rate policy at the International Monetary Fund. The key issue is whether China is complying with the requirements of Article IV of the IMF Articles of Agreement and, if not, what steps it should

---

[96] For a discussion of the WTO dispute resolution mechanism, see CRS Report RS20088, *Dispute Settlement in the World Trade Organization.*, updated December 28, 2005.

take to comply. Though other countries seem to have preferred that the United States take the lead and break the ice for them, they are also affected by China's trade policies. Arguably, international meetings where representatives of the major countries may speak with Chinese officials at the same time will be more persuasive than scattered bilateral talks where the only strong public statements come from the United States.

There continues to be debate as to what, if anything, the outside world can do to accelerate the reform process in China. In late September 2005, Treasury Under Secretary Adams demanded that the IMF crack down on countries that violate the prohibition in Article IV against currency manipulation, though it is not clear what tools he thought the IMF should use.[97] The IMF was, he said, "asleep at the wheel" and it should confront China concerning the deficiencies in its exchange rate policies. IMF Managing Director Rodrigo de Rato rejected that charge.[98] The IMF was addressing all aspects of the issue, he replied. The IMF had already investigated and rejected suggestions that China's currency policies warrant the use of "special consultations." Rather, he suggested, the United States should act more vigorously to straighten out its own budget and economic policies rather than blaming other countries for its problems.

According to IMF sources, special consultations between IMF management and a country have occurred twice previously in response to formal complaints by another country that it was manipulating its currency. In the 1990s, the United States made a complaint about Korea and Germany filed a complaint about Sweden. The two countries eventually adjusted their currency values, though they may have done this for their own reasons rather than in response to IMF consultations.

In January 2006, Adams maintained that the IMF should play a stronger role enforcing exchange rates and preventing currency manipulation.[99] The IMF should demonstrate strong leadership on multilateral exchange rate surveillance, he said. "A strong IMF role in exchange rate issues is central to the stability and health of the international economy," he remarked. The IMF's leaders "should endorse such an enhanced role for the IMF, restoring its central role on exchange rates." While Adams did not mention China by name, he said the IMF should identify countries "whose exchange rate policies might not be in accord with Fund principles" and it should "seek to identify problematic or inappropriate exchange rate behavior."

However, IMF Managing Director Rato told a session at the World Economic Forum in Davos, Switzerland that he does not consider China to be a currency manipulator. He rejected proposals that the Fund should put greater pressure on China. He said "there is a trade-off between our role as confidential adviser in our surveillance work and our role as a transparent judge."[100] He noted that the IMF had been the first international body to urge China to move from its fixed peg to a more flexible exchange rate process. Rato also said the IMF should not take a proactive role on exchange rates, in response to Adam's question what the IMF should do about countries "that are attempting to thwart balance of payments adjustments."

---

[97] Paul Blustein. "IMF Chief Pressured on Trade Imbalances." *The Washington Post*, September 29, 2005, p. D1.
[98] Ibid.
[99] U.S. Department of the Treasury. "Remarks by Under Secretary for International Affairs Tim Adams at AEI Seminar Working with the IMF to Strengthen Exchange Rate Surveillance." February 2, 2006, JS-4002. Available from the Treasury Department website at [*http://www.treas.gov/pres/releases/js4002.htm*].
[100] Chris Giles and Krishna Guha. "Interview with Rodrigo de Rato." *Financial Times* (London), January 28, 2006, p. 8

On February 9, 2006, Rato outlined his future plans for the IMF. He said the IMF should put more emphasis on surveillance but he raised several reservations about the Fund's taking the central policing role Adams had proposed.[101]

The IMF is a place where the views of affected countries can be presented to China and efforts can be made to press China to revalue its currency. The IMF cannot force countries to have exchange rate policies which mirror underlying economic conditions, even if they might be non-compliant with IMF rules. However, continuing discussion at the IMF and at other international meetings serves to focus attention on the issue. At the least, it puts Chinese officials in a situation where they need to explain or justify their policies and to respond in some way to international pressure. Arguably, it has caused them to take steps towards liberalization that they otherwise might be reluctant to take — or they might have taken more slowly — if these conversations had not taken place.

If the IMF were given the broader authority contemplated by Adams and others, the fundamental structure of the world exchange rate system would change and many countries, in addition to China, would have to seriously revise their domestic and international economic policies. China might not be willing to make fundamental changes in its foreign exchange and economic policies unless other major countries make fundamental changes in their policies as well.

Refer It to the WTO

The United States could petition the World Trade Organization (WTO) that it believed China was subsidizing its exports by undervaluing its currency. It could argue that China gains unfair trade advantages because of the artificially low value of its currency and it could ask the WTO to settle this dispute. Normally, arguments about subsidy reference individual products. In this case, however, the U.S. could argue that the subsidy applies to all Chinese goods. By undervaluing its currency, the United States could argue, China is artificially reducing living standards and prices in its domestic economy in order to stimulate and facilitate growth in its export sector. Arguably, subsidies do not have to be paid by governments directly to exporters for them to affect output. In China's case, the United States could argue, the lower production costs caused by the reduction in the standard of living would be the means by which the subsidy were delivered to Chinese export firms.

WTO rules do not permit individuals or private groups to appeal trade controversies to it. Under Section 301 of the Trade Act of 1974, however, groups and individuals may petition the U.S. Trade Representative for action concerning harmful foreign trade practices. In 2004, the Bush Administration rejected two petitions — one by the China Currency Coalition and one by 30 members of Congress — which proposed that the United States should refer the yuan-dollar trade issue to the WTO. The Administration expressed doubt, at the time, that the

---

[101] Rodrigo de Rato. *The IMF's Mid-Term Strategy: New Priorities, New Directions.* Remarks at the Aspen Institute, Rome Italy, February 9, 2006. Available from the IMF website at [*http://www.imf.org/external /np/speeches/2006/020906.htm*]. Some analysts speculate that, if the IMF was given the power to police exchange rates and BOP policies,it would probably start with the industrial countries whose policies have the greatest impacton the world economy rather than middle-income countries such as China.

United States could win a case of this sort in the WTO. It also said, in rejecting the petitions, that action of this sort might be "more damaging than helpful at this time."[102]

The WTO's dispute settlement process is a quasi-judicial process that is intended to resolve trade disputes between countries which cannot be resolved through conciliation or negotiation. A three member panel of experts is appointed by the WTO secretariat reviews the facts and arguments in the case and to render judgment based on principles embodied in WTO rules and international trade agreements. An appellate panel may review the initial panel's findings and, unless its findings are set aside by the WTO membership by consensus, the disputing parties are expected to implement the decision. If a country does not comply within a reasonable period of time, the WTO may authorize the complaining country to impose retaliatory duties on the non-compliant country's goods. Those duties or barriers remain in force until the country complies or until the disputing parties otherwise resolve the issue.[103]

The WTO has no authority to address exchange rate issues. However, the IMF and WTO have an agreement which requires the WTO to refer exchange rate disputes of this sort to the international monetary body and to accept the IMF's findings as conclusive.[104] By itself, a finding by the IMF that China is manipulating its currency would have no "teeth" that would require Chinese officials to change their procedures. However, in conjunction with a positive finding by the WTO, an IMF finding of this sort might have considerable affect. If a WTO dispute settlement panel found that China was gaining unfair trade advantage through a low valuation of its currency, it might authorize the United States to put special tariffs on Chinese products into effect until China raised the value of its currency.

It might be awkward for the United States to take a complaint of this sort to the WTO if it unilaterally imposed tariff restrictions on Chinese goods. Moreover, it would be risky for the United States to apply to the WTO for relief if it does not know how the IMF would rule on this. Support from the other major IMF member countries in the IMF would be critical. Unlike the dispute settlement in the WTO, decisions of this sort in the IMF are made by individuals representing member country governments. The G-7 countries and other members of the European Union comprise a majority of the voting power in the IMF. It might be helpful if the United States consulted with the other countries about their potential vote, if the issue were come to the IMF, before it approached the WTO with a complaint.

---

[102] U.S. Trade Representative. *Statement from USTR Spokesperson Neena Moorjani Regarding a Section 301 Petition on China's Currency Regime.* November 12, 2004 Available from the USTR website. Put quoted words in search box to locate text.

[103] For further information on the WTO's dispute settlement procedures, see CRS Report RS20088, *Dispute Settlement in the World Trade Organization: An Overview,* updated December 28, 2005.

[104] See Arrangement for Consultation and Cooperation with the Contracting Parties of GATT, September 9, 1948, and Guidelines/Framework for Fund Staff Collaboration with the World Trade Organization, April 21, 1995. Both are included in the IMF's Selected Decisions, note 56, pp. 546-9 and 552-9.

INDEX

D

E

H

I

J

K

L

M

T

U

V